The Birthmark Scar, Book 2
A Warrior's Path

Book 2 of:
The Birthmark Scar Trilogy
2024

By

P.E. Berg & Amanda Hemmingsen

© 2024 by P.E. Berg and Amanda Hemmingsen

All rights reserved. No part of this book, in part or in whole, may be reproduced, transmitted or utilized in any form or by any means, electronic, photographic or mechanical, including photocopying, recording, or by any information storage and retrieval system without permission in writing from Ozark Mountain Publishing, Inc. except for brief quotations embodied in literary articles and reviews.

For permission, serialization, condensation, adaptions, or for our catalog of other publications, write to Ozark Mountain Publishing, Inc., P.O. Box 754, Huntsville, AR 72740, ATTN: Permissions Department.

Library of Congress Cataloging-in-Publication Data

The Birthmark Scar, Book 2, A Warrior's Path by P.E. Berg -1970- and Amanda Hemmingsen -1988-

This book continues with the process of a group of characters coping with concepts regarding psychics, past-lives, religious dogma, and synchronicity of gods and goddesses.

1. Coping 2. Past Lives 3. Metaphysical 4. Synchronicity
I. Hemmingsen, Amanda, 1980, Berg, P.E., 1970 II. Metaphysical   III. Synchronicity   IV. Title

Library of Congress Catalog Card Number: 2025930501
ISBN: 978-1-950639-44-1

Front Cover Photo Credits: Madison Jewel Green
Cover Art and Layout: Victoria Cooper Art
Book set in: Amatic SC & Times New Roman
Book Design: Summer Garr
Published by:

PO Box 754, Huntsville, AR 72740
800-935-0045 or 479-738-2348; fax 479-738-2448
WWW.OZARKMT.COM

Printed in the United States of America

Table of Contents

Chapter 1: The Three Angels	1
Chapter 2: Kilas and the Green Man	3
Chapter 3: Lilith and Merc	9
Chapter 4: Dr. Angela Kapralov	12
Chapter 5: The Cemetery Visit	26
Chapter 6: Nera's Call	31
Chapter 7: Kilas Continues (Scrolls and Scarabs)	34
Chapter 8: Kilas and Angel	45
Chapter 9: Three Angels Visit Jamie	51
Chapter 10: Robert's Secret Library	56
Chapter 11: A Visit With Lena	63
Chapter 12: Iraq: 2003	71
Chapter 13: Angela and Nera	84
Chapter 14: Angela's Float Session	90
Chapter 15: Peter on 18th Street	96
Chapter 16: The Next Energy Session	118
Chapter 17: Jamie and Angela Connect	124
Chapter 18: Nera's Second Visit	128
Chapter 19: Kilas and Angel Depart	140
Chapter 20: Important Questions to Ask	150
Chapter 21: Jamie and Angela	170
Chapter 22: Inkeri (A Female Viking 876AD)	181
Chapter 23: Inkeri's Fight	191
Chapter 24: Lilith and Merc Revisit	204
Chapter 25: The Coven	210
Chapter 26: Kilas Travels	218
Chapter 27: Samael's Actions	226
Chapter 28: Angela and Lena	230
Chapter 29: The Coven Revisited	233
Chapter 30: The Tattoo	246
Chapter 31: Louis and Nera	248
Chapter 32: The Artifacts Secured	250
About the Authors	255

Chapter 1

The Three Angels

Senoy, Sansenoy, Semangel stood on the hill watching Kilas meet the Green Man. Each wore a stylish black suit, with traditional wingtip shoes. They were muscular and fit, their black wings partially folded.

Senoy said, "Think Lilith will be irate with us?"

Sansenoy smiled, "I hope she is infuriated. It is so lovely to get her all mad and watch her become who she is destined to be. I am not a fan of the nice Lilith. To be frank, I miss the woman whose wrath would devastate civilization and men."

Semangel chimed in, "We can't underestimate what Lilith will do. We did, after all, just mess up plans she has been working on for centuries. She will be pissed at us, just like the first time she met us when she was kicked out of heaven, depending on what version you reference. Remember that first time we all met?"

"I do not ever want to meet that pissed off Lilith again. I have to admit, I was scared of her. Oh how she was a scorned woman." Senoy mock sighed.

Sansenoy laughed, "Well, I so look forward to what will come next. The adventure begins now and we are going to be in so much trouble. So with that possibility, my friends, shall we all have a drink?" Sansenoy pulled out a flask from his coat.

Senoy said, "Well, well, well, is that a little bang bang?"

Sansenoy replied, "You know it is, want some?"

Senoy said, "Well of course. I think the last time we did this was in the 1400s?"

Sansenoy laughed, "Early 1500s, but who's counting. You know this would not feel so revengeful had Lilith not broken your heart. She probably still loves you—but won't after what you just did to her plan. Samael is not a fan of you, either. Lilith might someday have sex with you…but love is out of the picture. You are such a poor bastard; she is going to be pissed with all of us, but especially you. The only good thing you did was help inspire the witches' creed, but then—we crossed the line on that one, too."

Semangel raised an elegant eyebrow, "So, what are we going to do with Nera?"

Senoy quickly responded, "I have a plan to resolve that problem once and for all. It is time to call Jamie into the process. She has been quietly waiting to participate. Having been Paul's secretary for years, she deserves some crumbs off the table. Yes, it is time. The fireworks are really going to happen now. We have been quietly hiding Jamie for too long."

They each took a long swig from the flask. Each wore an identical, unrepentant smile. They all knew what they had just started…

Chapter 2

Kilas and the Green Man

Kilas stared at the Green Man. The Green Man smiled. "How do you do?"

Kilas did not know what to do, so she smiled in her confusion while gripping the dagger. She did not know if this was reality or a dream. The Green Man placed his armful of logs on the ground and reached his hand out. She shook his warm large hand. His hand was strong and engulfed her small hand in its grasp. He did not say his name formally, but just smiled with his whole face. He was a large man and fully green, with the most amazing tattoos on his muscular body. He just asked, "Tea?" Tea was the last thing she thought this large rigid muscular man would offer a woman, but she nodded and said, "Why not. Yes, please."

As Kilas followed the Green Man into his cabin, the three angels, watching from afar, all smiled and pulled their wings out as they started to walk away down the other side of the hill. They looked at each other with grins and started running to let their wings extend and took to the air, sailing like eagles catching a wind gust.

As Kilas followed the strange man into the cabin, she was not afraid, but more curious as she looked around. Then suddenly everything went black, and there was a bright light shining in her eyes and familiar voices speaking nearby.

Kilas said angrily, "What the hell is with the light?"

Her two humanoids, Craig and Greg, looked at her with concern and she blinked her eyes. She recalled that she had just opened a wooden box and found a blade on this barren planet. The blade still glowed slightly on the ground. Her thoughts were bringing her back to reality, where she is a Cardovian pilot on the outer rim, with two humanoid robots as her only companions. Her mind struggled to process what just happened—was it real or an illusion or a daydream? She looked at the foreign engravings on the blade again. For the first time in her life, she had been introduced to another 'green' person, but this man had tattoos that covered most of his body. There was comfort in her mind that there could also be someone else 'green.'

Craig kept asking, "Are you okay Captain? You fainted as soon as you touched that blade. You completely collapsed."

Greg, her other artificial companion, said, "I am still concerned about your health. are you okay? Your eyes are still slightly dilated. Your skin is pale."

Kilas snapped out, teeth gritted, "I will be okay. Just please put the dagger back into its box."

Greg complied, wrapping the blade with the old cloth and placing it back into the original box, securing it.

Kilas got up from the ground and tried to collect her thoughts. She was a pilot, she had fought as a commander for Independence in the Galactic Wars for two years, after the war she chose seclusion to work remote cargo ships in the frontier galaxies; she wanted the freedom of unchartered space. She had been severely wounded in the war, lost the lower part of her leg and foot, leaving her with a slight limp. She walked her own way of life on the outer frontier. She was trying to rationalize what happened. This had to be explained somehow, she kept telling herself. Maybe she fell and hit her head and then passed out and had this wonderful eclectic fascinating dream—or was it real? Her mind was trying to explain what she just saw to prove that it was not or was a reality.

Craig said, "Kilas, do you want to watch the video of what you did while you touched the dagger? I have it right here, right here, please watch; if you want, right here."

Chapter 2: Kilas and the Green Man

Kilas did not want to but she was fully interested in finding some validity to what she thought happened when she touched the dagger. The video was from the pilot's crew seat view from her ship's cockpit, which is always on to cover things that could and did happen in her profession. She reluctantly nodded her head.

Craig smiled and pushed a button on a handheld visual screen. The screen showed her unwrapping the blade, carefully gripping the handle to study the markings. The blade glowed; she remained standing as if in a trance. The clock on the recording had almost two minutes before Craig walked up to her, touched her shoulder, and she collapsed.

She decided to decompartmentalize and think about it later. Right now, she had this special prize—she made her living from finding unique occult magical artifact items which would give her a good price so she could stay out in the frontier; not have to have a normal job in one of the congested planets doing mundane work and living in overcrowded apartments. For security purposes and habit, she always felt her right leg to make sure her side arm weapon was still there, and felt for her left hip to make sure her small knife was still there.

Kilas now remembered her deal with Kobar. She knew that she gave her word to him, which was her ethical bond. She would have to inform him of her findings. She knew she could sell it somewhere else in the galaxy to get a better value over any deal with Kobar, who was a swindler and could not be trusted. She also wanted to keep it herself. There was something about it.

She carefully secured the blade from Craig and took it to her ship. She opened up her hidden safe inside the wall and placed it carefully in the hidden compartment before closing it back up. She recoded the lock so not even her humanoids could open it. Her secret code was JESS. She knew by keeping the code simple, it would make it too complex for her humanoids to figure it out. She knew why she liked the name Jess, because she had fallen in love with a beautiful young woman named Jess many years ago, but they could not be together at that time because it was forbidden. Kilas always hoped there might be a future when they could be together, but she really hoped to just be with anyone who could love her.

She knew she could never share this antique relic with Kobar and that she had to find something else in this terrain to keep him from growing suspicious. She was concerned about the whole situation. She quickly directed her humanoids onto her ship and sat them both down, de-activating both with a secret button on the their chest, before plugging them into her ship mainframe and slowly erasing the last 23 minutes of their memory. Once she was done clearing their so-called brains, or memory, she slowly turned them back on and rebooted them. Both Craig and Greg were brought back to life and said, "So what was that for, a new upgrade? A system upgrade was due?"

She looked at both and she calmly said, "My friends, you are my best friends, and for your own self-security and preservation, I have upgraded your memory to make you better, and deleted unneeded files so that you will be more efficient and much better servants to me. Thank you very much for letting me improve your operating system. You are such excellent companions."

Craig and Greg, both thanked her simultaneously for their friendship.

She felt bad purposefully lying to her humanoids; they were her only true friends, but she knew she must lie and protect them by erasing their memory. She didn't want them to pay for her secret with their existence.

Kilas sat back in her pilot chair looking at her dutiful humanoids. They were truly her only friends. They would give their android lives to protect her, but only because they were programmed that way. Suddenly Kilas felt alone in the galaxy. She had no friends and trusted no one. But, she did not live well in the large cities with so many people and she preferred to have her freedom to roam and explore. She looked back on her collective life and knew that she had been hurt, more than helped, by her so-called friends. The only person she could rely on was herself and she was perfectly okay with that. She was nearly tearful right now thinking to herself how alone she was. This blade was a find of a lifetime. She knew her life's future would depend on keeping the find absolutely secret. There was something about that Green

Chapter 2: Kilas and the Green Man

Man that she must pursue.

She sat in her ship's pilot chair and ran the terrain computer on the local region. She was looking for anything, any other type of relic she could retrieve to give Kobar so he would be pleased with easy money. She was hoping for anything of value, and she knew her computer terrain scanning system was exceptional, and she could find something. Within seconds the computer found something almost seven kilometers away from her current location. She did not know what it was, but knew it was old and odds on that meant it had some value. She plugged in the coordinates on her flight control guidance system and closed the outside hatch. The engines started coming online and she brought the aircraft to a hover and steered it in the direction of her new find. She eased the thrusters online to give her aircraft some momentum. As she did not have far to fly, she just gently let the aircraft slide on top of the air cushion it made on the terrain and cruised toward the new dig site.

She hoped this new artifact would be enough to keep Kobar off the hunt for the precious find that was now stored in her safe on her ship. She landed her ship within 100 meters of the identified dig site. She started to shut down the engines before thinking of her humanoids. She thought she should have them go down first and search for the exact dig site. She told Greg and Craig the coordinates and that she would be outside in a minute. She gave them direct orders to find the proposed object and start digging. She wanted to look at the unique blade alone again, one more time, for a few precious minutes.

She walked to the room where the secure container was and pressed the security code pad and the drawer slid out. She stared at the wrapped package. She knew that this blade was some kind of magical portal to some other dimension or something. And, she knew she had to protect it because she so wanted to go back and continue her meeting with the unique man who was green just like her. As she was about to reach for it, her humanoids pinged in on the radio that they had found the box and requested permission to open it. Kilas said, "Negative Craig and Greg. Wait for me to show up."

Turns out, she did not have time to touch the blade, so she quickly closed the secure container and relocked it so her humanoids could not access it. She got up and put on her holster and jacket and walked outside to check on what Craig and Greg had found for her.

Chapter 3

Lilith and Merc

Lilith and Merc were having lunch in a café in Berlin. It was a fine warm fall day and the clouds and cold weather had not hit the country yet.

Lilith was dressed casually, but stylish as always, and Merc was in blue jeans and his sneakers with hand-painted wings. Lilith hated those silly sneakers and thought it made him look foolish; he probably wore those silly sneakers just to annoy her.

They both had their sunglasses on since they were outside and drinking coffee. Lilith's cell phone went off and she answered.

Merc watched her face flash from happy and content to pissed off, then she slammed her phone on the table, "Those damn stupid angels are meddling in my plans. It's all your fault."

"I do not know which angels you are referring to. For it to be my fault, I need more details. If it is my fault, I will always be honest with you. There are just too many angels. Be more specific, please. Remember my travels between the sides, there are angels on both sides that might be irritated with me. It's just the line of work I'm in." With that comment Merc winked at her and sipped his coffee with his pinky high like the British style, which also thoroughly irritated her.

Lilith rolled her eyes and continued to fume, "Those three knucklehead angels, the ones with the nice suits that can't do anything on their own. Those oldest of ancient angels. Does that bring any clues? They just crossed time between the Green Man and the future warrior. She was not supposed to find it this early."

Merc realized who she meant and nearly spit out his coffee, "They didn't just do that? That messes up our plans that we have been working on with the chosen warrior. That really pisses me off. You know what we need to do immediately?"

Lilith asked, "What?"

Merc grinned, "We need to have some whiskey and cheer for what they just did."

Lilith said, "Are you just the stupidest Olympian god ever? What are you thinking? They ruined everything. Do you have any cognition left in your brain? What the hell are you wanting to have a drink for?"

Merc waved at the waiter and ordered two whiskies in German and the waiter quickened his pace, subconsciously absorbing the sense of urgency Merc conveyed. Within seconds, the waiter approached with two whiskies. Mercury handed Lilith a glass.

Lilith was still upset, "I do not see how you are in a good mood, but it is always charming to have whisky with you on a sunny fall day in Germany. You are still so kind. Okay, now explain."

Merc raised up his glass and wiggled it at Lilith, who rolled her eyes, but had a grin playing on the corners of her sensuous lips as she raised her glass for the formal toast, and Merc said, "To the rules that have been broken by our ancient three angels."

Lilith toasted with Merc and took her whisky in one gulp. "Now will you please tell me what the hell you are talking about."

Merc said calmly, "My lovely, the three angels broke the rules of time travel, because time travel can only be broken for the most important angelic missions—this stunt does not qualify. Talk about hot water—wait until the big boss finds out. She will take away their abilities, and most important, their wings. It will be so beautiful to see them mortal. Then, my sweet Lilith, our other plan will go into effect. You should be happy now, not upset. They lose everything once their wings are clipped. They become human. Then they can't interfere anymore."

Lilith looked at Merc, puzzled, and then she started to smile,

Chapter 3: Lilith and Merc

and slowly grinned at Merc. She looked down at the table, then looked up at Merc and said, "This changes everything. The three angels will not be able to interfere, except for their so-called angel-blood descendant woman. That beautiful child, she is walking around right now not knowing what angelic gifts she has. Does Jamie even have the slightest hint or know what she is?"

Mercury said, "No, that angel-blood woman is really our only unknown, but she has no idea what she is or what she can do. I think she needs a spiritual mother-figure to talk to her and work her charm on her. Maybe you can also use Dr. Angela to help you—remember Angela has that spiritual connection to Joe. Angela needs to connect with you again about that other loose item we have with Joe's untimely death. Remember, those damn mushrooms that he took were psychedelic, but also fatal? He wanted to talk to goddesses, gods, and most of all, you? Remember?"

Lilith smiled, deep brown eyes glowing, "Everyone thinks I am the unholy one, but you, my closest friend, who crosses over the worlds between heaven, the underworld, and the other astral worlds, you my friend are a freaking sneaky bastard. Let's have another whisky!"

"My love, that is why we are such good friends."

Lilith tossed her hair, "You are a historic sneaky bastard that history will never record or know. You non-hero god messenger. I wish someone would write a book about your dealings in both worlds. I would buy it."

They shared another drink and later walked out of the café and hugged one last time, then walked their separate ways and slowly disappeared into the crowds and into their realms, until they meet again.

Chapter 4
Dr. Angela Kapralov

Paul was sitting in a chair across from his therapist, Dr. Angela Kapralov, trying to explain the last couple of weeks of his unusual life following his father's death. Angela was his therapist, but she was also extremely sharp, witty, and sarcastic. Her eyes gleamed with interest as Paul talked, but she kept her neutral professional face through his stories of Lena, the inner temple tale, his friend Robert, his new friend Brynn, and their recent adventure to Scotland and Colorado. What interested her the most were the stories about the athame and Lilith.

Angela was petite and lean, with long brunette hair. She never wore a lot of makeup, but was a beautiful woman. Paul liked to make comments about her dolphin tattoo because, as she sat in front of him with her sandals, he could see it on her foot. Paul was still waiting for the day when she would tell him the entire story about it; she said she got after she received her doctorate, so there had to be a good story.

They had not had an appointment for almost two months, so Paul was on an extended session trying to catch Angela up. They had had a client-patient relationship for over a year, but they also were technically friends. Angela stayed calm and professional, gracefully poised in her leather chair, and taking it all in on everything Paul was saying about how an elegant, elderly person told him to bury this athame in a secret place on top of a mountain

Chapter 4: Dr. Angela Kapralov

in Colorado.

Angela knew that Paul had post-traumatic issues from his overseas combat zone work experiences and had severe bereavement, but they had not talked about his father's death in this session yet because Angela had to catch up with everything else. She was starting to worry about Paul and his new stories, and was seriously wondering if he was experiencing some kind of psychotic break because he was now hearing multiple voices and physically seeing people, or ghosts. He had never mentioned those situations, things, and people in any prior therapy sessions. She could not tell who was real or not in his stories.

Paul had also mentioned a tree of life and an inner temple lake house—classical metaphysical themes with ties to paganism and witchcraft traditions old, ancient, historic, and new. She knew all the references from her own experiences and was curious about his version. Angela had never told Paul that she was a practicing solitary white witch herself. Some things she never told anyone. That fact was one of those closely held pieces of the core of her heart that she would never tell a boyfriend or friends, let alone any clients. She had tried to deny her calling to witchcraft and spirituality as a teenager and her early college years, but during her late twenties she came to fully accept her witch-calling and psychic tendencies, and had been formally initiated four years ago during graduate school. She would never be in a coven publicly or participate in any public rituals because she was a future high-ranking psychologist working for a university hospital, and rumors of witchcraft would not be received lightly—however good of press witch stories were getting from Hollywood.

Angela had only four close girlfriends, who were also highly successful women in male-dominated fields, who knew about Angela being a practicing witch. They had a tight friendship, and her soul was nourished by the time that she could confide with them over bottles of wine in her basement once a month. An informal coven of women of sorts. They all had a story like what Paul was describing to Angela right now.

As Paul kept talking of his initial denial to believing in spirits, gods, past lives, and the metaphysical world, Angela was reflecting to graduate school experiences and was not listening to Paul anymore, as she was remembering her favorite psychology professor confiding in her that he was a witch.

Angela initially denied it, but eventually she agreed to start the process—a year and a day of learning and she would finally be initiated as a witch with several other women. She will always remember that she had to dance around a large fire outside, under the moon, fully naked, while other people in robes watched. She danced naked around the grand bonfire, each initiate and teacher also dancing, a strange mix of individuality and group cohesion. She remembered being in a trance with her spirits and that she was psychically not there, but her body was dancing, a spiritual out-of-body experience. When the dancing, singing, and music was over, everyone cheered in celebration and the initiates put on pure white dresses that they had never worn before, and were all accepted by all who attended.

Angela kept thinking of her initiation as Paul asked her, "Angela, did you hear what I said?"

Angela maintained her professional poise, "Of course Paul, I heard you. I am just comprehending it all. Please continue, I am taking it all in." She had been trained on that line for years with clients because many times her mind would drift when stories were not interesting. Though Paul's story was interesting, his first fifteen minutes of events is what she was still thinking about because it was so close to home to her personally. Angela had also had two so-called spiritual meetings with a woman named Lilith. Angela had met Lilith once when she was experimenting with LSD. A strange gentleman had been with Lilith, but she never got his name. She also had a small meeting with Lilith, which she unremembered when she was doing pot with a horrible past boyfriend she thought she might someday have a future with. Both times the conversations with Lilith were crystal clear, and both times afterward Angela had convinced herself that it was drug induced visions or hallucinations. She had compartmentalized those memories of Lilith for years, until now, when Paul was describing Lilith exactly how she acted, and exactly what she wore, when she had talked with her years ago.

Chapter 4: Dr. Angela Kapralov

Angela was now trying to logically explain her visions and conversations through her thousands of pages of psychology texts and research that she had read throughout her doctoral degree and practice. Now Paul was exactly describing a person she had...spiritually met. In what she had wanted to believe was a dream. This session with Paul validated her experiences which she thought would never be validated, or come up again in her conscious mind. She thought, what are the odds that one of her clients would have a talk with a goddess that was the same one she had within her own mind? How was this possible? There were no coincidences in life, everything happened for a reason, and now Paul was sitting in her office with a link to her personal spiritual psychological past. Angela acknowledged to herself it was time to start digging for the link, whatever it was. But how? She could never have anticipated this new connection with Paul, and it opened up a lot of implications and unknowns across the board.

Angela interrupted Paul, "Why do you think Lilith sought you out?"

Paul stopped to consider, "I do not know. The first time I met her was my first visit to my inner temple. Most of the visits were in my dreams or when I was meditating, but the last visit, she—was absolutely real. Lilith was as real at that national park as you and I are physically real here today. It freaked me out, but she was real. Brynn saw what I saw. Maybe there is a person living and breathing here on earth who is a goddess that looks exactly like Lilith. With everything else happening in my life, absolutely anything is possible."

Angela just sat back with the hair on her arms tingling and standing up and a chill down her back. *How could a goddess be also in human form and how is this possible?* It can't physically happen! This broke most the theories of science, psychology, religion, and physics, and this phenomenon also would validate that the metaphysical folks, psychics, and conspiracists have been right the whole time. That gods have been walking among us.

She quickly remembered as a teenager in the 1980s, when the famous actor George Burns portrayed God in the movie *Oh,*

God!, in which he came to Earth and talked with John Denver to prove that God was real and could be in human form. Could it be that simple? In regard to the movie, God proves that he is real, but as soon as he disappears, everybody goes back to not believing what he just said to them because they could not believe. It was just too much to comprehend.

She then thought of her favorite 90s movie about God, *Dogma*, where God was a woman. Angela just smiled and turned her full attention back to Paul sharing his amazing spiritual story of the past several weeks.

Paul was wrapping up telling about his meeting with the distinguished person at the Garden of the Gods. Paul described the last person he had met on his journey, a classical elderly man, with blue glasses, in an 18th century suit, with a cane, who definitively did not look like he was from around Colorado, but more Eastern Europe. Paul described the man exactly, and Angela was getting chills on the back of her neck and her arms again because she thought she knew exactly who that person was.

The time was getting short and Paul looked at his watch. He apologized for talking almost the entire hour of their session without her getting a chance to give him any intuitive open-ended Socratic questions that always had double meanings. They had more of a friendship than the normal client-patient relationship. Therapists were always going up to the 49 percent rule about guidance, but always allowing the patient to make the 51 percent decisions about their future. Angela was that 49 percent therapist and would guide the patient, but overall, it was the patent's responsibility to heal themselves. If they did not take responsibility for their actions, then they never really got healed, or learned, or recovered from their problems.

Angela told Paul, "Not to worry about the time. Go ahead and schedule another session in two weeks. I look forward to discussing your spiritual and metaphysical experiences more with you."

Paul got up from the chair and thanked her again for her friendship and guidance throughout the last several years of therapy. Angela walked him out and then buzzed him out of

Chapter 4: Dr. Angela Kapralov

the hallway. The clinic had added new security measures for all patients because some were having much more aggressive issues, and they wanted to protect the therapists. The clinic had also placed an armed security guard in the lobby to assure there was security, with a gun, in the building.

Paul walked to the receptionist, who was behind a protective plastic window, and scheduled another appointment with Dr. Angela for two weeks from today, then smiled and walked out the door.

Angela sat in her office watching Paul depart through her outside window. After a few more minutes of staring outside, she turned back to typing the notes of the session which she was required to do. This time, instead of being completely honest on what he said about the athame, Lilith, and Mercury, and their trip to Scotland and Colorado, she purposely left it out of her professional psychiatric notes. She knew there were certain people looking for certain powerful artifacts that she did not trust on the hospital records staff, who might have access to her notes. She was not going to put out notes of it on a database that could be hacked. Angela did personally write in her old-fashioned journal; some things she did not want on a digitalized document that could be searched, traced, or hacked. As she finished the journal writing and was going to return it to the back of her personal drawer, she decided this time to put the journal in her purse so she could take it home to reread tonight. She noticed a small package in aged cloth that she brought to her desk a year ago and had left and had almost forgot it was there. The package was wrapped in blue cloth with a broken seal on it and was tied with old cord. She slowly untied the cloth and unfolded the corners. There was her *Kila* or *phurba,* which was a three-sided stake, or knife, associated with Indo-Tibetan Buddhism with the practice of the yidam or the meditational deity Vajrakila. Angela had had this knife since graduate school when her professor-who-was-a-witch had mailed it to her the night he died.

She had an affair, as a young graduate student, with the professor. Which was wrong and they both knew it, but she was putty in his hands, and she just could not say no to him. His voice made her weak in her knees. Her professor had this psychic ability, developed from the metaphysical theory from Jung's work, which made angels appear and open up her mind. She remembered her first time visiting his house near campus, getting deliciously lost in his thousands of books, and cozy reading chairs, and everything on display from his world travels. It was like having your own library and private museum in a private home. He was truly amazing. Angela had this huge crush and full admiration of her professor; she was in awe of his expertise and his passion for psychology, and especially the occult. He was almost twenty-five years older than her, but he was an attractive 55-year-old man and did yoga and meditation every day to stay in good shape. His energy was electric, and he could just make people happy just by his presence. He was also an energy healer and students were always trying to inquire about his gifts in energy.

    When Angela was about six months out from graduating with her doctorate, Dr. Joe had invited her to come over to his house after dark, where no one would know who came over, and he would introduce her to energy healing. She was so nervous of the process and knew nothing of what was about to happen. His only real comment had been insisting she wear comfortable clothes. He came to the door without a shirt, but with loose yoga pants on. His house was completely dark except for candles. He took her hand and walked her over to his study where he had a massage table in the center of the room. He had sage burning on the side table under a beautiful shell, had calming Celtic music playing, and four candles in cardinal headings. She was so nervous and had never been in quite this situation with her professor, or any professor or older adult, like this. Dr. Joe told her she needed to share a drink of Scottish whiskey with him to work on her throat chakra before they could start. Plus, it would decrease the nerves and anxiety inside her. He poured them both a drink and they toasted for new psychic and metaphysical adventures and drank their small drinks in one swig. The alcohol burned Angela's throat deeply, but it felt good and smooth going down.

    Dr. Joe said, "Please lie on the table and just relax."

    Angela was so nervous, but as he said those words, she felt

Chapter 4: Dr. Angela Kapralov

calmed and ready for this new spiritual experience. Her heart still beat fast. She let her gaze lock onto the ceiling, waiting for Joe to come into view. She lay on the table not knowing what to think or do, but knowing that she just needed to lie down and breathe. She saw him take the sage, still pluming smoke, and walk around the table where she was; she could smell the sweet and natural sage and it was relaxing and comforting to her. Dr. Joe changed some music on his old CD player to some slower mediation music that quickly soothed her soul and calmed her mind.

Joe then identified the cardinal headings with words she could not hear clearly because he was whispering them to himself. He also laid something on the carpet around the table, but she could not see what since she was on the table. Then he was next to the table and took a warm scented cloth and covered Angela's eyes so she could not see. She was blind, she could not see what was happening and she could only anticipate his touch; she waited to hear his voice again. With his first touch, she became electric as soon as he laid both hands on her forehead. He mentioned slowly that he was opening her third eye, but she did not hear fully because she so enjoyed his physical slight touch on her forehead. She had been imagining this moment with him for so long after working with him for three years, and his small touch was electric on her body.

She visioned that she was transported to a meadow on a mountain, and she did not know if there were drugs in his sage or she was vividly dreaming. She wore a white flowing night gown as she walked in an open meadow with mountains surrounding a mountain lake, and then she saw a nice lake house with a huge patio on the lake. There was a group of people talking around a fire pit, so she walked toward the lake house and the people on the patio. As she got closer and stepped on the wooden patio, she could tell that they all knew each other as they were laughing among themselves. Suddenly, a woman turned and walked up to her before she could finish her first step onto the patio. The woman was middle-aged, but so beautiful and she was very kind, "My dear, you have been invited to the inner temple today. We have met before, but never formally introduced."

Angela felt and looked confused, not knowing what an inner temple was, and thought she was for sure dreaming now, or tripping, "I do not know what the inner temple is. Is this my inner dream temple or something? What is this beautiful place? It's incredible."

The woman took her hand softly, "Well, you shall be my guest to this inner temple in which Joe has invited you to share with him and us." There was an instant connection of fondness. Angela immediately liked this woman and felt she was so familiar due to the way she took charge with kindness. She was so attracted to this woman because she was so beautiful and charming. She would go anywhere this woman would lead her.

Angela looked at the woman, "My name is Angela. May I have your name? It feels like we have known each other for years. I believe we have met before."

The woman smiled back, which made Angela weaken in her knees. She moved her lips next to Angela's ear lobe and said, "My name is Lilith. So glad to meet you… again." She then kissed Angela's cheek, which drove her to being slightly lightheaded for this beautiful woman and her intoxicating energy. They walked hand in hand up to the patio deck where the rest of the people had made a circle of lounge chairs around the fire pit. Lilith said loudly and boldly, "Everyone, I need your attention, even you!" as she pointed to one of the men. Everyone looked toward Lilith and this new woman with her.

Lilith then said, "I would like to introduce everyone to Angela. She has been guided to us, for a reason we shall discuss. Now we shall all try and work it out to explain it all to her. But please, give her welcome to our inner temple."

Angela instantly became the center of attention; she felt like she was about to go on stage not knowing how to act. She took a breath and calmed her mind.

Everyone was now so interested in this woman that Lilith had brought to the inner temple. They all started to come over and introduce themselves. Angela met them one by one as if they all knew her and have been waiting for her for some time. The first one was a handsome middle-aged man with a touch of gray

Chapter 4: Dr. Angela Kapralov

hair, but very athletically fit, who wore a pair of gold converse sneakers that had a pair of wings drawn on them with a magic marker. He just said, "You can call me Merc."

Another woman then came up to her and gave her a hug like they were sisters and said, "Angela, just call me Samantha." She wore yoga pants and no shoes and a loose white Celtic shirt. She had so much confidence she did not care, and no one else did, either. Her brunette hair was curly and tangled and all over the place, but was just fun and full of energy.

Angela then met a quiet older man with a trimmed white beard, who simply shook her hand. He was more formally dressed in a suit and well-mannered and just simply said, "It is wonderful to meet you. My name is Sebastian." He had a gentle handshake, with tenderness and strength, and she looked into his crystal blue eyes and was getting lost in those eyes, when another person said, "My turn." There was a distinguished woman named Diana with glasses on and full gray hair in a bun. She wore a white dress that was full length, but flowing on the patio, with no shoes, and she had leather wrist wraps with foreign writing on them.

There were two others, a man and woman who stayed their distance and simply smiled and waved. Lilith came back and took Angela's arm and walked her off the patio, back to where they met. There was a path back into the woods that Lilith elegantly gestured to.

Lilith said, "Angela, this is only a glimpse of the inner world and your temple, but you do not truly seek this temple yet. Joe is only opening the door slightly to introduce you to this other side, or the other light, but you must want to pursue the journey to come back again and you must find another way to get here. It is time for you to awake. I need you to walk back to the present moment where you are receiving an energy session from our dear friend, Joe. Joe needs you to be safe before it is too late." Lilith hugged Angela, who was still confused by everything she just experienced. Angela then started walking on the trail into the woods. She waved back at Lilith and the others on the patio waved back to her.

As Angela was walking into the woods she tripped on a log

and fell. When she tried to get up, she could not. She was lying on the ground looking up into the trees and closed her eyes for no reason.

When she opened her eyes, she was back on the table in the dark living room and Joe was touching her forehead with both hands, chanting something under his breath which she did not understand. She was slightly scared and shocked when she found herself back on the table, and then tried to rationalize what she had experienced. She thought to herself that it must had been a dream or just an active imagination playing tricks on her. There must have been something in the sage…but it felt so real.

Her professor tapped her on the shoulder, assuring she had awoken, and then he said softly into her ear, "How was Lilith? Did you get to meet her?"

Angela looked straight up into Joe's eyes from the table and smiled and thought, how did he know? More important, how did he do this?

Angela thought she was in love with Dr. Joe because she just loved being around him and receiving his knowledge and his wonderful energy. His energy and passion were contagious. She kept thinking about him as she continued her studies, and she had no intention of stopping and was going to keep going and get her doctorate. She looked forward to the next two years working with Dr. Joe and was motivated to be as good as he was.

* * *

After hearing the news that her dissertation proposal was accepted and she could finally move forward into finishing up her degree this semester, Angela was so excited; the first person she was going to see was her beloved professor. As she went into his office there were people crying, and everyone was consoling everyone, and she asked, "Where's Dr. Joe?" and they all looked at the dean of the college; no one said anything, but everyone had tears in their eyes.

Dean Sampson asked Angela to step outside the office into the hallway and he informed Angela that Dr. Joe had died last

Chapter 4: Dr. Angela Kapralov

night. He was found dead, and naked, in his living room on his massage table. It looked like he was doing a ritual of some type. The medical examiner had said he died of natural causes caused by organic toxic mushrooms or something, and his heart just stopped. No one knew of any medical abnormalities that he had. He had dialed 911 himself and said he was dying. When the police showed up, he was already dead. They originally thought it was a suicide, but there is no clear physical evidence. Not your typical death, by any means.

Dean Sampson asked, "Are you Miss Angela Kapralov?"

Angela slowly said, "Yes, I am."

"Dr. Joe left you a letter. It was on his university desk, sealed." He handed the letter to Angela. Dean Sampson continued, "Would you please tell me if there was anything in that letter that would help us to know about his death. I know it's not a comfortable thing, but it could help."

Angela said, "Of course, just let me read it first."

Angela went into the department lobby and sat down in an empty chair. She could hear all the soft crying and the quiet personal discussions. She could tell that no one had expected Dr. Joe's death. One of the women asked who the girl was and the dean said, "Angela was one of Dr. Joe's students." And then the internal conversations went back to the normal death assumptions and rumors on why Dr. Joe had died and how. They were also talking about the condition of the body and how it was found.

Angela slowly opened the envelope with her shaking hands because she could not realize that Joe was gone. She pulled out the letter.

Dear Angela,

I am writing you this letter because I will die tonight, it is hard to fully explain, but you must finish my quest. I have done a quite unpolite thing by giving you this quest without telling you in person, but you were my favorite graduate student throughout my entire academic career. I need you to finish something for me, which I know you can complete. You met my inner temple of my dear spiritual friends and now you must reconnect with them and find another way. Someone who you have not met yet will help you to go back to the inner temple. Only by going back can you find my dearest friend, Lilith, who will assist you. Do not tell anyone of this letter, please burn it when you get home, there are people looking for this letter and something else that I have hidden. There is a second generic letter in this envelope, please give it to the dean (he is a nosy chap) to help with the investigation, but do not give this letter! You can't trust anyone! Do not tell anyone about this letter! I have left you notes along the way to assist and to find other people who will help you. You will receive a package today, there will be another letter in there, please just trust me. You and I were together in three prior past lives and you will learn each of the past lives in time. Trust me in this illogical subconscious nonsensical process.

I love you always like the river, through every past life and this current one.

Love, Joe.

Angela did not know what to do but followed his orders. She put the letter in her purse, but left the other letter in the envelope and gave it to the dean so he would have something to give up for the police investigation. She looked fully distraught, and the dean gave a generic condolence. Angela walked out of the office and the building quickly, her mind confused but focused. She walked into the parking garage and got into her car and drove out to clear her mind and head home in anticipation of the mail.

Angela drove to her townhouse, just a mile from campus, and went straight to her mailbox. There she found a key to a mailbox where the postman puts larger boxes. She took the key to the larger mailbox slot and opened it, and there was a box with her name on it. She looked both ways because now she was suspicious of all people who might be watching her. She had become paranoid since going to the office and receiving the letter. She took the box and quickly carried it into her townhouse and locked the door. She brought it to her dining room table and dropped her keys and purse next to it. She slowly found a letter opener and used it to open the box. A wooden ornamental box sat inside with strange markings and pictographs on it which she did not understand. She opened the ornamental box and found a unique knife...

Chapter 4: Dr. Angela Kapralov

* * *

While back in her private office at the current time, Angela was looking at the same knife, which she had researched was named a *Kila*. She had not thought of Joe in a while and her appointment with Paul had evoked many past emotions. She had compartmentalized his quest because it was still painful how Joe passed away.

She always regretted it, not pursuing the quest immediately, but she needed to graduate and then start her career. And then she was not ready for it even after finally getting comfortable in her first professional job. Maybe Paul's recent visit would restart her thinking on what she should have completed a year ago. She reflected back that the medical coroner never found any foul play in Joe's death. But her intuition thought that there must be a connection between his death, the letter, and the Kila. Maybe now was the time, and Paul could help her find Lilith again. She felt a longing for spiritual time with Lilith…

Chapter 5

The Cemetery Visit

As Paul was leaving Dr. Kapralov's office, he felt called to drive the 30 miles to visit his father's grave. As he drove to the rural Catholic cemetery, he relived the past couple of weeks of metaphysical adventures and his recent visit to Scotland. What a revelation had occurred in his mind. As he eased the truck up to the family plot, he could see the fresh ground still settling over his father's remains. He parked his truck and walked out to the pathway that led to the family plot of tombstones. He wanted to talk to his father alone.

He walked up to his father's plot and looked solemnly at the tombstone. Paul realized that it had been two months, almost to the day, that he had died. "Dad, there has been a lot of stuff happening, but it is all for the good. I will remember everything you have told and taught me. I promise to be a good man, too, like you. You raised me well. Thank you."

He knelt down and patted the tombstone. He saw a family also visiting, but their gravesite was much more recent because it was still piled high with fresh dirt. The burial must have happened in the last couple of days. There were two parents, and he guessed a daughter in her early 20s. It seemed to be a brother and son that had passed away. He felt sadness for that family. The pains of his father's death were still fresh. It seems death has a way of eventually winning all the time and no one gets to live forever.

Chapter 5: The Cemetery Visit

He looked back down at his father's tombstone, stood up, and then walked over to his truck to depart. He opened the door and got in. He turned the key on to start his truck, remembering the last time that he had seen his father alive. His father had been in the hospital for a couple weeks and had just been diagnosed with Alzheimer's. His dad did not know himself. But the doctors had informed Paul he was in a wheelchair with a red bracelet on his left wrist which said "flight risk." He was 87 years old, how far could he go with his wheelchair, Paul wondered. His dad's mind had been coming and going in their last conversation. The doctors told Paul that he tried to leave last night because the Viet Cong were after him for what he had done to a village during the war. This fully convinced the staff of his state of mind.

The doctors were concerned with him committing suicide or doing some damage, but Paul had to explain that his father was a south Vietnamese advisor and taught soldiers how to kill the enemy. Paul was sure these vivid combat traumatic images were coming through as he was fighting against the disease in his mind. He himself had felt the same way after going to multiple combat areas in the world and had had too much of the multiple horrors of war. There was always a true madness of killing another human being. Once you get used to killing, it becomes like cleaning the toilet and had no effect on the brain anymore. In combat, you had to be strong, because the weak would always be killed. The strong survive, the darkness will always be darkness, and once you have lived in the darkness, you find your way through the darkness of death. Everyone is afraid of the journey through the darkness, even scared to go there, but once you have gone to horror and returned, it is only a temporary thing, and you know your way out. The thing is, the consequences of walking through darkness has its toll on the mind. One too many trips can reformat your own thinking and make you numb. There were always unique characters he would meet on his mental trips.

As Paul was coming back to the reality of the present, the young woman walked over to him, "Sir, did you recently lose a family member?"

Paul nodded his head yes and smiled sadly back to the young

woman.

The young woman said, "You know he is in heaven, your father."

Paul said, "Thank you, I think he is in heaven also, but how do you know?"

The young woman walked closer to Paul and slowly grabbed his hand through the window of the truck and looked into his eyes, "Well sir, he told me, and he wants you not to fuss or worry about him."

Paul held her hand and kissed the top of it and with full tears in his eyes he said, "Thank you for telling me that, but how did you hear from him? Do you hear spirits and voices, too?"

The young woman said, "Yes, I can hear the other side and spirits, but please do not tell my parents. They do not know that I have this special gift. They are very Catholic and would not understand. They would misinterpret the voices from angels as from demons. My priest knows and he tells me they are secret messages between God and I, and that I should not tell anyone because it could lose its meaning in society and this small community."

Paul smiled at her, "Do not worry, I also hear voices from the other side. You should also think of the idea of gods and goddesses and not just a singular god. It makes it easier for me to communicate with the voices."

She smiled back and started walking back to her parents and said aloud, "The black-haired woman in the dark sunglasses is still looking for you. She will come back with more power and more anger very soon." She smiled and waved and walked up to her parents and they got into their car and started to drive away. The young woman pointed in a direction and winked to Paul before she got in the car.

Paul knew Nera was the woman in sunglasses, and also knew Nera would approach him once again, only further angered from being thwarted at their last meeting. But he knew now that he had the advantage with the help of his spiritual friends that had intervened that night in his backyard. He hoped he would be just as lucky next time.

Chapter 5: The Cemetery Visit

As Paul was waving at the young woman, she smiled and yelled, "You will win again. There are new alliances and friends coming to aid you for this new challenge. Do not doubt yourself. You will have so much fun and adventure." She waved and smiled a sweet smile that makes your heart warm. Paul just sat there in dismay at how visiting his father's grave led to running into another spiritual clue for the future. Paul just smiled and turned on the engine. He rubbed his howlite bracelet that Nera gave him, which he initially did not like, but was now accustomed to its additional power to his spiritual connections.

As he looked at his truck engine lights and began to shift his truck to drive, he knew he was going to face new challenges. He felt reassured that he would receive new friends and new alliances that would support him. He thought that if he still had Merc and Lilith by his side he would be fully protected. As Paul put the truck into gear and started to pull away from the cemetery parking lot, he looked in his rearview mirror, always looking for someone to be watching him. He had become more aware of people watching or observing him, because now there were entities, and spirits, and people who were looking for him due to the athame. The elderly distinguished man had told him to be careful, because there were others looking for the athame, and when he truly needed assistance, all he needed to do was to request help and he and others would be there soon. It was a reassuring comment after taking so much risk in protecting the athame.

Paul just smiled and looked at himself in the mirror and said, "You are too paranoid, relax a little."

Just as he did so, a white sports car came roaring down the street. The sports car screeched to a halt within a foot of his truck. The engine roared and Paul knew it was Nera. The car door flew open, and Nera stepped out with her large dark sunglasses, a tight black dress, and high heels, and she sauntered toward Paul who was sitting in his truck. "Paul, you will tell me where you put the athame. I need it. You may have won last month, but now I will make the playing fields more equal. You can't win this time. The friends you think you have, really are not. You are being played for a bigger prize, you just do not know it."

She looked at the howlite bracelet, remembering that she gave it to him to connect with the athame. She realized something and then looked straight into Paul's eyes. "Paul, this is not over. We have unfinished business and there are still things you do not know. Be careful. You do not need to fear me, but the one who comes after me, for they are more dangerous than I can ever be. My curse will be released from me one way or another. I promise you that." She looked down and then smiled, "I have missed you." She gave him a wink and kissed his cheek, then walked back to her sports car and waved like nothing happened. Then she screeched out of the cemetery.

Paul sighed long and calmly smiled, and shook his head. He looked over at his father's tombstone, "You never prepared me for this." As he talked to himself, he put his truck into drive and a blue jay landed on his father's tombstone. He suddenly felt calm, because blue jays are signs of family spirits and angels. He smiled a full smile and knew he had entities, spirits, gods, and probably some haphazard ghosts giving him advice and protecting him. He drove out of the cemetery feeling more relaxed and confident. He truly believed in synchronicity, that everything happens for a reason and there is no luck or coincidences.

Chapter 6

Nera's Call

As Nera departed the cemetery, she knew she needed more assistance in this magical and metaphysical revenge. Samael had helped her in the past and she owed him, well, she had made a loyalty to him like a contract. The agreement always sounded more like a mob thing, "I will do this for you today, but someday, I might need your help on something, and I will ask you to return this favor" type of agreement.

Nera drove to her townhouse and went into her office. She pulled out her crystals and stones so she could establish her circle. She wanted to communicate with Diana. Meeting Paul had flustered her, let alone how upset she was about having to keep this curse, which she did not deserve. She had only been doing the dirty work for the angels, gods, and goddesses in her past lives and never by her choice.

She lit her candles and placed her crystals on the floor in the four cardinal directions, chanting for each direction before sitting on the floor cross-legged and putting her hands together to pray. She pulled out her blue amulet from under her shirt and held it between her hands. She prayed to enchant Diana or Samael to speak to her and give her guidance.

There was no answer. Frustrated, she called out to them again and no answer. She closed her eyes, "If you two will not call to me, maybe I should pray to other gods who actually care!"

All of a sudden, the room chilled and candles flickered and Samael walked in, "That's not the best approach to ask to talk. Do you need a lesson on spiritual manners, my dear?"

Nera pouted, "I just wanted to talk to you and receive guidance on what I am supposed to do next. I do not know what to do and it's driving me crazy."

Samael sat across from her on the floor, crossed his legs like her, and looked straight into her eyes. He kept silent for a moment to irritate Nera some more because she wanted communication immediately. She was such a snot.

He said, "Why don't you become what your instincts and past lives say you are? Why do you not have the courage to do what needs to be done? Your immaturity and indecision are getting tiring. It's time to play the final game."

Nera looked back scornfully at Samael, "I seek the courage to do what needs to be done, but I have trouble hurting the people that I still love. I still have strong feelings for Paul, I mean, William in the past. I regret murdering him multiple times in our past lives. I want to do what needs to be done again, but I can't find the courage to be that evil and dark again. There is still goodness inside me. You have not scraped it all out of me. I am still weak, so help me. Show me the way again."

Samael said with a devilish grin, "You will find the way, because the curse is continuing and will enter your dreams more and more now, since you failed the mission. You must find the athame. I assume you have secured the other artifacts out of the warehouse, because they were not there when I went looking for them. You must know that Angela has the sacred Kila. Befriend her. Use her. Get the Kila. There is another woman now in the picture, whose name I do not know, who you need to be worried about. She is more powerful than we both know, but she does not know her power yet, so don't waste time. Angela is the most important key right now; this you can't fail. Do what you must to connect with her. Use all your so-called charm."

Nera said, "What can I do to break the curse now that the athame is gone?"

"There is nothing you can do until someone uses that or

Chapter 6: Nera's Call

another magical instrument on you to hurt you. That person must also be an innocent. Only when that happens, are you released from the curse."

Nera said, "Paul would never hurt me. Just like last time. Someone will always come in and change his mind."

Samael said, "If someone is going to hurt you to release the curse, it has been foretold that it will be a woman. I have visioned it. I want you to close your eyes and think of how to create a plan and what your actions will be when you find it. Then open your eyes again once complete."

Nera closed her eyes for a few minutes and thought of a way. When she opened her eyes, Samael was gone. She wondered if he was actually here or just her imagination. It really did not matter, because she knew what she had to do.

She got up from the floor, picked up her crystals, blew out the candles, and put everything away. She walked over to her bar, poured herself a glass of Malbec, and sat on her couch and pulled out her journal. Her cat, Tabitha, jumped up with her and snuggled next to her leg.

Nera drank some wine as she tried to compose her journal statements. She always wrote in her journal when she needed to analyze her options and thoughts. She wrote about what Samael said and what she agreed to. The last words she wrote were, *Paul needs to feel my pain, but not death yet. I must break the curse in this lifetime. I must.* She put her journal on the coffee table and grabbed her wine. She talked with Tabitha and petted her slowly for comfort. She laid down on her couch and cuddled with Tabitha and brought down a blanket from the side arm.

Within minutes they were both asleep on the couch. There was a chill in the air again. Tabitha woke up and saw a stranger in the room and jumped off the couch to quietly go to the next room. A woman was standing over Nera, looking at her, and shaking her head. She touched Nera's forehead without waking her up and smiled, "My sweet, you will do what you must do for us. There is no turning back now. You will not hurt Paul yet, but you will try... and you will kill another innocent woman." She then walked out of the room and disappeared.

Chapter 7

Kilas Continues (Scrolls and Scarabs)

As Kilas moved her ship to the new finding a few kilometers away, Craig and Greg got the equipment ready and waited for Kilas to find a safe landing area for their ship. Kilas said, "I found a good spot to park, get ready to depart immediately."

Craig and Greg were ready by the exit doors as Kilas's landed was slightly rough. Greg pushed a button to open the landing door so both droids could exit the ship and secure the area before she came out. Kilas shut down the engines and pulled out the tracker device to find the next artifact their computer had identified. She walked off the ship with her goggles on and her weapons out. She started walking toward their new dig site and Craig and Greg followed to protect her. Her tracker was beeping and soon was at a steady tone.

Kilas stopped walking, "Start digging here."

Craig and Greg started to dig and within a few minutes found a solid sound, which meant they had found a box. Craig and Greg felt for the edges of the metal box and used their fingers to move dirt away from the box so they could pull it up out of the ground. They found a grip and handles and pulled it out and put it next to

Chapter 7 : Kilas Continues (Scrolls and Scarabs)

the hole. The box was metal with stencils on it that looked like military names. The stencil said, "Property of U.S. Government. Top Secret" on the sides and top.

Craig said, "The box has been welded shut and we will need to get the blow torch to cut it open. Someone did not want us to find or open this box."

Kilas was now intrigued by what was so close to the other artifact, but was more secure. She kept wondering when this box was secured and why it was buried so close to the other artifact. She thought that it was mere coincidence, but in her line of work, nothing was coincidence and everything was connected. She heard Craig turn on the blow torch, but Kilas stopped him and wanted to examine the large metal box and the stencils on the box one more time. She got on her knees and looked at the stenciling and noticed that the cover was welded shut. No one does that unless they want to make sure no one gets in the case. Kilas said, "Greg, pull out the x-ray sensor. Let's make sure what is inside of the box. Then if safe, we will cut it open."

"Affirmative." Greg departed back to the ship and came back with an x-ray sensor. They moved the box, placed the x-ray machine, and looked at the video screen to see what was inside. Kilas asked, "What does that look like?"

Greg said, "I think it looks like a scroll, several scrolls. The computer says it's a paper product, but papyrus and old. There is a smaller box inside which the camera can't see what it is inside."

Kilas said, "Okay, Craig, cut it open."

Craig turned on the blowtorch again. When the seals were cut open, he turned the torch off and picked up the top of the metal box and lifted it off. There was a breath of air inside that quickly escaped into the desert. Kilas, Greg, and Craig looked inside and saw the scrolls. They were in good shape. Kilas noticed a small wooden box. There were no markings on it at all, but the wood was brittle. Kilas reached down and picked it up. As she was holding it, something inside of it moved which surprised her. Could something be alive in this small box? "Greg, put the sensor over this wooden box. Let's see what this is?" Greg put the sensor on it and the screen showed a bug, like a scarab, moving. How is it still alive? It's a bug.

Kilas said, "Let's not open this until we do more research on it. Bring the other box into the ship and let's do an initial analysis of the scrolls. We might have something to give up so we can depart this simple planet."

Craig and Greg placed the box inside the ship and let Kilas look at the manuscript scrolls. She looked at how brittle they were and was afraid to pull them open because they could fall apart, so she thought to call an expert on this type of thing. She knew that conversation would be monitored by other organizations and it might cause more people showing up looking for other items. This conversation could drop the pebble that starts a chain of events that could be her ticket out of here.

Kilas knew she needed to contact Kobar before she brought attention to this sector. Attention to his domain might upset him, but he could be interested in profit by all the visitors and their requirement for food, gas, and entertainment. She decided to call him first and let him know that she kept her promise to tell him if she found anything. She walked up to the cockpit and turned on the electricity for a video call. After several seconds, Kobar answered, "What do you want—oh, hello Kilas! Did you find anything?"

Kilas said, "I found some old scrolls and something I am afraid to open because it is moving inside the box. I wanted to let you know about it and wanted to communicate on high frequency with a scientist that I know who might know what it is. I wanted your permission first, because I assume other organizations might be listening to the unsecure interstellar communication. I know you like your privacy, but I also know you like to make a profit from visitors."

Kobar said, "I want you to bring the artifacts to me and I want to look at them myself. I might have a woman here who works for me that could decipher what it is. Bring it to me now. Do not talk to anyone. Do not let anyone know. Let Angel look at them. She is a spiritual witch—or she claims to be. I have known her since she was a teenager and she knows antiquities." He leered at her then hung up.

Chapter 7 : Kilas Continues (Scrolls and Scarabs)

Kilas told Greg and Craig to get the ship ready to go back to port so they could show Kobar what they uncovered. The two humanoids did what they were told. They sat in the pilot's chairs and got the ship ready and the engines on. When everything was ready, they asked Kilas if they had permission to depart. She said, "Affirmative. Fly her nice and slow. We are not in any hurry." The two humanoids flew the aircraft back to the station, where Kobar was waiting for them on the landing pad. He had a security force of four soldiers with him, which Kilas thought was curious. The aircraft landed safely, the ramp was lowered, and Kobar entered the ship with his security force. "Where are the scrolls and the case?"

Kilas pointed to the open case. The soldiers quickly picked it up and departed with it. Kilas was upset with this treatment and knew she needed to take a stand. "Where are they taking it? Where is my cut of the profits?"

Kobar said, "Once we know what it is, we can discuss the financial arrangements.

Now please, tell me exactly where you found it."

Kilas quickly asked Greg to give Kobar and his assistant the exact quadrants and grid where the box was found and recorded. Then Kobar looked at Kilas and asked, "Did you find anything else?"

Kilas said, "That is what we found. And as I promised, I informed you first when we found it."

Kobar told the assistant he had to plug into the droids and ask them the same question. He knew humanoids were programmed not to tell any lies. The assistant said, "The humanoids only know about the scrolls. I searched their database and Kilas is telling the truth."

Kilas asked, "Kobar, you don't trust me?"

Kobar said, "I do not trust anyone. That is why, and how, I have survived so long on this planet." He moved his hand to listen to his earpiece, "They are taking it to my witch, Angel, for authentication. What you found could be valuable The initial tests estimated it at 5,000 years old. You have done well, Kilas. Thank you for your honor and keeping your promise."

Kilas had no idea of the importance of the scrolls, but if it took Kobar off the scent of the knife that had transported her to the Green Man, that was really all she wanted. She wanted to explore, again, the man who was green like her. She knew that the knife had special powers and just wanted to get off this planet to touch it and meet the Green Man again. There was something special about meeting him and about her identity. She had never met anyone else green like her in her natural life, and maybe it was some portal for her to meet another green person. Kilas asked, "Could I see the scrolls and meet the witch? I have never met one before?"

Kobar said, "I do not know why you would want to meet Angel. She's a strange one. Never much to say, but go ahead. No one has ever requested to meet her. I do not mind. You did bring in the scrolls for me and it's the least I can do. She is in the basement on the east wing of sector twelve. There will be a guard at the door."

Kilas left the room knowing that Kobar was happy with the discovery. He wasn't really interested in what the witch said, but was now looking toward the future and how much he could sell the scrolls for. Kilas continued with the directions, now interested in meeting a true self-proclaimed witch. She had always been interested in the legends of witches, but had never met one. She really had never been given the opportunity to meet one in her life, so she took the opportunity. Maybe she could ask some discreet questions about green men, and portals, and blades without raising any suspicion. She walked down the corridor Kobar said the witch was located and found a lazy old guard sitting in front of the door. She approached him and said, "Kobar said I could visit the witch."

The guard only waved at her to open the door and she walked into the room where she assumed to find an old woman in a cloak. She was surprised to find a young attractive brunette reading the scrolls on a desk, in a room that was comfortable and with many books along the walls. It was not what she expected to see when she thought of meeting a witch. The woman looked up from reading the scrolls and asked, "May I help you? I am kind of

Chapter 7 : Kilas Continues (Scrolls and Scarabs)

busy."

Kilas said, "I was the one who found the scrolls and the other box that had something move in it. I was curious what you transcribed and wondered if you opened the small box. I was too afraid to open up the small box because I thought it was alive."

The woman said, "My name is Angel and you must be Kilas. Yes, I am a witch, but not what you normally think. I am an expert in antiquities and actually an expert researcher. But, I am on loan to this place for several months of every year. I am in debt with Kobar and he is letting me work it off. You are the first person in months to find any valuable relics. How did you find this piece? Please tell me the details."

Kilas walked closer to her and sat down on the stool next to her and watched her look at the scrolls and said, "I have good sensory equipment, slightly modified. Digging up antiquities helps me pay the bills when the shipping business slows down. Do you know what the scrolls are?"

Angel said, "They are around 5,000 years old and it's amazing the papyrus is still intact. I would have thought the paper would have disintegrated with the air, but they are holding together. I am unable to unroll them because they will fall apart, but I'm hoping my instruments help read the writings. I am about to take the first photos if you want to watch and help?"

Kilas said, "Sure, I would like that." As Angel was moving around the table, gently moving the scrolls to take a photo with her equipment, Kilas noticed a bar code on her neck. She thought that was peculiar because only non-humans were tagged with the barcode tattoo. Angel's outfit was simple and most of her skin was covered. She wore work overalls that were loose on her. Kilas also noticed two scars on Angel's wrist. That could mean she was injured severely, or she tried to commit suicide, which was against the code in this sector, because they were too short of humans for reproduction to keep ahead of the humanoids and machines. She wondered internally what this backstory of Angel was, but for right now needed to find out more about the scrolls.

Angel moved the scanner over the rolled scrolls slowly and in multiple directions to capture as many scans as she could. After a while she said, "I am going to turn off the lights and do an ultraviolet look." Kilas acknowledged and Angel turned off the lights and then turned on the purple light. The scrolls seemed to be glowing. Angel ran the light over the paper trying to find any hidden writings that could not be seen with the naked eye. Angel said, "It looks like there is blood on the scrolls. You can see with the ultraviolet light...that is interesting. Like these were being protected and there was harm to a human because you can see the splatter on the paper." She pointed out the small dots of color to Kilas. "Tell me, Kilas, what else did you find out there in the desert? Was this the only thing you found today?"

Kilas said, "Yes, this was all that I found. You can even ask my humanoids."

Angel said, "This will stay between you and me, but I checked your humanoids. They have no recollection of any other findings because their memory had been erased for twenty-three minutes today. Do you know how that could have happened? Do not worry, I have not told Kobar. But personally, I am interested in what you found that was so precious that you would wipe out the memory of your most trusted humanoids."

Kilas went pale and did not know how Angel could have known unless she was also a humanoid. She tried to deny it, "Angel, I do not know what you are talking about."

Angel said, "Okay, we can play your little game. But I just want to know the truth. I am not what you think I am, working in this shit hole. I am much more and I know how to keep secrets and never tell. I have many secrets myself. But I am also a witch and practitioner of what some people call the dark arts. I prefer to call them the natural arts of the universe. You never know, you might want a witch as a partner in your future." She winked at Kilas.

Kilas smiled, "Thank you. I will consider that." She thought it over and needed to ask her something before she could trust her. Her intuition told her to trust this woman, even though she just met her, and it was not logical. But her heart told her to trust her, too. There was something there that she knew could be trustworthy. Kilas asked, "May I ask you a question?"

Chapter 7 : Kilas Continues (Scrolls and Scarabs)

"Yes, anything."

"What is the bar code on your neck?"

Angel smiled, "That? Well, I was a young soldier, or really a spy, about ten years ago in the Sand War in the Qualich sector. I was only fourteen years old and both of my parents had been murdered in the war. I was too young to fight, but could pass through enemy lines and find secrets because I was smart. I was so young that no one was suspicious of me. But, one day I was caught and I was caught by young, thin Kobar, not the sloth that he is now. He caught me, but instead of turning me into the prison where I would die, he worked me and I became his pet spy, playing both sides to his profit. The bar code tattoo was his idea. No one would question humanoids as possible spies, so he did it to me. I acted like one to make it out alive for the years that I worked for Kobar during the wars. Some of his friends abused me, but he never did. He has a heart somewhere in that unhonest body of his. He is a bastard and I never trusted him, but he helped me survive. I portrayed a humanoid, but was a real girl. I had to play the role just to keep living. I still return here every year for a few months of free work to keep the charade up and to watch over Kobar. He does not trust anyone, but he does slightly trust me. Everyone here talks freely in front of humanoids because they are not afraid of being rat on. So even though the war is over, I am still a spy, but more of an internal spy for Kobar. But he pays off my debt well, so I can do my real passion, which is spirit work, or what some call, witch work."

Kilas was lowering her guard, "So, are you being a spy right now with me to get Kobar secrets?"

Angel smiled, "No. You see, from the moment you came here, I knew you and I were connected spiritually. I can feel it and it has only happened a few times in my life. But you seek something which you need help with. I am not afraid of your beautiful green skin; you are one of the most beautiful women that I have ever met or seen. I know I am making you blush inside, and you are not used to words of flattery, but it comes from my soul, so it is true. I want you to trust me because I know there is something you are hiding." She walked over to Kilas and touched her hand with both of hers, which made Kilas shorten her breath. She took her hand and put it palm up onto her heart and whispered, "Can you feel that I am human? Can you feel my heart?"

Kilas was blushing and somewhat lightheaded. She could feel Angel's heart pounding, but it was like a trance, and she was now looking into her cold green eyes and getting lost. Kilas had not felt like this for years. She had not felt another human being in many years. She had not had human touch in so long. Angel moved closer to Kilas's face, and was getting closer to her lips when a beep went off on her desk and the results were coming back. Their moment was broken, but not forgotten. They both looked at the printer sending out the report. Angel let go of Kilas's hand and walked over to the printer. She walked over to her desk drawer and pulled out her glasses so she could look more thoroughly. She had a puzzled look on her face.

Kilas said, "What does the computer say?"

Angel said, "The language is not in our recorded history. It seems to be a new language that has never been recorded. That does not make sense. It has to be recorded. There is no reason that the location you found this could have any historical significance. This place is nothing. There has been nothing here in thousands of years." She looked over at Kilas and said again, "Is there anything else you found out there in the desert? I must know."

Kilas walked over to her and looked at her eyes and kissed her on her lips for several seconds. Then there was silence if they should continue or stop temporarily. She gently put both of her hands on Angel's face, looked into her eyes, and kissed her one more time and said, "I will trust you because it feels right. There was something else that I found, but it is on my ship and you must go to my ship to look at it. I will not bring it here. It is a portal that can transfer you to another world. It is a knife or a dagger that glows when I get close to it. I will show you because I trust you right now. But if you cross me, I will kill you painfully, because I never trust anyone."

Angel kissed her back with the last statement and whispered into her ear, "I trust you and I will never betray you. Please show me the object…now if possible. Let's not look anxious as we

Chapter 7 : Kilas Continues (Scrolls and Scarabs)

walk to your ship."

First thing, Angel secured the scrolls carefully into a vault and tapped the code into the digital safe. They walked out normally and headed toward Kilas's ship. They talked minimally, trying to not show any affection between the two of them as they walked side by side; wanting to touch each other again, but they had to keep their physical emotions and facial reaction normal as they continued to walk through the hallways to Kilas's ship. They entered the hangar and the two security guards looked at Kilas and Angel as they walked in. Angel told the guards she was ordered by Kobar to search the ship one more time. The guards knew Angel and waved them onto the ship and continued their conversation.

As they walked into the ship and were finally alone, completely alone, they dropped the backpack and kissed each other again, which was revealing passion inside both of them that had been suppressed. Their kisses were passionate and caring, and they started to giggle, trying not to get caught kissing. They both knew they had crossed the line emotionally and were committed to each other's mission. They just knew that they were committed to each other.

They stopped kissing and Kilas said, "Let me show you what else I found in the desert." She took her hand and walked her to the hidden safe. She opened the safe and pulled out the cloth that had wrapped the dagger and she put it on the table. She slowly opened it up and exposed the knife to Angel. Angel looked at it without touching it and Kilas said, "Don't touch it, because it takes you to the Green Man. That is what it did for me. It transported me to another dimension or time. It is still hard to explain."

Angel looked up to Kilas, "Let's do it. If we hold hands while you touch it, do you think it will take both of us?"

Kilas said, "I do not know. It scared me on the first trip, but it felt so real. It must have been real. I saw this beautiful green man. But then my humanoids, Greg and Craig, interrupted me and I was brought back and did not even have time to talk with the Green Man."

Angel said, "I have researched these portals in ancient texts, but have never actually seen one. Can we try to travel together? We have nothing to lose. I have heard time in the present does not change as time changes through the portal."

Kilas did not know the answer but said, "We can try it together if you want to. I do not know what will happen. That is why I did not tell Kobar and erased the memories from my humanoids. It was just something too complicated to comprehend. I did not know what to do but to keep it secret until I understood it better."

Angel said, "Please, let's try it together." The dagger was on the table unwrapped, waiting for them to make a decision. Angel grabbed Kilas's hand and smiled and said, "I trust you with my life. I have waited for you to enter my life for years and have visions of you coming into my life. So I trust the synchronicity of this moment."

Kilas felt the same way, but did not know how to say it back. She only tightened her grip with Angel and touched the blade....

++++

...In an instant, they were both next to the cabin by a lake where she had left the Green Man. They were still holding hands. They looked at each other in disbelief. They had transported to another plane, or dimension, or time.

Angel said, "It actually happened. I have never experienced anything like this."

Kilas said, "Follow me. I think we shall have some tea."

They knocked on the door and the beautiful Green Man, without a shirt, opened the door and smiled at both.

The Green Man said, "You disappeared, but I assumed you would be back soon. You brought a friend with you. You are both welcome into my home and I shall protect you against any evil. I give you my word. Would you like some tea?"

Kilas and Angel looked at each other and continued to hold hands as they walked into the Green Man's cabin.

Chapter 8

Kilas and Angel

Kilas and Angel walked hand in hand into the Green Man's cabin. He walked outside as if he was looking for someone else to show up, and then came back inside and locked the door behind them.

The cabin was warm and had natural light streaming through a large southern window. The Green Man had dark black tattoos all over his skin, and was muscular and quietly confident, with his long black hair with shades of gray coming through. He walked over to the fireplace where he had some water boiling. He grabbed the water and prepared three cups for tea. Angel and Kilas still stood holding hands and just watched the gorgeous Green Man make them tea, which was the last thing they expected from such a warrior-like person. The Green Man said, "Please sit down by the table and we shall talk once I finish everything here with the water and the tea."

The Green man said, "Would you like some sugar in your tea?"

Angela and Kilas both looked at each and said, "Yes."

The Green Man came back with a wooden tray with three cups of tea to serve. He handed each one their tea and said, "It is hot, be careful."

Kilas said, "Thank you for your kindness, but we have a question for you."

The Green Man said, "Your question is where are you and

how is this possible? Is that close?"

Kilas smiled back at him, "Yes. What is this place and are we here in our imagination? And, how is this possible?"

Angel said, "Are you the fabled Green Man who journeyed up the great mountain to find and save your teacher? You also found the great evil one, but did not pursue. Our group worships your story on your honor and patience. Your legend tells that you protect the trees, the forests, and the animals. It's still in the ancient text which are currently outlawed by political parties to read, but is now only passed along by people through stories and folklore. Our current politics do not want critical thinkers."

The Green Man said, "I will answer your questions in order. The first question is, where are we? We are in a spiritual mutual place and the athame is a portal to this inner temple, only accessible to a few people because it is also magically protected. But the athame, also, can go to another inner temple through the woods. Time is parallel. The future, past, and present all move together in circles and sometimes they cross lines, which is happening right now. Time in the physical world has slowed down so you can be here with me in my inner temple. We are also in each other's minds right now. You are here in this inner temple because you needed to come to this secret place where I am. And only here the other gods and goddesses can't get to you, or listen to this conversation. This is a secret and magically protected spiritual place. You have had many past lives through your ancient soul with Angel, and there is unfinished work from a past life which you are destined to finish in your present life with Angel. I know that is a lot for the first answer, but you have always known that you are more than what you are. You have that old soul and you see things differently. You were meant to meet Angel today and you both are meant to be here together, because we will need both of you to complete your quest in this lifetime. You instantly knew each other at first sight, like you have known each other your whole life. That is because you have multiple past lives together and you are spiritually connected. You have finally met and will be together for the rest of your lives. I guess I should not have told you your future, but you already feel it."

Chapter 8: Kilas and Angel

Angel and Kilas squeezed each other's hands and Angel said, "I felt it immediately. As soon as she walked in my office today."

The Green Man said, "You two will get closer, but you are destined to be together. In addition, your talents will complement each other." The Green Man took a breath, closed his eyes, and opened them and said, "In regard to the second question; I am who you regard, but I will talk more details at a later time. Yes, it all happened as you have heard and have spoken. My teacher, when she died, gave me her powers and transferred them with her tattoos. That is why I have all these tattoos. I helped my village for many years after being banished for something that I did not do. I traveled the world before returning to my village to build a school. One day, I was spiritually called to leave my village and come here and build this cabin to await the person who I will help, and eventually teach and train to carry on my legacy. You two are the warriors that I will teach. You both have been chosen."

There was a knock on the door. The Green Man placed his index finger on his lips, a signal for quiet. He got up from the table and walked over to the wall and picked up an axe that was mounted. He opened the door and walked outside to see three angels in black suits, with their wings exposed, who he knew too well.

The Green Man walked outside with his ax on his shoulder with full confidence. He said, "So, who has ordered you three to cross over the forbidden boundary and come and disturb me while I am having tea with guests. You know you can't be here; it is against the code. I am protected, and this realm is protected. You three have some nerve."

The three angels were just standing there staring at the Green Man. Senoy, the oldest of them, said, "We are the ones who started the chain of events that assisted Kilas to find the athame in which brought her to meet Angel, and then brought her to finally meet you here and now. You see, we are the ones behind this plan, because we need some permanent changes around the house. We would like new management, if you know what we mean. We are here as outlaws who have broken the code and other things, all to achieve change. Sometimes a revolution is good for everyone, except for those in absolute power."

The Green Man smiled, "Thank you for being honest. I was a bit perplexed because I did not have visions of this happening, but now it makes more sense. So, tell me, what do you need Angel and Kilas to do for your revolution?"

Angel and Kilas were huddled under a window trying to keep listening to the conversation since they were involved in it.

Senoy said, "We need them to take the athame back so a woman can kill Lilith and help Samael."

The Green Man said, "Killing a goddess and a direct creation of God, and then assisting a fallen angel, a former servant of God, will get all three of you killed yourself. You will spend your eternity in the otherworld with many friends that you sent directly there and I am sure they would enjoy your company."

Senoy said, "We know what we are doing, but we need the athame to go back. And since you and the three of us can't travel through time with the athame, because it is against the code, we need Kilas and Angel to deliver it to a woman."

The Green Man said, "So why should I help you?"

Senoy said, "The evil one who killed your teacher was Lilith. You can finally get your revenge. Remember how you found your teacher after so many weeks of torture? Remember how she looked? And remember how much anger you had for someone who hurt the only family you ever had, the only person who saw your spiritual potential? You can finally settle the score. Yes, Lilith was the evil one who did that. She was much younger and eviler back then, and now she is somewhat different and not so much fun."

The Green Man said, looking thoughtful, "Well, I never knew Lilith was the evil one. Let me touch your hand to see what you say. I have the power to read your mind and thoughts. If you are saying the truth, I will help you in your plan. But I must see for myself."

Senoy walked up to the Green Man. They were the same height and looked eye to eye. The Green Man was much more muscular and looked more rugged. Senoy offered his hand for the Green Man to touch and to read his thoughts. The Green Man

Chapter 8: Kilas and Angel

grabbed his hand with both of his and closed his eyes. It took only a few seconds and then he let go of his hand and said, "I believe you; I saw what you said. I saw that Lilith was the evil one and I now know the truth. Thank you for letting me see your visions. I will help you."

Senoy and the other angels smiled and Senoy said, "I knew we could count on you to assist us in our change of the hierarchy. You will get your revenge as you wanted many years ago. We just need you to help get the athame back to a person named Nera. We think she will be trusted the most from Lilith to pull this off. Nera is working closely with Samael right now to get the athame and to release a curse on her. And to get a certain Kila, that is now in the picture, to release several demons that are trapped in it. The one named Boutros is also in the picture."

The Green Man looked down at the ground as if remembering something important, then he said, "Boutros is not one to be messed with and that will make it more difficult. What is your plan for this revolution that you want to start?"

Senoy said, "We will not go into details right now, but the most important thing is to make sure Kilas and Angel depart immediately with the athame to a new location. There are others looking for the athame, too. You have made enemies throughout your time and others know that the athame will transport them back here to you. Give them what they need in skills to be safely away quickly. They only have a few hours before the enemy at the gates arrive to find the athame. There are other angels breaking the rules, too, for other reasons. We must go now, before someone finds us. We will talk later." Without any further discussion, the three angels opened up their wings and flew away in large movements on their wings, flying quickly away, close along the ground.

The Green Man smiled and said, "I assume you two heard everything from below the window?" He was looking at both of them through the window as they were sitting with their backs to the wall, listening to everything without being seen.

Angel said, "We did, but we do not understand it all."

The Green Man said with a smile, "That is exactly what I

needed you to do. Let's discuss what you need to do immediately and then we will meet again for the next stage." He walked into the cabin and they all returned to the table. "You heard you will need to depart soon before someone finds out what you have found. So, I want you to go back now and return to the ship. I want you to make up some story that you need to depart and smuggle the athame out. Angel must be onboard. She must come with you. I want you to go to a more barren place then you have ever gone to before, where no one can find you. And then once you are there, you both touch the athame again and return here. Do you understand?"

Kilas said, "I can figure out a way to get off the planet, but I do not know if Angel can pull it off. They watch her pretty close."

Angel said, "Don't worry about me. You just tell me when you are departing and I will be on your ship."

The Green Man said, "Good. You do not have much time."

Kilas asked, "How do we get back?"

The Green Man said, "Hold each other's hands and then you both touch my arm."

They held each other's hands and then nodded to each other and touched the Green Man's arm. They were back on the ship immediately, as if nothing had happened. They looked at the clock and it had only been three minutes; the Green Man was right about time. They looked at each other and knew what they had to do.

Kilas looked Angel in the eye, "We depart in two hours, do what you have to do."

Angel nodded and gave her a quick kiss on the lips and left immediately to prepare.

Chapter 9

Three Angels Visit Jamie

Jamie was pregnant and starting to show; she was drinking tea, sitting on her hammock on her back porch. Three strangely dressed men appeared out of nowhere. They looked like characters from *The Matrix* or *Men in Black* or something. She thought she was dreaming in her hammock, with her running shorts on and a T-shirt, when they arrived on her back-balcony deck. The men sat on her wooden deck chairs like FBI agents with sunglasses and they started a normal investigative conversation with her.

She had been drinking some hot organic mushroom tea that she bought in Colorado. She looked at her tea and thought maybe it might be loaded with hallucinogens and she was having a really bad trip, but the tea label was perfectly clear of no additives.

She had not had any of her good psychedelic mushrooms since she found out she was pregnant, so she must be really being visited by three strange men, all dressed in black suits—or she was in an absolutely wonderful dream and she wanted to dream more with these three mysteriously handsome men. One man said, "We are three angels here to visit you with a proposition. Do you need a metaphysical spiritual adventure?"

Jamie said to them, due to her high and bravado, "I don't believe you. You must show me your angelic wings for me to believe you are angels, and then I will show you mine." She never thought that they would show their wings at all.

The three angels smiled, and the one on the left with a light blond beard said, "I got this one. You two got the last one, after all." He stood up and took off his jacket and placed it neatly on the chair. Then took off his dress shirt and dropped it on top. All Jamie could notice was his physique and chest muscles and muscular arms. Then all of a sudden, he stretched out his arms and these gorgeous black wings appeared out of his back, about ten feet wide. They were full and feathered and strong. Jamie was taken aback and was slightly turned on by the power that stood in front of her. She was becoming lightheaded as she took him all in.

The angel said, "My dear, you said if I showed you mine, you would show me yours."

Jamie came to her senses quickly...more or less, "Oh that. Okay." She stood up and could tell they were all looking at her. She was not wearing a bra and she turned around and raised the back of her shirt to show her full back, "My wings are only tattoos, but aren't they beautiful."

The three angels fully admired her full tattoo wings. It must have taken over sixty hours and the artist was extraordinarily talented. But her shorts covered up the tips of her wings, which went onto her butt cheeks. The angel with no shirt said, "May I see the last part that you are so lovely covering up, so we can take in the magnificent tattoo artwork that took hours of labor to ink?"

Jamie had heard many lines from many men to see her butt for the rest of her wings, but those words from the angel had an enormous effect on her emotions and she lowered her shorts to show her butt. The hidden tips of her wings go down her butt cheeks and end on the outside of her hips. She was catching her breath. She did not know how powerful it was to have three angels look at your bare back and ass. She needed to keep herself together and to remember to buy that type of tea again, because this might be one of her best teas ever in her mediocre, mundane life.

The angel with no shirt walked over to Jamie and put his finger on the outside lines of the tattoo and ran it across her back and along her butt and ended on her outer hip, which melted poor Jamie with goosebumps. And then he grabbed her shorts

Chapter 9: Three Angels Visit Jamie

with both hands along the elastic and pulled them to cover her; a perfect gentleman. He also pulled her t-shirt back down to cover her back. He then took his dress shirt that was laid on the chair and placed it over her shoulders and said, "You look cold so please wear my shirt for the time being. You will find that silk shirts have wonderful effects on warming the skin."

Jamie turned around buttoning up the shirt, but not buttoning all of the them to keep the attention of the angels. "Now, what are you doing here on my deck and how can I assist you? Because this seems like fun." As she finished the sentence she sat down on her chair and propped her feet up.

The three angles introduced themselves as Senoy, Sansenoy, and Semangel. They were about as real as real can get, for Jamie. Senoy was the angel with no shirt. Senoy said, "We require your assistance to help Paul on his next journey, and we need you to keep us updated on his progress to make sure he finds what he is destined to find."

Jamie said, "Why don't you ask Professor Robert? He is the one who always goes with Paul on his spontaneous adventures and does the sacred rituals with him. He is much more experienced in that sort of thing."

Senoy leaned in within a foot of Jamie, "We need you to help us, because you are more powerful than Robert."

Jamie always thought of herself as the student compared to Dr. Robert. She was curious and quietly said, "What do you mean that I am more powerful?"

Senoy got up from his chair and walked up to her and looked into her eyes sincerely and said, "You have angelic blood in your veins. You are a descendant of an angel."

Jamie laughed, "This must be really great tea, but I do not believe it that I am an angel."

Senoy smiled, "I said you had angel blood, not that you were angel, yet." He gestured at himself and his companions, muscles rippling, "We are the first three angels of the true story of Adam and Lilith. We were called down by God to convince Adam's first wife, Lilith, to return to heaven. So we are the original three of the religious Judeo-Christian origin histories, which is not at all in the Christian bible. We were also misinterpreted in the Jewish Tarot. We are angels who failed in our mission to bring Lilith back to the Garden, if you believe in that origin myth. Dear Lilith fully refused to be a subject of a man, but only an equal, especially to Adam. We tried with our biggest charm and savviest wiles and bargaining, but we were much younger back then, and failed. You see, we tried to drown her in the Red Sea when we initially found her, but Lilith swore in the name of the Lord she will not harm any infant who wears an amulet bearing the name of the three angels. So, she made a deal with us and God, which means she is also divine. Without getting too deep, Lilith later partners with Samael."

Sansenoy said boldly, "There you go dropping Samael's name again. You just don't like him, do you? You are skipping major parts of the myth like always, so just get to the point of what you are trying to prove."

Semangel then looked at Jamie, "Lilith partnered with Samael, who is associated as the leader of the fallen angels. Lilith and Samael formed an alliance."

Senoy interrupted and said, "You can't skip that God found out and castrated Samael due to his evilness. How many times have you told this story and you still get it wrong?"

Sansenoy said, "Please let me finish! Naturally not every detail can be shared, don't want to overwhelm the girl. He smiled and bowed to Jamie. "Then there is the folklore of Lilith that talks about her having a pact with the Bible's serpent, or snake, from Eden. She convinces the snake to loan her the snake shape, and as she was disguised as a snake, she returned back to heaven and Eden. She convinces Eve first, and then Adam, to sin and eat from the forbidden tree and God had great sorrow about the events. Lilith was also one of the most beautiful women on Earth. If you are still lost, I want you to remember C.S. Lewis. In the *Chronicles of Narnia* he used the example of Lilith as inspiration for the White Witch, one of the evilest persons in any of his stories."

Jamie said, "Can you please get to the point? I have to agree with your angel friends."

Chapter 9: Three Angels Visit Jamie

Sansenoy said, "You have actual angel blood in your veins. It's from a generation ago, but you have angelic powers inside you. What that means is, you are powerful and you do not yet know how powerful you can be. We three angels could teach you. That's why we are here. But you first must make sure that Paul visits the reader, Lena, in three days."

Jamie was stunned with this information. She always had this feeling that there was something quite unique inside herself, but she could never put her finger on it. She could never figure it out. But right now, even though it was absolutely the most bizarre and unbelievable thing she ever heard, she fully believed it. She believed what these angels on her patio were saying, or she was on the biggest non-drug trip of her life just imagining it all up herself. That Colorado tea was exceptional.

Senoy stepped up, calmed his breath, and decided his words slowly and looked her straight in her eyes and said, "You are partially divine. You have insight no one can compare to, you have the ability to see the future which you have not been trained on yet, and you have the ability to feel other people's emotions. You, yes you, are partially divine. With our training, you can be quietly powerful here on Earth. You will also receive your true wings someday."

Jamie just looked at all three angels and started to cry like a heavy load was just released from her shoulders. It was like she had believed in something for years, for her lifetime, but everyone convinced her that she was wrong. Not until these three angels revealed the new truth, did she finally know the full truth. Jamie cried and immediately hugged Senoy and he also fully hugged her back like a good father figure.

As they started to depart, Senoy said, "I can feel you are with child. Is that true?"

Jamie smiled with a blush while touching her stomach, "Yes, I am about through my first trimester."

All three angels looked at each other.

Chapter 10
Robert's Secret Library

Paul parked in front of Casaneta's. The restaurant had been open over 140 years. Originally built during the Civil War and shut down during the prohibition era—although there are stories of an illegal speakeasy built in the basement that was said to look like a bank vault. Paul had never seen it, mainly heard rumors about it from Robert, he thought.

Paul walked into the library as always, but tonight would be a conversation with Robert over an excellent dinner, and probably two bottles of wine or several exceptional Scotch-Irish whiskeys. As he sat down in his favorite dark red chaise, his phone pinged. Looks like Robert was running late and was bringing someone with him. Paul laughed to himself. Typical Robert chaos, asking for a tête-à-tête, then surprising him with some mysterious stranger. Given their deep friendship and the depths to which Robert always had his back, Paul found himself looking forward to discovering what Robert was up to now.

Paul occupied a nook with three chairs, ordered a bottle of Merlot, poured himself a glass, and took a seat on the antique chair by the fireplace. He saw Robert's convertible pull up to the front; Jamie—his secretary?—sat in the passenger seat. He had brought out the 1969 Jaguar, so Paul knew he was in a good mood because he never brought it out except for special occasions, and when the weather was perfect. Paul could hear Robert's voice as he walked

Chapter 10: Robert's Secret Library

in and was still surprised that he was bringing his secretary. No doubt Robert's new scheme still had many curveballs, not least of which was getting to know Jamie outside of a professional setting.

Paul welcomed Robert, as always, before turning to Jamie with a smile. Paul realized he had never once seen her in a non-work setting, where her hair was always up and her clothes were always cool distant prim neutrals. Tonight, she was in blue jeans, and her hair was loose and almost crazy curly, and she had a loose shirt that draped so one shoulder was bare. Jamie walked over to Paul and gave him a hug and whispered in his ear, "Thank you for letting me attend tonight. There is so much we have to catch up on, spiritually." She kissed him on the cheek as they embraced.

Paul smiled back to her with a wink, "What happens in the library stays in the library."

Robert grinned, an impish gleam in his eyes, "Paul, what is spoken in this room can't be repeated. We have important things to do." As he said this, he nodded to the bartender, Woodrow, who was a trusted friend. Woodrow came in and closed the main doors of the library, drew the curtains, and posted a sign outside the room that read, "Private party. Do not disturb." Robert then pulled out his cell phone and hit a button and the doors' top latches locked. He hit another button which turned off the security cameras in the library and they all pointed downward. Robert then texted the bartender, confirming that everything was secure.

Jamie smiled at both of them, "I have many things to catch you up on which will affect your future spiritual adventures."

Robert said, "We must go to a more secure area than this room before you indulge Paul in your latest experiences." Robert walked over to a Greek figurine of Mercury, with his winged sandals. "Paul, what I am about to show you, you can't divulge to anyone. Once we all go down to my other room, I will explain more. Now follow me. Jamie, could you close the door behind us."

Robert turned the Greek figurine counterclockwise and a bookcase clicked and jarred forward. Robert walked across the library to the bookcase and opened it up to an old masonry staircase. He merely said, "Follow me." He switched on a light and there was a row of old candescent light bulbs that led down to an old stone basement. Paul had known Robert for years and he had never divulged such a room to him, and now wondered what else had Robert withheld.

The cut masonry of the steps showed years of a worn path of footsteps. Robert smiled and walked to a large wine cellar that also looked like another library, but this was much more 18th century looking. There were hundreds of old books along the library walls. It looked like an expensive private collection. First editions by the covers and the leather, and the names and authors were not ones you could find readily in a normal university library, or on the internet. This was quite a unique collection.

Paul said, "Robert, I have known you over twenty years. What is this place, and why did you never tell me about it?"

Jamie walked behind a classic wooden bar, pulled a bottle off the shelf and three glasses from under the bar for them to welcome the new visitor to this special place. Jamie looked like she had been there many times with Robert. Jamie poured herself a water and stiff drinks for the two men.

Robert walked over to Jamie and smiled, "Jamie, you always know the right decision to make before awkward comes around." He smiled at her and she winked back as he picked up a glass for himself and one for Paul.

Paul was still looking at all the books and the architecture of the cellar library. He looked down at Robert across his glass and said, "My dear friend, please explain. I am so curious at this new part of you."

Robert said, "First and foremost, a toast to friendship and future adventures." Jamie came from around the bar with her glass. Robert raised his glass and the other two followed and he said, "*Gus càirdeas!*" They all touched their glasses together. Robert added "When translated in Scot Gaelic that means 'to friendship'. My friends, we now make a bond for our friendship on and forward. Blessed be."

It was old, smooth whiskey and left that nice burning feeling in the throat when it went down.

Chapter 10: Robert's Secret Library

Paul then said, "Robert, now that we have toasted our friendship, would you please tell me about this unique wine cellar, or library, that we are all standing in."

Robert pointed to the chairs and the couch next to the shelves of hundreds of books lining the wall. Robert sat down on the couch, Jamie sat next to him, and Paul sat across from them with an end table between. Robert gestured grandly, "This room was first built as a storm cellar in the 1860s, during the Civil War. The hotel was built on top of it. This cellar was forgotten about, except for a secret group of people that used it during the underground railroad to help slaves escape to the free states of the North. It was most notoriously used as a speakeasy during prohibition. In the 1960s, I worked here as a busboy and stumbled across some of the other tunnels between buildings and found unique historical artifacts. I kept most of the artifacts for myself and did not tell anyone. During the Carter years and the 1970s recession, the entire place was put up for sale, and I, as a new assistant professor at the university, with no business background, bought it. Throughout the years, I was a silent major owner and have added business partners to help out financially, and more spiritually, but eventually they all departed, and I bought them out as I became a full tenured professor. My friend, I own Casaneta's, this entire building. And this is my private library, where I am most nights. Do you ever ask yourself how I found you after you walked out of here drunk with Nera that night? Well, Woodrow called me because he knew you were in a vulnerable situation, and he did not trust Nera at all. Woodrow is one of my most loyal employees. and he is also a solitary witch and protects the place spiritually. He was right about you, that you were a drunken mess and collapsed in the gutter that poor cold rainy night. I was working down here when you were with Nera upstairs; I heard the conversation, too."

Paul sat back in the chair and finished off his drink, remembering that evening with Nera. After a spell, he started to get up to refill his glass. Robert immediately said to Jamie, "Jamie will you be so polite and just bring the bottle to the table so we can more easily refill our glasses." Jamie slowly got up and walked over to the bar, picked up the bottle, and brought it over. She refilled Robert's glass and filled it up higher, knowing they were going to need more alcohol as the rest of the story was told.

Jamie returned to her seat; her legs curled up comfortably on the couch. Robert continued, "Paul, this place is secure to speak in. No listening devices can penetrate the three-foot thick rocks of this cellar. This is as safe as a bank vault. We can say anything and any secret needed, and then also know who was here, because it is just us. Who knows might be trying to listen in upstairs." Robert shrugged and leaned back in his chair with his typical nonchalance. He took a sip of whisky, visibly savoring the drink. He knew his audience. Suddenly, he grinned. "You have known Jamie for over a year as your secretary, but now she needs to be seen in a different light. Time for you to know her other side. No worries. She has never lied to you, just omitted certain things, per my requests to protect you."

Jamie smiled, "I can be quite professional at the university. I think we all understand the need for a work slash life balance and the circumspection required for that." She deadpanned and raised one eyebrow ironically. Then she gestured at the room. "Looks circumspect to me! Robert and I have been friends for years spiritually. I give him energy healings and he taught me the old ways of spirituality, witchcraft, religion, paganism, and all the eclectic occult topics. I have been hearing voices since I was a little girl. I was a strict Catholic, and during my teenager years I thought the voices were from God, or saints, and I was destined for a life of faith and the church. So, at eighteen, I went to become a nun." Paul almost spit out his scotch, seeing how beautiful and free-loving this woman was—thinking of her as a nun was too much.

Jamie's voice was rich and playful in its sarcasm as she continued. "As I was saying, I heard these voices and I followed them. When I divulged the voices during weekly confession to the bishop in my training, he said I was only a child and just dreaming. That only true "honorable *men* of God" can hear divine voices. Those men who receive voices have had proper training to interpret the words of God. No woman has the ability to interpret

Chapter 10: Robert's Secret Library

the word of God properly." Jamie shrugged, "I was furious, because why can't a woman hear God?" She leaned forward and lowered her voice. "But what I realized was that the voices were not from the almighty God, but from multiple goddesses, the other side of religion, which is not discussed. The gods and goddesses of pre-Christian times, the older gods of humanity. So, I quit the convent and got into yoga, Buddhism, Reiki, and everything else. I have no regrets. When I moved here to Kansas, I was drawn to Professor Robert immediately after he visited you in your office. We were instantly connected by past lives. I approached him, trying not to act or seem crazy, and well, Robert fully understood me and my voices and my visions of the goddesses. And he said that I was not alone. That there are more like us in the world, walking among us, but unknown."

Jamie smiled fondly at Robert. He ruffled her hair, and she rolled her eyes and gave a playful toss of her head. "For the first time in many years, I did not feel alone. I did not feel like a freak. I truly believed in myself and my purpose. I finally believed in these unique abilities of mine. I have this unique power of touch, which makes me an excellent energy healer. I follow my intuition, I see colors of auras, I can feel everyone's emotions and energy in a room, and well, I follow my intuition. I am a free spirit. So, to get to the point, the main reason I decided to share our unique relationship with you is that now I am connected to your personal story. I had three angels visit me two days ago on my back patio. And they gave me an assignment to help you in your journey, and a task to keep them informed and to make sure you see Lena."

Paul looked stunned and confused, but truly believed her. He picked up the bottle and poured himself another drink and poured Robert a refill. "Jamie, please continue. I believe you fully."

Before she started again, Robert picked up his fresh drink and took a large gulp.

Jamie said, "I had just had some mushroom black tea and was in an excellent mood. These three angels just arrived and started to talk to me, just like you and I are talking right now. One of them even showed me his gorgeous wings, but I will continue. They said that I had angel blood in me and that I was a descendant from one of the oldest angels. They then told me a story how they found the one who was supposed to find the athame in the future. You buried it correctly, in the right spot in Colorado. And it will be found by a chosen spiritual woman. But, they also said the athame is a special portal for her to meet the Green Man. Do you know who this Green Man is?"

Paul looked at Robert with confusion, "I have no memory of a green man, I have never been told I had a past life regarding a green man, and I haven't had any dreams about a green man, either. Robert, do you have any memory of a green man?"

Robert looked puzzled, "I do not either. The reason we risked making you aware of Jamie's true past, and her new angelic potential, was that if she gave you the firsthand witness explanation, it might bring out any known or subconscious memory that you might have, because, I guess, we were grasping for straws. The whiskey is excellent and should help us open up our minds. Let's have just one more for the road and then Jamie will drive us both home safely."

Paul fully agreed and started to bring his whiskey to his mouth, and then stopped with a thought. "You know what we could do."

Robert and Jamie both looked at Paul.

Jamie quickly jumped in, "We should go see Lena tomorrow. She could help us in this process."

Robert and Paul both smiled and knew that Lena was probably the best gatekeeper to these newest clues. Robert said, "I may have heard of Lena and met her once many years ago. Would you mind properly introducing me tomorrow, if we can get in to see her?"

Paul smiled, "Sure, that will be an introduction to remember. Jamie, you must go with us."

Jamie smiled, "I would not miss it for the world." She was subtle not to mention that Lena and her had had multiple readings in the past year. Jamie did not want to divulge all her cards quite yet. Jamie also remembered that during her meeting with the angels, they requested that Paul meet the reader within three days. So she guessed she fulfilled their request.

Chapter 11

A Visit With Lena

Paul had woken up and was getting his coffee. The plan for the day was that Robert and Jamie would stop at his house early for his famous microwave breakfast burritos, which they would eat on his back balcony before visiting with Lena. Paul loved mornings, especially when he could watch the sunrise and drink his coffee on his porch. Paul was still in his pj's when he heard a knock on his front door. He got up and went to open the door with his coffee in hand. He could see it was Jamie and Robert through the door window. They were giggling, and when he opened the door they both said, "Someone said they might have coffee." They both had brought their coffee travel mugs and held them both toward Paul.

Paul just laughed, "I might have coffee for true friends, but you must answer one question."

They both looked at him with a puzzled look, and in a joking matter he said, "What is your favorite color?" He was referring to an older classic movie and everyone laughed, and he welcomed them through his door.

Jamie walked up to Paul and gave him a hug and said, "Blue."

Robert patted Paul on his shoulder and said, "Violet."

They were both doing a poor attempt to replicate a classic movie quote. As they both made their way to his kitchen, Paul just smiled and then shook his head on what good friends he had with these two.

Robert said, "My friend, where is breakfast? I am also hungry."

Jamie said, "I request only a bagel."

Paul laughed, "Whatever's in my kitchen is yours. If you want breakfast, please make it. I am a one dish breakfast person—microwave breakfast burritos that cook up in two minutes."

Robert said, "Jamie, would you be a dear and find me an apron and I shall make breakfast for us so we are ready to see Lena. It is always best not to see her on an empty stomach."

Jamie and Paul looked at Robert with puzzled looks because they thought he did not know her. Robert said, "Well…I might have known her in my younger days, when I had a different occupation."

They looked at him again with raised eyebrows. "Okay, okay, we know each other from twenty years ago, when we were much younger and more adventurous. We had a falling out, so I have not seen her in a long time. And you gave me a perfect excuse to mend broken fences, to say it plainly. That's why I shall make each of us breakfast, because I might have had a few readings from her years ago and know these lessons learned of her psychic ability."

Jamie and Paul were hungry and agreed to allow breakfast to be cooked and to start another conversation.

* * *

As they drove up to Lena's shop and parked across the street, Robert said, "My dear, it has been a long time since I have seen her and I am a little nervous. It's been so long, I wonder if she remembers me?"

Paul and Jamie just smiled and looked at Robert, "Of course, she will."

Robert said, "You two please walk in first and I will follow."

They exited the truck and walked across the street and opened door to the antique store where Lena did readings in the back. It was a day full of winter chills on the streets and everyone had their coats on with collars up high.

Chapter 11: A Visit With Lena

The small bell attached to the top of the door chimed as the door opened. Paul led the way toward the back of the store. Lena waved them toward her table. You could tell she was waiting for them.

She was looking down at the cards, shuffling them while the three sat down. She looked up and saw Robert.

Lena said gruffly, "Paul, what are you doing with this terrible untrusting man? I had such high regards toward you until you brought him with you." She looked at Jamie, "Dear, please sit down. You are always welcome. There are reasons you are here today, and we must talk all about it."

Jamie said, "Yes, ma'am," and promptly sat and made herself at home.

"Robert, I have something for you." Lena looked down toward her huge purse and started digging for something and said, "Here it is." She pulled out a .45 caliber revolver with an eight-inch barrel, pointing it toward Robert.

Robert instantly raised his hands, "Lena, please....do not do anything stupid. It's been a long time. Did I really upset you that much on our last adventure?"

Paul and Jamie were just shocked about what they were seeing. Lena is a petit woman, but she was holding a large caliber pistol, which took two hands to hold, pointing it at Robert.

Jamie looked at Lena to distract the current situation and said, "Three angels with black wings visited me and we need your help. You are the only one who could help us. They said I have angel blood in me and there is a spiritual confrontation about to happen over a spear, and some athame, and some other new blade."

Robert, Lena, and Paul all looked at Jamie as she said that new clue, which she had been holding back from them all.

Lena lowered the massive pistol and laughed, "Thank you for that information. We should start our session as soon as Robert says he is sorry." She pointed the gun back at him with a fierce gesture.

Robert said, "I do not know what I am saying sorry for."

Paul and Jamie said, "Just say you are sorry!"

Lena pulled the trigger back, which audibly positioned a

round in the chamber.

Robert said, "Well, if you are going to be like that, I am sorry."

Lena said, "Say it again, Robert, but with meaning. You can do better with all that fine and dandy education you have."

Robert took a deep breath and looked straight at Lena, "Lena, I am sorry how things turned out on our last adventure so many years ago. It was my fault, and my ego got the best of me. Could you find it in your heart to forgive an old friend?"

Lena said, "I accept your apology," and she put the gun back into her purse. "Now let's do this reading and see what the cards say. This should be exciting."

Lena pointed to all of them to sit closer around her table and she started to shuffle the cards thoroughly. "So, tell me about these three angels. Were they well dressed, with black wings?"

Jamie was surprised, "Yes, exactly. How did you know?"

Lena said as she handed her the cards to cut the deck, "Well, Jamie, you found the angels Senoy, Sansenoy, and Semangel. Under Jewish history, the most valued amulets to protect women while giving birth had the three angels' names on them. Adam and Lilith are not in the Christian Bible, but in the Talmud."

Jamie handed the deck back to Lena as Lena continued. "Lilith was Adam's first wife, but was banished before she could have children because she insisted on being an equal, and not a subordinate, of Adam." Jamie snorted. Lena raised an eyebrow as if to say, "yup". "Lilith and Adam were both—by myth—created from dust by God and she saw herself as an equal. Jewish mythology believes that Lilith revenged on Adam and all his offspring by harassing newborn children and their mothers. She is called a demon from this point on, since she was against God's intentions of being Adam's subordinate. And, is said to strangle young children in their sleep and seduce men. The myth says she had sex with men to have demonic stepchildren." Lena sighed dramatically, shaking her head at human silliness. "All propaganda and stories to frighten young mothers and keep the oppression of women going. The three you describe come into the story now. Really, all this confusion boils down to Lilith preferring to be on top during sex and let her body set the rhythm,

Chapter 11: A Visit With Lena

and Adam refusing. So, she left the Eden, and Adam, and the myths were created. It's the same smear campaign by men that happened to Mary.

"The three angels were sent to Lilith to return her to Adam. Instead of bringing her back, they made a deal with Lilith. She had already aligned with Samael, who is said to be a source of evil and wants to defeat God, but that is not my interpretation. Since Lilith was now with Samael, she could not go back to Adam. The three angels did make a deal with Lilith, and that deal was that she could not harm any children from Adam and his second wife, Eve.

"This deal between the three angels and Lilith is the key foundation of the most desired amulet used by Jewish women after childbirth. Lilith is the first woman, but has been lost in history. Some include that the three angels were guardians against Lilith, but that is an opinion. The names of Senoy and Sansenoy are mentioned several times in the first century Hebrew texts found in modern day Iraq. In Christian versions, the names of the three angels have become saints—really freaking saints—where Senoy became St. Sisoe, Sansenoy became St. Sisynios and Semangel became St. Synidores. So, depends on what you finally believe of the three angels. But overall, they are protecting humans against Lilith or, some witches say, they are hitmen for God because Lilith is now the beacon for women. I know that is a lot tonight."

Jamie said, "Lena, I had no idea of the background of these three angels. I am now more concerned about what they said. One of them said I had angel blood."

Lena asked, "May I see your hands?"

Jamie moved her hands toward her and let her lightly touch her palms and fingertips. Lena held one hand between hers, looking at the lines on her palm. She ran her fingers along the lines.

Lena smiled and said, "Well, Jamie, you probably do have special characteristics. You have the potential to be powerful and you are gifted with a strong ability to clearly perceive the emotional state of others. But you can also change the mood of people. Have you ever been able to make a room of gloomy people happy, or changed the mood of the room with just your presence?"

Jamie nodded solemnly, "Yes, I seem to have an energy that lights up the room."

Lena said, "We will leave it at that until we look at the cards, okay?" She started to lay down the cards into a circle and then placed one card in the center. She set the deck to the side of the table and then started to touch each of the cards individually. "Jamie, before we start, have you had experiences with gods or goddesses before?"

Jamie said, "I do not know. Sometimes I dream of something or someone. In my dreams, sometimes there is this well-mannered beautiful woman, who is always comforting and kind to me, and always encouraging me to further explore."

Lena said, "That sounds like Lilith." As Lena was moving the rest of the deck of cards to the side of the table, she immediately stopped. Lena looked up with fright on her face at Robert and said, "*Avizvasya,*" and looked right at him with a nod.

Robert stood up, "Paul, Jamie, we have to go now. No questions asked." Lena pointed to the door to a storage room. Paul and Jamie were confused, but Robert said, "We have to go now!" and they followed his cues and went through the door to the rear storage room. Lena remained at her table, gathered up the cards, and reshuffled calmly.

Robert went to the back of the room. He turned a light fixture upside down, a click sounded in the wall, and the wall popped open. Robert opened it and walked in. Paul and Jamie followed, still confused. Robert sealed the door behind them into complete darkness and then turned on the light, which illuminated a staircase that was old and made out of stone, with worn rock steps. Robert led them to a barren room with occult books, a table, and an old bar.

Paul asked, "Robert, what is going on?"

"Well, one of our key words for danger was *avizvasya* which means "dangerous one" in Sanskrit. On our adventures, Lena would get signals from her spirit guide when danger was

Chapter 11: A Visit With Lena

approaching, and she would use Sanskrit to emphasize that an enemy from old is approaching. She saved my life three times in our adventures with that codeword. She would also use Navajo when needed." Robert was looking for something behind the bar as he was talking and he finally found it.

Paul asked, "Robert, are you going to tell us how to get out of here if someone is going to come down here looking for us?"

Robert said, "I have a plan, just give me a moment. This was a bar during the days when all the drinking was underground. All of these basements are connected by tunnels and I am trying to remember the hiding place for the key to the connecting tunnel."

"Here it is!" Robert pulled out what looked like a medieval skeleton key and then approached a hole in the wall and inserted and turned the key. There was another click and another door opened.

Paul and Jamie followed Robert into a tunnel and he closed the door behind them and locked it from their side. He turned on the light and it looked like a hotel room hallway, with doors on each side. Robert said, "Each of these doors goes to the buildings up above us on the street. But most of the owners do not know this exists and we like to keep it that way. The red door is to my tunnel that goes to my bar to the secret room under the library. You catching all of this?"

They walked the hallway and found Robert's red door. It looked like a medieval door with the artwork, but this one had a digital keypad and was heavily armed. Robert put in the keypad numbers and the numbers clicked the door open. All of a sudden, they were in his secret room below the library in Casanetta's.

Paul said, "I had no idea these passageways existed."

Robert said, "That is the idea. To not let anyone know about them for safety to all."

Jamie said, "What about Lena?"

Robert stopped and closed the door after they all entered, "Lena can handle herself, she is quite powerful. Plus, she has several guns in that big purse of hers. She also carries a big bowie knife for fun. She will be fine."

As Robert, Paul, and Jamie were all leaving the secret

basement to go upstairs to the bar, Lena was preparing for the dangerous person to enter her establishment. She could feel the person getting closer. The door opened, the small bell rung, and Lena looked up from her table as she pulled out her handgun and put it on the table.

Lena said, "Nera, we have not seen each other for some time. What are you doing here? We had an agreement."

Nera smiled and took off her jacket, "Now Lena, we will not be needing that pistol right now. Help me. Could I have a reading from you? I will pay three times the money for it. What do you say, for old-time's sake? I know you want to read my cards and see what my future holds. You are more curious than I."

Lena smiled, "Sure, please sit down. What has it been—two years since the last historic 'Nera' reading that had you running out of my store to not return again until now? You must be really jonesing to see what the cards will say today. I am sure you have tried to read your own cards, but are not satisfied with the results. So you come to me."

Nera said, "Yes, I now must come to you. Shall we begin?"

Lena nodded to the empty chair across from her, "You are invited officially to my table."

Nera sat down at the table and Lena started shuffling the cards. They both smiled at each other. Lena said, "Remember when we used to be close friends? You were an excellent student."

Nera said, "Yes, I do. I miss our friendship. I am sorry we had a falling out."

Lena said, "The falling out all started with your friendship with Samael. He is a real evil bastard."

Nera said, "Well, so is Lilith."

Chapter 12

Iraq: 2003

As Jamie, Robert, and Paul found their way out to their cars, Robert told them both, "Please keep your phones near and lock your doors. If there is anything unusual, please give us a call and we can be there in five minutes." Paul made his way home and confirmed through text that he was home secure, and read the other texts that everyone else was home. Paul sent an emoji smile back. Jamie was now in his small secret circle of close friends. The conversation all day had been easy, real, light-hearted, and fulfilling. He just shook his head and walked to his bar. He poured himself another whiskey, though he already had too much to drink, but made his drink anyway, with some ice and heavy on the whiskey.

Paul took his drink over to his desk, turned on the desk light, opened one of the drawers and rifled through the contents. He found what he was looking for. A black and white photo that he took over to his leather couch and turned on the side lamp to better study the people in the photo. It was a photo of Robert and him almost twenty years ago, shoulder to shoulder, in the middle eastern desert sand, looking much younger than what they are now. Paul turned it over. He had written 'Robert and I, 2003, Iraq.' Paul sat there looking at the photo, reflecting on when he had first met Robert in Kirkuk, and how he did not know at the time that it would be the start of a wonderful friendship. He just laughed to himself and slowly thought of that first day.

* * *

Paul was a contractor for the US military. A human terrain analyst, studying human relationships among the Iraqi populace, families, and the politicians' networks. He was only thirty-two at the time, and had spent time in Bosnia in the 90s, and spent time in Mongolia and Russia in the 2000s. But now he was in Iraq during the war. He had been embedded with an infantry division. The day he met Robert, he was riding in a UH-60 Blackhawk helicopter, with a Kevlar helmet and full body armor that weighed too much, everything he owned in a large rucksack, too heavy to carry, sitting on his lap. The heat was exhausting. Paul felt like he was sitting in an oven. Over twenty helicopters headed into northern Iraq. Paul was a brand-new PhD, wondering what he got himself into when he volunteered to be over there when they were looking for PhDs in psychology and education to do human terrain analysis. The pay was so excellent, better than anything—especially any post-doctoral position that he would find in any university in the states right after graduating, so he took the jump onto this special opportunity.

The Blackhawk landed on the helipad at the airfield in Kirkuk. Paul felt like they were herded like cows into the cramped hot waiting area. There were hundreds of folks that looked like they arrived a couple days too early, because it was as barren as the desert in terms of infrastructure to support life, let alone a war.

Paul felt like a lost lamb in the sand with his rucksack when an older man in a straw cowboy hat, walking with an umbrella, and rolling a huge trunk with stickers from all the countries that he had visited, came up to him. Paul looked like he was lost, but this strange older odd-looking gentleman looked like he was in the wrong era. He looked more like he was out digging for tombs in Egypt, circa the 50s or 60s. Paul looked at this older man and all of a sudden he knew, or felt, his intuition that he needed to be friends with him to help him calm his anxiety of his first real war experience. This strange older gentleman seemed to not be fazed at all by being in a third world country during a military invasion. Paul looked at him and asked, "How are you so calm right now? You know there is an invasion going on?"

The strange man looked down at Paul and said, "By what do you mean?"

Paul was all confused by his response, "This is somewhat scary. There is combat just a few miles away, based on the noise. So how are you so calm right now, like going for a stroll in a park in autumn with that silly umbrella?"

"Well, before I answer that comical inquiry, we must first introduce ourselves. We can still have manners in an almost war zone. My name is Dr. Robert Anderson. What might you be named?" He politely took off his hat and tilted his head and pushed his hand out to Paul to shake.

Paul felt like he was getting lectured from a professor. As if he were a first-year grad student, "Well, okay. My name is Dr. Paul Chastain...so can you please answer my question?" They both shook hands in the formal male fashion.

Dr. Robert said, "Well Paul, this is really not war, yet. Just some combat until it becomes a war—soon I hope, as we are in the confusion of an invasion of one country not really believing what is happening. Just trust me on this. This is quite entertaining."

There was another small mortar explosion a couple of miles away. Paul felt himself annoyed, and then confused, and irritated slightly. He looked fully in disbelief at Robert. Robert could feel his annoyance, "Paul, would you like to go get some tea? We could move out of this heat."

Paul was highly irritated, "What the hell are you talking about, tea?"

"Paul, calm down. Look at me. Would you like to pick up your rucksack and follow me to that small tin building over there and have some freshly brewed British tea? I know the manager of the shop over there. The tea is excellent. Though the chairs and tables are plastic, it is one of the only places in town that has authentic Darjeeling. So, would you like some tea?"

Another mortar fell; people dove for cover, but Robert just stood at total ease, as if they were standing on the street of a small town in Maine. Paul's little voice in his head said to follow Robert and get the hell out of the open area, away from the mortars. So, Paul said, "Okay, let's have tea."

They both picked up their bags and slowly worked their way toward the tea store while there was panic and fear in other soldiers and civilians, who were taking cover in local bunkers. Robert's gait betrayed no hint of tension or awareness of being in a war zone. "The Iraqis have such poor mortar systems and the soldiers are poorly trained. Your chances of being hit by their mortars are the same as being hit by lightning, and I choose not to worry about them. If you do the statistics, your chance of living is statistically within two standard deviations. What kind of tea do you prefer? The type of tea a man chooses can tell a lot about a person."

Paul was slighted scared, irritated, confused, and just kept dragging his bags through the sand toward the tea store, sweating to keep up with Robert's pace. All he could think right now was really about tea? Paul just replied back and said, "I like black tea, no sugar." He was just grasping for straws to try and participate in this unique tea discussion without feeling silly talking about tea during a mortar attack.

Robert just laughed, "Paul, you are a civilized man with an education. You need to have one or two blocks of sugar like the finely educated entity you are."

Paul was confused by the choice of the word entity, but did not have the time to think about it as he sweated profusely in the heat.

Robert just kept dragging his old trunk with those huge wheels on it, so it was easy for him, while Paul was struggling because he had brought the wrong type of luggage for a war zone. They both finally made the last 100-yards to the tea shop. They dragged their bags into the tiny shop and placed them in the corner and found a plastic table with two plastic chairs that you would find outside at a picnic. A young Arab boy came to them with two bottles of water and asked what they wanted.

Robert said, "Chai, shukraan lak," which means *Tea, thank you*. Robert also raised up two fingers to mean two teas.

Chapter 12: Iraq: 2003

Paul was confused, "Robert, do you know Arabic?"

"I just spoke in Arabic, what do you think?" He started laughing. He then said, "Paul listen to me, say *Marhabaan sadiq* please. Go ahead." He pointed to Paul to repeat the phrase.

Paul attempted back poorly and Robert laughed, "Paul, we will have to teach you Arabic in your time in this ancient and historic country. We will be good friends. Look, our tea is here. You will also benefit from learning Aramaic…might come in handy later."

Robert thanked the young boy who brought the tea and he gave him a few dinars for his trouble. The boy smiled and went back to the kitchen. Robert said, "Well, Paul, let's discuss this Kirkuk tea. You really must add some sugar to it, It's quite intense, even though it is in a small glass cup with these tiny dainty spoons. The saucer of the cup always tells the story of the tea owner's background. These saucers are handmade and hand painted, you can tell by the lines." Paul looked at the artwork on the saucer, but could not tell the details that Robert was describing. Paul just put sugar in the tea and used the tiny spoon and stirred, and was now ready to have a drink of the long-awaited, and much, discussed tea.

Robert drank his tea and Paul quickly followed, observing carefully to be sure there was no other ritual or custom to follow. Paul was just amazed at how his first couple of hours in Iraq were going; he felt the heat that was like an oven, he smelled the jet fuel while he walked off the helicopter that took him there. He also dragged his bags almost a half mile in the sand, and he met the most unlikely new academic friend who seemed to not be afraid of anything. This new friend kept his full manners while in a war zone, but had this sense of inquiry of knowledge. Paul just smiled and thought about what the hell had he got himself into. Paul had to laugh at his current situation. Drinking tea in a shack with plastic chairs with his new friend Robert. It was going to be a good year he hoped, and adventurous for sure.

* * *

Several months had passed. Robert and Paul had been becoming excellent co-workers in the villages of Iraq and found a way to get used to the heat, the sand, and the danger. Robert was an excellent mentor to Paul in the local customs and ways. They used their degrees to intellectually research the human terrain in this combat zone, which allowed them both to go outside the wire into the cities and villages freely and explore the societies, culture, and especially the unique dynamics of the people.

They would travel among the populace almost every day, learning the culture more and more each day. Paul's Arabic was improving significantly every day and their chai drinking was now an almost daily ritual. Their respect from the people in the Iraqi cities was increasing and they were helping the local people more and more with their needs through the transitions of the new governments.

One day Robert said, "Paul, Easter Sunday is in a few days and we should go to the Chaldean Catholic church in downtown Kirkuk. I have always wanted to visit that church again, where the famous Carmelite missionary, Father Benedict, started a mission in 1743."

Paul said, "Robert, I don't think that is a good idea. We would have to drive through IED alley to get to the church. There is so much violence on that road. Are you feeling, okay? That's really dangerous!"

Robert said calmly, "Paul, that is why we should walk without body armor and without any weapons or have a security team; we shall be true pacifists and be able to walk in the worst neighborhoods and the market. Also, our good friend from the community, Jaleel, invited us and will meet us at the gate and we shall walk hand-in-hand with him as a show of friendship. It is the best way to travel, with a local sponsor. You just have to trust me on this one. It is the safest travel when you walk, just like my time on the road to Santiago. Just trust me. What do you have to lose?"

Paul, in his usual way, just shook his head and smiled. He fully trusted his intuition and his gut saying that Robert knew exactly what he was doing, and he should trust him.

Chapter 12: Iraq: 2003

* * *

Paul and Robert received clearance to leave the military base and Jaleel knew when and where to meet them. The three of them had worked together for months. This was a quite different experience with no military escort and no body armor. Paul felt completely vulnerable and somewhat afraid. He felt like he had no backup and no security. If he were kidnapped, no one would know how to find him.

Jaleel waved at them as the gate closed behind Paul and Robert. As the gate finished closing, the sound of metal on metal rung out behind them, affirming they were on their own. Jaleel hugged them both and gave them a kiss on both of their cheeks as a sign of respect. "My friends, now we will walk to the cathedral that you want to visit. They are awaiting you and have some guests for you to meet and some new artifacts, which you have not seen."

Paul looked confused, but Robert said, "That is wonderful news. And will we get to tour the new section in the catacomb tunnel?"

Jaleel said, "I had to pull some strings. We can get the private tour, but you both must not tell anyone about the catacombs or the excavations."

Robert quickly said, "Of course we will not say a word. We give you our honor with God."

Paul was even more confused and thought Robert was not telling him the whole truth. Robert said, "Paul, I guess I should tell you that I have been to Iraq several times throughout the years and not just in this war, but Desert Storm, and the Iraq-Iran War, and other times. I have many unique friends and stories and it helps with my discoveries in my professional field of philosophy, especially the occult."

Paul was thinking about his last words of 'discoveries and occult' and was now wondering what the other side of Robert consisted of.

Robert smiled at Paul as Jaleel told them to hold hands as they walked down the last street to the cathedral. Jaleel looked up at the buildings and at the rooftops for people, and also along the alleyways as they continued to walk. He started to talk Kurdish more loudly as they walked closer to the church. He talked loudly enough so that the people on the street could understand the dialect and accent. Robert said softly, "Jaleel is Kurdish and lives in Kirkuk. He is a simple, honorable man, which you know, but he is also a retired military officer who helped defend Kirkuk from assault of the Iraqi forces, and Saddam on his siege of the city many decades ago, and has a strong reputation."

Jaleel overheard the soft conversation. "That was a long time ago when I was younger. I have not killed anybody in a long time. Maybe today will be the day. I miss killing people, especially infidels." Jaleel then laughed loudly to the both of them as they walked up to the church. There were two priests waiting for them at the steps of the cathedral who noticed Jaleel and waved. As they approached each other, the customary kisses on each of the cheeks to greet with friendship happened between them all.

The older priest said, "My name is Father James McIntosh. Before anyone asks any questions, yes, I am a Scotsman in Kirkuk. It's a long story for another time. Welcome to our home. Robert, always so nice to see you again. What has it been, ten years? Jaleel thank you so much for escorting our friends to our home." He gave Jaleel a hug and then came up to Paul. "You must be Paul. Welcome to the Chaldean Catholic church of Kirkuk. We are two of the priests here." He pointed to the priest next to him and said, "This is Father Robert Francis, and he is from the Benedictine order, but has taken a year of silence and will start speaking again in four months. He is not being rude, just not talking. It is quite awkward to drink with a silent priest." Everyone laughed slightly, thinking how you drink anything quietly. Father Robert pulled his hands out of his cassock and waved at them both and then put his hands back in his robe.

Father James said, "Let's come inside before the neighborhood changes its mind about these new strangers." He opened the doors and everyone walked inside the cathedral. Paul was amazed at the beauty of the church from the inside, because on the outside, there was nothing ornamental like the churches that he had seen

Chapter 12: Iraq: 2003

in Europe. The first thing Paul noticed was the Arabic writings on the walls and the stained glass windows. It was a beautiful church and so like the many Catholic churches he had seen throughout his life. The only difference between this church and his own church was the writing and the smell, but so much was the same, especially the altar.

Father James said, "Robert, I would like to go straight to the tunnels if you do not mind. I need to show you our progress since you have not been here in so long."

Robert smiled, "You read my mind, my friend." Robert patted his shoulder as they walked and you could tell they were good friends, even though they had not seen each other for a long time.

Paul was even more curious when Father James said, "Robert, we have made good progress finding the ancient tunnels, but it just takes time not to make noise and disturbance in our work that suspicious, or clever folks, could hear in the streets or the buildings above the tunnels. Since we are a church and holy land owned by Rome, no one can dig under the church. We just don't let anyone know that we have been digging for decades. Now, Paul, you are forbidden to say anything about what you are about to see, or we shall have Jaleel kill you. Okay?" Paul just looked shocked and quickly nodded his head yes to acknowledge he understood.

Father James took them past the altar to the far-right side and walked into the sacristy in the back of the church where the priest got ready for mass. Then Father James knelt in front of a statue of Mary, pressed a small button, and the wall behind the statue opened up. Father James said, "Robert, we have made improvements on the tunnel and excavations since the last time you were here. We think we have reached the tunnels that date pre-Christian times, or at least pre-dates the Council of Nicene in 325 A.D. The artifacts are amazing, but we are keeping them secret to protect their historical identities and to protect the church, as always. Some of the most recent finds you will find most interesting."

They continued to walk through a natural cave with lights attached to the ceiling and the cave continued downward by the slope of the ground. Then they approached a larger cavern, which made Robert and Paul look in full amazement at the natural cavern, about two-hundred feet below the church. It looked like a natural underground church or temple, with carvings and drawings along the walls. The ceiling must have been forty feet high. There were benches that had been cut out of the rock. It was like nothing that Paul had ever seen.

Robert said, "Father James, what is this place? It looks like a gathering place, or might be an underground church?"

Father James said, "Our top archeologists think this was an ancient church or gathering place, or a place for ceremonies. The language scratched on the walls is not known in our human history. It's not a known language. This language is something completely new. We have a few people who are working on deciphering it, but I would like your expertise on what we have found, if you are able and willing."

Robert and Paul were in awe of the underground church and Robert said, "I will help as much as I can but, deciphering ancient pre-Christian text is not my area. I am more of an anthropologist and occultist."

Father James just said, "We need you to look at something more on the occult side, not ancient text." Father James continued to walk through the great cavern, and toward the end of the room was another smaller cave in which the light was turned on. This tunnel was much smaller and looked much older. They came upon a smaller cave room with colored carvings and painting on the cave walls. Father James stopped and said, "Let me get the rest of the lights on." He walked to a homemade switch and the room was lit from the ceiling to the floor with spotlights and Robert could clearly see the ancient paintings on the cave walls. The wonderful primitive paintings showed a man who was 'green' with a sword and shield, facing a woman in a dark cloak. And there were men with wings next to the green man and men with wings next to the hooded woman. All of them were painted like they were in a cave, just like the one they were standing in. Then the next scene showed the woman gone and the green man with tattoos on his face. Then the next scene showed a large tree with small figures

Chapter 12: Iraq: 2003

along the limbs and markings all over the tree next to a lake. The next scene, to the right, showed a sword inside the tree. And then it looked like the green man went inside the tree, or became the tree, or transfigured into something. Robert was explaining his interpretation to the group as he looked at the primitive paintings and Father James and Jaleel both nodded as he was interpreting it. Father James said, "The last scene is what we need you to look at the most Robert. It's something quite different. It's really why you and Paul are here."

He pointed to the last scene, which was much more recent based on the colors, and the style was definitely not from the same era. This scene was much more detailed and showed a man with a sword, but also with a small knife stabbed in his back, fighting a woman with brown hair, with three beings with wings behind her, and also a black figure with yellow eyes. The man with the knife in his back had a woman next to him that had a beam from the sun shining down on her, that created a glow around him for protection. It looked like she was protecting him. Next to the man was a male-like figure from the sky, with wings on his feet, and several other god-like figures behind him, helping to defend the man, too.

Robert looked at it and said, "This looks like an epic battle between gods, working through humans to fight their battles. This is like nothing I have seen before. But it does not fit the other three scenes in color, or technique, or time period. It has to be younger than the other paintings, by the advanced technique."

Jaleel said, "That was our hypothesis, also. Our new twist was this more current stone carving in the corner, over there in the bottom. It is carved in Gaelic."

Robert responded, "Gaelic? That does not make sense. These carvings and paintings are much more ancient, except for this newer painting." He looked at the words scratched into the cave *tha Dia annad, tha an spiorad a-staigh* and Robert recognized as Gaelic and said, "Well, it means God is within you and the spirit is inside you." Robert read the second line which said *dion Dia agus gheibh thu duais* and he said, "Defend God and you will be rewarded."

Father James smiled and said, "That is also how we interpreted the Gaelic carvings. What we need to know is, what does it mean?"

Robert smiled, "First question is, how did Gaelic get in this cave in Iraq under a Chaldean church? Given how historically unique this is, it is impossible to explain without further evidence. But the words mean that God is within you, which is covered by the Gospels of Thomas and Mary Magdalene, which never made the full Bible back in the Council of Nicene. It's a theory of individual divinity, which means we are all divine; it's more eastern religious thought. This also means that certain humans have more divinity than others. In the lost gospels, it also refers to the idea that the kingdom of God is within you and outside you, once you come to know yourselves you will become known, and you will know that it is you who are the children of the living father. It's a state of consciousness. It is all about gnosis, which means living spiritual knowledge. It is a question of knowing yourself—when you know yourself, you will know God, because in the end, you will discover that the divine is within you. All of these gospels were found at Nag Hammadi, which were more the original historical words of Jesus, than our four gospels. The church will never recognize the gospels and will never accept them, because their canon remains strictly based on the four chosen by the council. The church does have scholars working on the authenticity and several priests are still trying to link the gnostic gospels historical background. But the church isn't exactly interested in changing over two thousand years of church law and theory."

Jaleel and Paul looked confused.

Robert elaborated, "What this means is that when one truly knows oneself, one will understand that they are divine, but also that one is mortal. Mortality is meaningless, as a physical existence is meaningless. Death is no longer a problem, but death is a solution because past lives do not depend on physical existence. But when you know yourself, you are no longer dependent on physical existence. You live forever through your soul. You know past lives let you live forever, through your soul."

Chapter 12: Iraq: 2003

Father James looked at Robert, "That is good insight which we had not thought of. The inscription is still somewhat unidentifiable as the other lines can't be read yet. What this means is the Scot-Irish British Druids were in Iraq somehow, which there is no prior evidence, or historical written proof that suggests they were, except for these carvings. Why were they here? How did they get to this region of Iraq? How did they find this cavern?"

Robert said, "Just think what the historical community would say if they knew of these discoveries and these carvings."

Father James said, "Our plan is for them to never find out until we can solve the mysteries first. We have other caves and other tunnels to explore and do not want to share our findings with the world yet. The Church and the Holy See want their chance to solve it before the critics, and prevent all those treasure hunters and media getting any wind of it. We've only explored around 30 percent of the caves and tunnels so far. You know if this was public, we would have every treasure hunter trying to dig in our tunnels, even though we are in an ancient city in Iraq and also in a combat zone."

Paul was still looking at the painting of the man with a knife in his back. He could not interpret it, but something about it looked and felt familiar.

Chapter 13

Angela and Nera

Dr. Angela Kapralov sat in her leather armchair, reflecting on what happened with her last session with Paul, which triggered memories about Joe. She only called him Joe in private, so she was always accustomed to refer to him as Dr. Joe. She did not have any patients this next hour and had pulled out the ruby Kila that Joe had left her the night he died. She still had not done his quest that he had asked her to do for him. She was rereading the letter he had left while she had a break between patients. She never burned it as directed.

She kept looking at the letter and the statement, "I will die tonight", and was wondering how he knew he was going to die. There was no evidence of any foul play, he had just died naked on his massage table. The other sentence that she reread was about giving her a quest and, "I need you to finish something for me, which I know you can complete." Angela was remembering the energy session that she had with Joe and how spiritually unique it was, especially the inner temple scene. She remembered the meeting with those wonderful people to include Lilith and Merc, but she had not been able to return since, and didn't know how to return. She knew that Lilith would help her find her way, but she had no connection to her, either.

No one had ever asked her if there was another letter and no one ever investigated for anything more. She stored the letter in

Chapter 13: Angela and Nera

her office in her patient files under an imaginary patient named Sebastian Jones. The best way to hide something is to have it non-hidden right in front of you. She never found what Joe was implying about the something else he had hidden. She had kept her secret and had not told anyone about the letter, but she never found any more notes, or clues, that Joe said that he left for her.

Since she had not told anyone, she had not met anyone to help her on this journey that she was tasked to do. Paul was the first person who had ever mentioned or fully described Lilith. If anyone asked about the knife in her desk, she would say that a patient gave it to her. But no one snoops around other doctor's offices, it's a therapist code. Angela had never discovered the three past lives that she had spent with Joe, and she had no clue what he was talking about. She had never really thought about past lives and did not know anyone that she could actually talk to about the unique subject. In the psychology field, the idea of past lives and regression are not well liked, and you can get dismissed by your peers if you pursue it publicly, and even privately.

There was a call on her phone and the receptionist informed Angela her next client was here. Angela let the receptionist know she would be down the hall to the lobby to pick up her new patient. Because there was so much security, each doctor had to buzz in their patients. This was her client's first time to see her, so Angela always wanted to be as polite as a possible as part of building trust with a new patient.

Angela put the blade and the file into her cabinet for safe keeping, got up from her desk, and opened her office door. She took her security key and walked down the hallway to the lobby to pick up her next therapy patient.

Angela walked up to the receptionist and she handed Angela the new patient file and pointed to a young woman with long brunette hair sitting in the corner. Angela took the file and walked over to the woman typing on her cellphone. Angela walked up to the woman and said, "Good morning, my name is Dr. Angela Kapralov."

The woman looked up from her chair and smiled and stood up, "My name is Nera. It is so nice to meet you." They shook hands and Angela walked her back to her office and closed the door. She sat in a leather chair by her desk and Nera sat on the leather couch.

Nera said, "Angela, thank you for meeting me on such short notice. You were highly recommended."

"Thank you. Who recommended me? I am curious."

Nera said, "My friend, Paul. He said you were absolutely wonderful."

Angela maintained her professional smile, but internally was immediately cautious because she knew that Paul had never divulged that she was his therapist to anyone. It was one of the tenets of their friendship. No one knew she was his therapist and no one knew he was her client. It all fell under doctor-patient privacy. Angela knew that there was something to be warned on with this new client. "Nera, what brings you here? How may I help you?"

Nera looked down at her phone and then put it away, "Angela, I have a problem with something very personal. Paul has hurt me deeply in his inactions a couple weeks ago and I am having issues with dealing with it. It involves past lives, Lilith, a couple of stupid angels, and a cursed athame, which still curses me to this day. I was cursed due to my past lives. Seems I keep killing, or some say murdering, the same person over and over again."

Angela turned white because this woman knew almost everything about Paul's last session with her; almost word for word. She knew she had to compose her emotions, but she was scared, and needed inquiry, and knew the negotiation therapy game of questions and answers. She knew if she followed her role as a therapist and asked the right questions, she could find out how Nera knew so much about Paul. Angela said, "Nera, please tell me more. How did this all happen?"

Nera said, "I will start at the first, it's better that way. Well, Paul and I shared multiple past lives together. Sometimes we were lovers and sometimes hated enemies. In several of our past lives, I may have killed him and some of his best friends with an athame and other blades, or whatever was available. But they burned me in one of those lives, so they thought. Anyway, there were other

Chapter 13: Angela and Nera

past lives where we were married and he so adored me. I died of natural causes in only one. Well, a couple weeks ago, it all came to a climax when he was supposed to release me from my horrible unfair curse of the athame. The bastard didn't because the spirit of Anna, the woman he loved and I had killed, came back into the situation and she talked him down. And since he did not harm me, I still have this horrible spiritual curse. Paul is such an honorable man. Why do some men never cross over and become evil?"

Angela said, "Well, all men are capable of evil, it just depends on the situation. We are wired that way. It's whether they choose to be evil and action it."

Nera looked up, "How do you get someone to turn evil or to kill?"

Angela was nervous about the subject and said, "That is not my specialty. I mainly deal with trauma and depression."

Nera looked frustrated at that. "Well, maybe we can discuss it next time. I would like to be a regular patient. Maybe every two weeks."

Angela said, "I usually see patients once a month, but we can always make exceptions for unique situations. I will never turn you down."

Nera and Angela continued to discuss Paul, the athame, and meeting Diana through astral projections for the next forty-five minutes. They both realized the time and stood up at the same time. As she was leaving, Nera looked at a photo on her bookshelf, of Angela and other students standing with Dr. Joe at the university during some social event. Nera said, "That is such a lovely photo you have with Joseph. Too bad he was sticking his nose in other people's business."

Angela said, "Do you know Dr. Joe?"

Nera said, "We knew each other. It is such a shame he passed. He was so talented, don't you think? He had such a promising career. Did they ever find any leads on his murder? I have not heard that the police ever found his murderer."

Angela was shocked by the statement and said, "As far as I know, the police thought it was a suicide and could not find any evidence of a murder, or even looked for a murderer."

Nera said, "How interesting. That's good to know. Everybody gets what's coming to them someday or another. One last thing, Angela, does the name Samael mean anything to you?"

Angela said, "I do not have any patients named Samuel and do not have any acquaintances named that either." Angela did not divulge what Lena had told her about Samael, but she thought Nera was digging for something else.

Nera said, "That's too bad. He is an amazing person to know in a time of need. Well, I better go. Thank you so much for listening to me. I believe this shall be the start of a beautiful friendship." As Nera was walking down the hall, Angela buzzed her out and she turned back to Angela, who was standing in her office doorway and said, "Tell Lilith hello for me the next time you see her. And one last thing, I promise. You must be careful with magical blades, you never know what might happen."

She then continued to walk down into the reception area thankful and smiling, then she exited toward her car. Her car was already running and a man was sitting in the passenger seat waiting for her.

As she opened the car door and sat, Nera said with a smile, "It all went as planned Samael, it all went as planned. We made headway on finding the Kila that we know she has."

Samael smiled back, "Excellent work, Nera. I never knew you were such an excellent actress."

Nera said, "I have been trained by the best and Dr. Angela is going to be easy to manipulate. She has no idea what's coming during our next appointment."

As Angela went back into her office, her receptionist informed her that her next patient had just cancelled, so she had an hour break. The last statement from Nera bothered Angela the most. How did Nera know Lilith? There was something cold and evil about Nera. Angela's intuition was saying Nera purposely sought her out for some reason she could not comprehend. Nera also mentioned the power of the blade, and she was wondering if she was referring to the athame, or the Kila she had stored in her office. Angela walked over to the file cabinet and opened it and pulled out the Kila. Still safe in her office. She was still thinking

Chapter 13: Angela and Nera

if having Nera as a patient today was an accident, or purely intentional to get to the Kila. What was so valuable about this Kila? The one thing she did know was that she needed help, and she decided to give Paul a friendly text to see what he was doing tomorrow night. She needed help and this was beyond her scope. Nera knew way too much about Paul for her comfort level.

Chapter 14

Angela's Float Session

After the troubling meeting with Nera, Angela needed a float to decompress her psyche. The spa she regularly visited held three sensory deprivation chambers, and she loved lying in the Epsom salt water in complete darkness and total silence. These floats were therapeutic and relaxing to many people who had stressful days—it was a little like returning to the womb—and Angela used them to reset her psyche on a regular basis. She had first come to the float because Paul recommended it to her, and she had kept going monthly because of how much it helped her psychologically and physically.

As she sat in the waiting room, Lawrence, the manager, came up to her with a warm smile, "Angela, we are ready for you. Please follow me as usual. It's always nice to see one of our best customers."

Angela knew the routine and Lawrence led her to a changing room. After closing the door, she started to take off her clothes and put them in a locker and pulled out the key. She stood there, completely naked, and smiled. In her life she had never taken much time for herself, but these floats were her alone time, her absolutely alone time. She looked at the plush robe that was hanging, waiting for her to put on, and to put her locker key in the robe pocket. There were also the adorable plush slippers that she liked to wear. She walked out to the meditation room, waiting

Chapter 14: Angela's Float Session

for her massage chair time before her float. Lawrence opened the curtain and waved her into one of those really expensive massage chairs. She sat and started to melt, because she knew what would happen next. Lawrence turned on the massage chair, and as it measured her height and leaned back, the ceiling twinkled as if covered in stars and Angela felt her body settle in to relaxing and letting go. These massage chair session lasted twenty-five minutes and then she would have her float time.

Angela was so relaxed from the massage chair, that when the time was up and her chair started to move back to normal upright setting is when she realized that it was time for her float. She stepped out of her chair and slipped on her slippers. Lawrence walked in and smiled and signaled float room #2 for her. He knew it was her favorite room. He opened the door and knew she did not need any directions and started the five minute timer before bowing himself out of the room. She had five minutes to take a shower and get in the float before the light and sound would turn off in the float tank. She took her robe and slippers off and walked into the shower and turned it on. She quickly cleaned her scalp, hair, and body and turned off the shower. There was only fifteen inches of water in the float tank, but there was over two hundred pounds of Epson salt. She opened the door and stepped into the water, which was the same temperature as her skin, by design, and she slowly lowered herself into the water and leaned back. She was instantly floating and she allowed her head and neck to relax into floating on the water. The lights and music were still on and she knew in less than a minute the lights and sound would fade out and she could be alone with her thoughts.

The floats always calmed her down and got her brain into the theta brain state, especially when the only sounds were of the water when her body moved, and her heartbeat.

As she was going deep into relaxation she was starting to dream about things, and during these dreams she would always have conversations with her mind, or spirits, or other entities. As her heart rate lowered and her relaxation deepened, she saw herself in a white night gown, walking along a pale glowing path at night. She was approaching the inner temple that she had traveled with

Joe during that special energy session she experienced before he passed away. This time she was walking to the patio by the lake and the moon was a horned waxing crescent, low and vibrant on the horizon, and the fire pit was roaring, but there was only two people sitting in the Adirondack chairs. As she slowly approached the back patio, Lilith looked at Angela, smiled, and put her wine glass down. She got up and hugged Angela like a favorite aunt would hug a favorite niece. Lilith was so happy to see her.

Angela smiled and Lilith took her hand and said, "It is so wonderful that you are visiting us tonight. You know it is the spring equinox, don't you? Well, if you don't, then let's celebrate with my most-dearest friend. My dear Angela, this is Merc. You have met him before, but this time more intimate. I hate when he gets stiff with crowds and find him much more fun in small groups."

A most attractive middle-aged man stood up from his chair and took Angela's hand and kissed the top of it. He looked straight into her eyes, which gave Angela warmth in her heart and her heart jumped because she was getting lost in his crystal blue eyes.

Lilith took her hand back, "Merc, she is my friend and you need to behave."

Lilith smiled and gestured at a chair, "Angela, please sit down and talk with us. This is a special night, but most folks who are usually here are with their human connections, so it is only Merc and I tonight. We are so happy you came to join us while you are doing your float today. Everything aligned for all of this to happen right now."

Angela was cautious in her questions, "Lilith, can you help me with Joe's death? He gave me a letter the night before he passed away, but did not tell me what to do for him. It's been almost a year and I have done nothing with the Kila or told anyone. I loved Joe. I loved him so much, but I never told him. He was my hero and my mentor; I loved just spending time with him. He asked me to go on a quest for him, but I never did; I was afraid. I am so lost and do not know where to start. He did tell me if I found you, you would help me."

Lilith said, "Angela, would you like to talk to him?"

Chapter 14: Angela's Float Session

"Of course I would, but he died. He's dead."

Lilith smiled, "No one really dies, they just transform into spirit and light. Let me see what we can do." She looked over at Merc, "Merc, we need your special communication skills with the other world. Please help us in this special circumstance."

Merc was standing next to them, texting on his phone, and finishing his drink. He put his phone in his back pocket and looked at Lilith, "My dear, how may I assist the two of you?"

"Merc, Angela here needs to communicate with her professor who passed away almost a year ago and left her a special knife, a Kila, in which she has told absolutely no one about. I think you might remember the Kila?" As she finished her words she winked at Merc.

Angela said, "I do not know how Merc can help because you can't talk to the dead."

Merc smiled, "My dear Angela, do you know who I am?"

"Your name is Merc. I have no idea who you are."

Lilith interfered, "Angela, Merc is short for Mercury, who is actually the messenger of the gods and guide of dead souls to the underworld. He is also known as Hermes."

Angela smiled, "Really? This man in front of me is Hermes, the son of Zeus? I thought he would be taller."

Lilith started laughing and Merc looked frustrated as hell and put his hands up and tilted his head to the right. She said, "Angela, you just made my decade and gave me lots to tease Merc about for centuries." Lilith gave Angela a hug and laughed again. "I so adore you; we will be friends for a long time. Well, yes, this rather short man"—she was jeering at Merc again—"is a god, a small god"—at this they both started laughing, "—but he is a messenger of the gods and has access to the underworld to speak to the dead. He can help us speak to Joe if you want?"

Angela looked at Lilith and then at Merc, "I would so much like to speak one more time with Joe. I need his encouragement to finish his task. Please."

Merc, somewhat frustrated at the shallowness of the height comment, looked into her eyes and her heart melted, "Angela, I shall help you speak with Joe again, but it will be on your next visit. I need time to find him. You will need to come back and visit us soon so you can talk with Joe. In three days, find a new way to this inner temple, a way you have never tried before, with a stranger you have never met. Find a man named Peter. He has a shop on 18th Street. Tell him that Merc and Lilith sent you and that he owes us a favor. If he is still a jerk to you, please use the word, MacGregor, and he then must help you. It's one of our secret codewords."

Angela said, "How will I get here again? Will Peter help me? This is my second time to visit, Lilith. How do I find my way back?" She paused her babble and sighed, "Okay, I will look for Peter."

Lilith said, "He has a new age energy office inside a yoga studio downtown on 18th Street. Most people do not know it exists because there is no sign. Tell him you need the special energy session to meet Lilith. He will know exactly what to do so you can return to the inner temple and meet Merc and I, and hopefully Joe, also. Do you understand what I just told you? Peter is one of my oldest friends."

Angela nodded, "Yes, I must find Peter and tell him I need to meet Lilith."

Merc smiled, "If Peter doubts you, you also must tell him that it is time for him to get a haircut. If you say that, he will know you are a messenger from us. He hates sarcasm."

Angela looked at Lilith for confirmation asking if it was a joke and Lilith said, "I agree. If you say that about his long hair, he will know it is from Merc, who always teases him about his hair. But only use that phrase if he does not believe you on the word MacGregor."

The lights came slowly back on in the float tank, which meant her float was complete and her visit with Lilith immediately ended, since she was now awake. She slowly started to stand in the tank and let the saltwater drip off her body. There was a small towel near the door of the tank to wipe her face to make sure no Epson salt burned her eyes. She loved the way the water was the same temperature as her core body temperature so her senses never knew where the skin ended and the water began. She was

Chapter 14: Angela's Float Session

just a part of the water element.

As she stood there, the lights turned fully on and the music started back to awaken the person fully, then she opened up the door and stepped out into the shower room. She walked over to the shower and turned it on. It was one of those huge rain effect showerheads with warm water to help rinse off all the salt.

After every float she was always in this relaxed state for several hours, and in a complete state of mellowness for the rest of the day. She found her locker and put on her normal clothes to face the world again. As she departed, she waved at Lawrence at the front desk, "Same time, two weeks!" and Lawrence gave her the thumbs up because he knew words did not matter right now. She kept a journal in her car so she could write everything down as she sat in her car, getting her senses back, so she could drive home coherently.

She opened her journal and wrote *Peter on 18th Street.*

Chapter 15
Peter on 18th Street

Angela's next work day at the clinic ended and she was so done with her patients' sessions that day. She locked her filing cabinet and locked her office door. She waved to her receptionist on her way out, walked into the parking lot, and got into her sports car. As a doctor, she made an excellent salary and was conservative on everything except her BMW, which was excellent and could hit 100 mph with no problem. She settled into her leather seat and just let the car warm up a little before she made the drive home. Something was bugging her since her appointment with Nera the day prior, so she pulled out her phone to text Paul and wanted to confirm that he could meet her tonight. She then decided not to text, but to call Paul and had Bluetooth on in her car so she could talk to him if he answered as she was driving.

Paul answered, "Hello."

"Paul, this is Angela, do you have a minute tonight? I think I need your help. Could we meet somewhere and have a drink?"

Paul was in jeans, in his home, had not showered all day and had on a T-shirt that he slept in the night prior. "You caught me by surprise, and I am really not dressed to go out. Do you want to come over here?"

Angela said, "Okay, but I need a glass of whiskey if you have any."

Paul leaned back and smiled from his couch, listening to

Chapter 15: Peter on 18th Street

Blue Swede's *Hooked on a Feeling*. He was tapping his toes to the music and looking at the five o'clock whisky he was already drinking and chuckled, "I think I can provide you whiskey. Do you need directions to my house?"

Angela said, "Thanks. Hey, are you listening to *Hooked on a Feeling*? That's a great freaking drinking song. Be there in fifteen minutes."

Paul took a big gulp of whiskey, "Why yes it is. The garage door is open. You can pull in and close the door and no one will know you are here."

Angela smiled, "Paul…thank you for always thinking about me and protecting me. See you soon."

Paul was going to get off the couch to open his garage door but remembered he had an app that would do it for him. He then opened the app and looked for the open the garage button, found it, and hit it. He then heard the garage door open and smiled. He might have had two whiskey drinks as he looked at his empty glass. He decided to sit on his couch and wait for Angela. He smelled his shirt and then decided he should at least change shirts, so he got up and went to his bedroom to find a clean T-shirt. Paul loved T-shirts and preferred to wear them, over anything else, except a flannel in the cold. He pulled out the next clean shirt in his drawer and it was his *Journey Departure Tour 1981* shirt. His original shirt was way too old and too tight and this was bought online through a classic 80s website. He was always a sucker for good classic T-shirts.

When he walked back into the living room, Angela was already barefoot and holding a whiskey bottle at his bar. Paul merely said, "Make yourself at home."

Angela said, "Thank you for letting me come over. I have gotten myself into an interesting situation and you are also in the middle of it." She poured herself a double in the glass with ice.

Paul said, "Well, let me make myself a drink and accompany you so you don't drink alone."

Angela asked, "You mean your third drink?"

Paul replied, "What do you mean?"

Angela said, "Well there are two glasses on your coffee table that are empty, but still have condensation, so they were recently drank. Don't fib. Just get your drink and come over here and sit on the couch right now. We are in so much trouble together."

Paul just smiled and followed orders from his doctor. He got himself a drink and quickly joined her on the couch and said, "How may I help? I doubt I am in trouble."

Angela looked at him hard, "Tell me everything on a woman named Nera."

Paul almost spit out his drink. He said, "Well, remember that woman who gave me the athame a couple months ago, that was cursed and we have had multiple past lives together, that end up always bad for me, mostly? I think I have died in three or more of them. Yea, that's her."

Angela said, "That was what I thought. But what does she want from me? Why did she come to my office as a client? I just know it was intentional. I just know it!"

Paul took a drink and thought for a moment, "Well, my best guess is she is trying to get to me through you. That, or you have something she might want. But I doubt you have some ancient artifact in your house or office."

Angela finished her drink in one gulp, "What if I have something that is quite unique, that my college professor gave me after a healing session he did on me, and well, the next day he died."

Paul just looked at her in disbelief, "I never knew you did energy healing; you never talked about it in our sessions. What did he leave you?"

Angela smiled and said, "Our sessions are about you and not me and I hardly divulge important things about me in our sessions. It's not professional. Oh yea, during my energy session with Dr. Joe, I met Lilith and she was exactly how you described her."

Paul looked at her again in full surprise and said, "No shit, and you never told me. Well, that's a revelation. Did you go to an inner temple?"

Angela said with a guilty grin, "Yes, I went to a large cabin with the deck facing the mountain lake."

Chapter 15: Peter on 18th Street

Paul slugged his drink down and got up to pour another and she handed him her glass, too, "Well, is there any other key information that I should know about while I make us another drink? By the way, you can sleep on my couch if you drink too much." He finished making the drinks and headed back toward the couch.

Angela said, "If I stay the night, you will be a gentlemen and sleep on the couch. I will have your bed to sleep on."

He just smiled back, "Nope. You will just sleep in the guest room."

Angela threw a pillow at him for the comment by not offering her the guest room in this teasing banter. "There is one more thing. I had a sensory deprivation float yesterday after work and I had a vision from Lilith and Merc, who instructed me to find Peter on 18th Street who does energy sessions and other things. They both said that Peter would help me and that he knows Lilith and Merc and he owed them a favor."

Paul said, "You did not tell me that you met Merc also." He rolled his eyes again and smiled with consternation at her. He said, "Is there anything else you are holding back?"

Angela smiled, "Nope. I think that is it. I tried to look up this Peter guy on 18th Street, but there are no businesses on 18th that have an owner named Peter from what I found on the internet."

Paul smiled back at her and said, "This is your lucky day. I know exactly which Peter they were referring to. He has a secluded office inside a yoga studio and does not have any advertisement or business phones to it. There is just a door there with 'Dr. Peter: Energy Expert' on it. I have walked by it going to ashtanga yoga and have never seen the door open and never met Dr. Peter, but I know where it is."

Angela toasted drinks with Paul, "Let's have another drink. And do you have an old T-shirt that I can sleep in in your guest room?"

Paul said, "Well, let me get another drink first for us and then I have a plethora of T-shirts for you to choose from. You need to tell me your style and genre and I will find one."

Angela just said, "I need the softest one you have in a large so it covers my panties if I walk around at night."

Paul nearly dropped his glass with that comment, "Okay, I have the exact one you need." Within thirty seconds, he came back with a simple cotton blend large white shirt with simple words "Be Excellent to Each Other" on it. The letters were not scratchy and the cotton was soft to the touch. He handed it to her with her drink and she laughed.

Angela said, *Bill and Ted's Adventure* was a great movie with George Carlin."

They both laughed and then talked for another hour on miscellaneous things. Then the alcohol made them both tired, and they were glad that it was Friday night and neither one had to work in the morning. They decided to head to bed, and Angela hugged Paul to thank him for listening to her and helping her in the morning. He merely said, "No problem."

* * *

When Angela woke up, she almost forgot where she was as she looked at the guest room that she was sleeping in, but she could smell coffee brewing, and also something cooking in the kitchen. She got up and went to the bathroom, then looked for clothes to put on, but decided walking with just his shirt on into his kitchen would be more fun. As she walked in, blowing hair out of eyes and saying "I am ready for the coffee," she was surprised to find an older man and another woman in the kitchen with Paul. Paul handed her a fresh cup of coffee and she was trying to see if she should put some pants on, but the company felt comfortable and the other woman lounging at the kitchen bar also looked like she had just woken up. Paul pulled out a chair for Angela and said, "I would like you to meet some friends." She just nodded and grabbed her coffee with both hands and sat down. Paul pointed to Robert and said, "That distinguished man cooking breakfast is Robert. He is a professor with me at the university."

Robert said, "Pleased to meet you, my dear."

Paul gestured to the woman next to her, "This is Jamie, who has experienced three angels. She works at the university, also."

Chapter 15: Peter on 18th Street

Jamie shook her hand. "I have brought them here this morning so the three of us can brainstorm about Nera and help you find Dr. Peter."

Angela sipped her coffee, "That's cool. The more the merrier. What's for breakfast? That smells delicious."

Robert brought over a spoonful of eggs and wanted her to taste it. She did and instantly smiled. He said, "This, my dear, is my morning after breakfast. It has crumbled bison sausage, organic onions, cheese, jalapenos, mushrooms, and scrambled farm eggs that are put between two slices of French toast. After the night of drinking you and Paul had, I thought it would help this morning."

Angela said, "You know, men cooking is quite sexy."

Robert smiled, placing a plate in front of her that smelled divine, "My dear, I am old enough to be your father. But, I am single and always looking for an intellectual equal who likes to travel the world." He said this with a jest and a jaunty bow, not knowing if he was kidding or being serious.

Angela took a bite of breakfast and said, "I might take you up on that, pending your dinner cooking abilities."

Everyone laughed at the razzing between them and Robert also put a plate in front of Jamie and Paul.

Angela, with her mouth full of food said, "How are all of you going to help me with Nera?"

Paul said, "We are first going to help you find Dr. Peter, who is a recluse and quite odd. Robert knows the rumors about him, so I will let him explain."

Robert sat at the bar with everyone and sipped a cup of coffee. "Dr. Peter is a unique and odd gentleman. He is brilliant. He has a doctorate in sociology and also spent many years in the military, and overseas, since the 80s. There are years where he just disappeared and there were rumors he was in the CIA, or even the KGB, and then there are rumors that he went mad. He has plenty of money because there are times when he does not work and disappears. He opened up an energy shop on 18th, but he does not advertise and has so few clients. And they all meet at odd, unpredictable hours. He is a real recluse. We met in the 80s when he used to teach at the university and then he got so odd. He is still carried as an adjunct professor for the department. The one thing I know about his change was when he spent time in Russia and Mongolia in Shaman training, and when he came back, he was quite different. I have never met anyone who has ever had an energy session with him. I have no idea how to contact him, but know where his office is."

Angela smiled at Robert, "I was messaged through a dream I had during a float to find Peter on 18th Street and he would know what to do."

Jamie said, "Who messaged you this?"

Angela said, "It is going to sound crazy, but Lilith and a guy called Merc that I met in my dream state due to the float that I was doing."

Jamie said, "I have met angels, but I have not yet met her. But I believe you and let's head out to 18th Street and find this Peter guy."

Paul started collecting the empty plates and looked at Angela, "Looks like we are all ready to depart, but you are the one who needs some pants on."

Angela had completely forgot she was not wearing pants and still had on Paul's T-shirt from last night. She smiled, "Give me two minutes to get dressed."

Paul finished all the plates and cups and put them in the dishwasher while the rest of them put their coffee in travel mugs, because coffee is too precious to pour down the sink if you had not finished the mug yet. As Paul was turning on the dishwasher and finding his keys, Robert said, "I shall drive. We are parked behind you and it's just easier if we all fit in my Jeep."

Paul laughed and Angela hopped out of the guest room with her hair in a ponytail, ready to do this challenge with this group of new friends. She had more confidence now that she could try and finish what Joe wanted her to do. They all left Paul's house and climbed in Robert's Jeep and headed downtown to 18th Street to find Peter.

* * *

Chapter 15: Peter on 18th Street

Robert parked the jeep across the street from the yoga studio. The building was old, built in the 1920s, and the yoga studio was on the second floor. They walked across the street, entered the building, and walked up the stairs to the yoga studio. The door to Peter's office was inside the studio and right behind the counter with a sign that said 'Dr. Peter: Energy Expert'. There was no telephone number, no office hours, no way to communicate with him. Robert touched the door knob and the door was unlocked. So he turned the doorknob and opened the door.

Paul said, "Robert, should we be snooping in his office without permission?"

Robert merely said, "If Peter did not want anyone snooping, then he should have locked his door."

They all walked into the empty reception room and there was nothing on the walls and no furniture in the room. It looked like no one had been there for weeks. They continued to walk to the next room and there was a drastic change. There was a massage table in the middle and prayer flags, candles, and alters on every side of the room. It looked like an occult or a witchcraft room. Everyone stopped and was looking around when a voice from a speaker on the wall said, "Robert, what are you and your friends doing in my office?"

Robert said, "Peter is that you? If so, we need help that only you can provide. This young woman next to me had a vision from Lilith and Merc to find you so that she could get assistance to the inner temple for another message. She even has the proof to convince you."

The speaker said, "Robert, I do not believe you. It has been years since anyone was directed to find me, and that was an emergency case due to a curse. What is the message?"

Robert pointed to Angela to speak and she shyly said, "Peter, I was told to find you. That Peter on 18th Street would help me. Lilith and Merc said you owed them. Merc said to comment about your long hair, that you would know it is was from him, because he would always tease you about your hair. But if you do not believe that, then Lilith said I could use the word 'MacGregor'.

That is what Lilith told me. She said you were the only one who could assist me back to the inner temple."

Paul looked at Robert when Angela commented about 'MacGregor' and then looked at Jamie and they both had blank looks on their faces.

Robert pointed toward a video camera in the corner and a speaker in the ceiling and said, "Peter, are you spying on us? That is not like you."

The voice came back on, "Please describe Lilith for me."

Angela said, "She was a beautiful woman, with simple casual clothes, but elegant, with a smile that would calm your soul, and a touch that put goose bumps on my neck She was divine to be within feet from. She was like a sunset on a beach in Hawaii."

All of a sudden, an attic ceiling door with stairs dropped down and there was a voice from the attic that said, "Please come up to my loft."

Robert pointed to Angela to go up first on the ladder to, what was assumed, an attic. They were all surprised by the room. There were books on every shelf. The room was circular, with weapons from old to current, and flags, and old bottles of alcohol and wine. It looked like an old cigar library with fine leather chairs. And there were three skylights in the ceiling that let the light in and only one lamp on. There was a gray-haired man with his back to them pouring himself a drink. He said, "Robert, it's been a long time."

Robert replied, "Yes, it has been too long. But you are the one that can never be found. There is trouble brewing and Angela is in the middle of it. Lilith and Merc trust you, and so do we."

As he turned around, he had long gray hair, a trimmed gray beard, full weathered skin from too much sun, and piercing sky-blue eyes, with a scar on his cheekbone. It looked like he had been through a lot of life throughout the years. He turned around and had four wine glasses and an open bottle of wine. He said, "Well, my name is Peter. Before we discuss anything, it is my tradition to have a glass of wine with new friends, as a Pagan custom, before we talk business. So will you all partake? It's a ritual."

Chapter 15: Peter on 18th Street

They all looked at each other and nodded yes.

Peter handed them each a glass and poured them some wine, then he poured himself a glass and said, "Before we drink we must make a toast. That toast is to fellowship and to follow through on the quest no matter what it takes." He put his glass toward his new guests and they all toasted together. He then said, "I will only help you if no one speaks about my room above my office. This is my private office that no one in the building knows about and I want to keep it that way. Do you all agree to keep this promise?"

They all nodded yes. Then everyone had a nice sip of wine.

They finished with the toast and agreeing not to talk about the office. Then Peter said, "Well, let me pull out my table so we can help this young woman get back to the inner temple. Robert, will you help?"

As the table was being put together, Peter said, "Who had the message from Lilith?" Angela raised her hand. He said, "Come here and let me look at your hands." Angela came to Peter and he took both of her hands and looked at them closely, then put them side by side and read both hands. He then looked directly in her eyes and said, "Was Merc annoying and somewhat of a jerk?"

Angela said, "I think so, but I did not have that much time with him. He was annoyed by my request to help communicate with Dr. Joe who died and left me a task and an artifact."

Peter said, "What artifact?"

Angela said, "He left me a unique knife that my research says is an ancient Kila. It's quite old by the style and markings and something odd happens when I hold it. The blade glows purple and I get visions."

Robert and Paul looked at each other and did not know any of this exact information before, and were amazed by the similarity to the athame.

Peter said, "Okay, thank you. Now I will need you to take off your jeans and your shirt and get on the table. There is no time to be shy. We need to all have skin contact with you and get you to the inner temple. Take your jeans and shirt off now." He patted the table indicating her to hurry up.

Angela looked at Paul, who shrugged and nodded. So,

Angela unbuttoned her jeans and took them off, and took off her shirt. She was only in her bra and panties and Peter said, "Lay on the table. We have to all work together to get you to the inner temple." Angela laid down. Peter lit several candles and dimmed the lights, and then took out some sage. He took a lighter, lit the sage, and walked around the table and let the smoke go around Angela. He then said, "Robert, Paul, and Jamie, I need you all to stand around the table and when I tell you, I want you to put your hands on Angela. Only when I tell you, do you understand?" They all nodded and took positions. Peter went to a black bag he had on the table and poured some large crystals in his hands and placed them on Angela's body; one on each thigh, one on her stomach, one on her sternum, and one on her throat. He then pulled a healing bowl from the bookcase and hit it once by her head, then rang it by her side, rang it again by her feet, then again by her other side. He then placed the bowl on Angela's stomach and started to circle the bowl, in which a unique vibrational sound occurred. It had an instant effect on Angela, as she completely calmed down and relaxed with the vibrations. He continued to run the wooden handle along the rim of the healing bowl, and the vibrations and sound were getting more intense in the quiet room.

As all of this was happening, Angela was first scared to be almost naked on a massage table with people she hardly knew, but instantly thought of Joe and her experience with him in their healing session. Peter was doing some of the same things that Joe had. The crystals felt comforting and the sound bowl brought all the inner energy into focus. She had her eyes closed and was starting to see colors in her mind, mainly purples and blues. She heard Peter tell them all to put their hands on her, and as soon as they all did, she was transported to a new place. She was traveling in her mind, but did not know where.

Peter had told all of them to touch Angela with full palms down and he said, "Do not let go not matter what she does or says. Only let go if I tell you to let go. Do you all understand?" They all nodded and could tell they had an effect with all their hands on her at the same time. She started to calm down and to twitch slowly. Her breathing calmed.

Chapter 15: Peter on 18th Street

Angela was visioning a wooded path and there was snow on the ground. She was barefoot, with just a robe on and that T-shirt that Paul let her borrow last night. Angela had never been to this path and was scared, but knew she needed to keep walking. She could hear her bare feet crunch in the snow, but her feet were not cold, but warm. She kept walking down the snowy trail and could see someone in an opening of trees, standing next to a fire, with a black trench coat on and a walking stick, just monitoring the fire. She was walking closer to the person when the person turned around to look at her and it was Peter. Peter smiled back at her and said, "It is good that you made it here, back with me this time."

Angela said, "How are you in my dreams right now?"

Peter said, "This is not a dream, but a different realm. You are astral traveling. You are having an out-of-body experience with me. This is how you have separated your physical body from your spiritual body. This is an ancient way to commune with your consciousness, spirit, or astral body. So, let's take the walk together to continue to the inner temple. I will walk with you to meet Lilith. You just have to trust me."

Angela said, "I do trust you."

Peter said, "Well, let's start walking to the temple together. It is not far away from here." Peter took ahold of her hand and they started walking hand in hand down the trail. Angela was not cold, even though she was barefoot in the snow, and Peter's hand was super warm. They continued to walk the wooded snow trail together. Peter had a walking stick in his left hand and holding Angela's hand with his right.

Peter said, "Angela, we are close to our destination. What do you seek most of all?"

Angela looked over at Peter and said, "I would want one more time with Joe. I never got to tell him what he meant to me, and I need his help to finish his quest. He told me to find people who would help me, but never told me what the result or end state was supposed to be."

Peter stopped and looked at her, "You know he might just want to go on the journey of explorations, because life is about the process and not always about the end result. The result may not be the goal at all."

Angela looked back, "Yes, that is exactly what Joe would have said." She looked down into the snow and looked back at their footsteps in the snow and asked, "Will I get to see him again?"

Peter smiled and said, "That depends on our friend Merc and if he did his duty." They started walking through the trail that was frozen. They continued in silence for a few more minutes, until they came to a meadow where the lake house was and the porch that faced the mountain lake. This time snow covered the house, but there was a chimney with smoke coming through. The mountain lake was frozen solid and the mountains were covered in snow. The patio was empty and it looked like no one had been there in a while.

Angela said, "I did not know that my dreams would have seasons. Like this inner temple, I thought it would be the same weather all the time, each time I would visit."

Peter smiled, still holding her hand, "Well, everything has changes and like the seasons, it is good for our dreams to go through a death and rebirth for the process of knowing where and who we really are. Since Mother Earth and Father Sky must change, why not in our dreams, too?"

Angela took the comments in to think about, and with her psychology background and her experience with Joe's guidance and the framework, it made sense that the process of dying and rebirth is essential in the cycle of life.

They reached the patio, but it was empty and full of snow and had not been swept or cleaned off. It looked like no one had stepped out into the snow at all. Peter continued to hold her hand and walked her up to the back door of the house. There were small lights on she could see through the back windows. As they came near the door, Merc opened it and said, "Thank you, Peter, for helping Angela back to the inner temple. It is good to see you. I still love your long gray hair."

Peter looked down at Merc's shoes and said, "Merc, I can see you still wear middle-school kid's shoes, but always nice to see

Chapter 15: Peter on 18th Street

you again my friend. It's been a long time."

Angela was surprised to see Merc in the house and then she saw Lilith getting up from the couch. She had been talking to someone in a chair. Lilith was dressed for winter, and had a beautiful sweater and winter boots on, always elegant in whatever she wore. She walked up to Angela as they all stood just inside the door and said, "My dear Angela, Merc did his part as promised, and I have talked with Joe already. You will have only about fifteen minutes with Joe before Merc has to take him back. Merc bent some rules, but we did not break any of the big rules. We will be outside. Ask what you must ask, and we have to move on." Lilith gave Angela a hug and whispered, "Ask and tell him everything. You don't have much time. This is the only time you will be able to talk with Joe."

Lilith then gave Peter a hug and kissed him on both cheeks, "I have missed you Peter. Now let's go outside and give Joe and Angela their brief time together. Come on Merc. We need to get Joe back before they find out he is missing." Lilith, Merc, and Peter departed the house and closed the door behind them. Angela realized it was now quiet, except for the sound of the fire going on in the large stone fireplace. She stood frozen, slightly scared to move forward toward the chair. She could see a man facing the fire in a chair. but she could only see his back.

A voice from the chair said, "Angela, please sit next to me."

Angela felt chills and knew the voice of Joe. She started to slowly cry, but walked toward the chairs. She was trying to look closely at the man, but could not fully identify him, but he sounded just like Joe. She was shaking due to her emotions. Then she sat down in the chair next to the man, and then he turned his head and looked at her and smiled. It was Joe. She started crying and got up from the chair and went over to him and gave him a hug. She was unable to keep trying to restrain herself and cried fully with her whole body. It was really him; she did not have the time to rationalize how he was there in her arms right now. She just wanted to feel him next to her again and she was crying so much her tears fell on his cheeks. He had his arms around her, too, while she was crying on his shoulder and cheek.

Joe said, "Now dear, no time for tears. We do not have much time." He pulled her close to him, took his hand and touched her chin, and had her look at him in his crystal- blue eyes. He leaned forward and kissed her on her lips with a soft comfortable loving kiss. Her tears were still rolling down both cheeks as he kissed her.

Joe said, "Our love between us is entwined between multiple past lives and this present life. My life was cut short so that I can meet you again in your next life. I had made a treacherous deal in a past life with a goddess to save someone and she called for her paid due."

Angela said, "That's a lot to think about. You could have written that in your secret letter you left me." As she said it she smiled and laughed a little.

Joe smiled back, "Yes. I left you a letter to do something with not enough information to do it and my best graduate student editor did not help me with it." He was implying that she was not there to help him write the letter that he left her, in a teasing, gentle way.

She ended up sitting on his lap sideways and her feet dangled off the side, but he held her tight and they started to talk about the letter.

Joe said, "Angela, do you still have the Kila in a safe place?" Angela nodded her head, and was just soaking in Joe's words and that he had his arms around her. He also said, "I need you to match it with its staff."

Angela said, "What staff?"

Joe said, "That staff over there in the corner. It is waiting for its partner."

Angela said, "I am in a dream, I think. How am I supposed to bring something from my dream back to reality?"

Joe said, "Carry it with you. When you depart in a few minutes it shall return with you. Now, you will need to attach the Kila to the staff when the time comes. When you need protection from evil. You will know when you need it. It will give you hints. You will just know. I want you to trust in your intuition. I want you to trust Peter and the group. They are your allies and will help

Chapter 15: Peter on 18th Street

you on this quest."

Angela said, "What is the quest?"

Joe said, "There is a woman who is seeking the Kila. She can never have it, because she wants to use it to undo what the Kila has done spiritually. The Kila, or also called a Phurba, is a 3-sided stake associated with the meditational deity *Vajrakila* who bears three faces; one joyful, one peaceful, and one wrathful. The blade's power transforms the negative energies known as the "three poisons" of ignorance, greed, and aggression. It is a ritual knife and the energy is fierce. The blade that I gave you, this one is for shamanic healing and energy work. Show it to Peter and he will know what to do with it. This blade is also connected to Hermes, or you know him as Merc, sitting outside right now. The Kila holds demons and has been used in exorcisms for millennia. This Kila is a spiritual weapon that you must respect. When you need the power of the Kila, you must stab it into the ground. That is how it is the most powerful. This blade is used for the destruction of demonic powers. I want you to remember that. The energy of the Kila is fierce, wrathful, and piercing. It holds many demons in place once exorcised from a human host. That is why the strange woman wants it back. She wants to release the demons because Samael was the one who brought the demons to Earth. Well, you will find out sooner than later, but Samael and Lilith used to be married and now they hate each other. It's quite a little family feud."

Angela said, "Why did they not tell me?"

Joe said, "They are not allowed to give information to humans that could cause them physical harm, or to do their own business for them. There are certain rules of the universal godly domain."

Angela said, "You never told me why you had to die?"

Joe kissed her forehead and said, "I had to pay dues with a goddess that I made an irreversible deal with. I had to give myself to save someone. Somewhat like playing with the devil, and she came calling my soul a little early and that is why I need your help to finish my tasks. Our current time is over and I must return to the underworld. I will visit you again, either in a dream or another healing session. I promise you."

Merc entered the house and said, "Our time is up and we must get back before anyone finds out you are missing."

Joe got up from the chair and gave Angela a long hug and kiss on her cheek. He whispered in her ear, "Make sure you remember to take the staff back with you and use it with the Kila. I also put a stone in your pocket. Do not reach for it until you get back. That stone will give us a verbal connection to talk when needed." He hugged her again and left the room to meet with Merc. Merc waved back at Angela, winked, and sauntered out.

As Joe and Merc departed, Lilith walked in to console Angela. Lilith walked over to the couch where she was sitting, still dumbfounded. As she sat down and held Angela's hand, Peter walked in and said, "Angela, it is now time for us to go back to the present moment, to the now, or whatever we want to call it."

Angela looked at Lilith, "What do you call this if it is not the present? Are not we in the present moment?"

Lilith looked at her and said, "We are in the cosmos, your mind, the metaphysical, the space between the spaces, the subconscious mind. But I agree, it is time for Peter to take you back."

Angela got up with Lilith and looked at her, "Joe said things about you that I should talk about. When will we ever meet again?"

Lilith said, "Now that you know Peter, and where he is located, he is one of the historic ways to always find me. But you can work on your own way to contact me, too. That's quite a powerful stone there in your pocket that Joe gave to you, after all. Now, my dear, don't forget your staff."

Angela walked over to the corner and picked up the plain staff, which was only about five feet tall, and walked over to Peter and said, "I guess we better go."

Peter walked over to Lilith, "I miss you, and I will always love you." As he said this, he gave her a romantic kiss on the lips, like the kind of kiss you would give an ex-lover. Their kiss stopped and he winked at her and she blushed slightly, He turned to Angela and grabbed her hand, and they walked outside, back to the snow and back to the trail. Peter said, "Keep tight and hold

Chapter 15: Peter on 18th Street

onto that staff when we pass over. We can't afford you to lose it now." Peter grabbed her hand tight, and as they started to walk through the snowy forest trail he said, "Hold my hand tight and hold the staff high, then strike it to the ground hard."

Angela looked at Peter and he smiled, encouraging her to do it. She raised the staff in the air and then touched it to the ground. There was a bright flash of light and Angela opened her eyes. She was back on the table, with all of them with their hands on her, and she was looking at the ceiling in Peter's secret attic office. Peter said, "You may all release your hands from Angela. We have both returned from the inner temple."

Angela was still in a daze from the experience and she heard Robert say, "Well, that only took a few minutes. I hope they received the messages they needed." Angela knew that she had spent over an hour or two on her journey and in the lake house, but could not explain how it only could have been five minutes in normal time.

Peter looked at Paul, Robert, and Jamie, and said, "It was a successful visit, and we have brought back the staff." He pointed to the corner of the room at the staff that Angela had successfully transported from the inner temple.

Robert said, "Peter, how is that possible? We have never been able to bring things back. How did you do it?"

Peter said, "Secrets of the profession, my friend Robert. I can't tell. But I did not bring it back. Angela was the one authorized to bring it back. A gift from her dear friend."

As Robert was looking at it and moving forward to touch it, Angela said, "Please do not touch it. It is not ready to be handled by other people. It has just spoken to me and needs to be connected with the Kila."

Paul said, "I'm sure I don't have to tell you to be careful with the Kila. When it is time."

Angela was slowly sitting up from the table and realized, again, that she was half-naked, but really did not mind anymore, "Just to catch everyone up, Joe gave me a Kila in the mail, after he died. It has been used to expel demons from humans across the centuries and still has many demons trapped in its blade. The Kila is what Nera is looking for, because she is aligned with Samael and he needs it."

Peter, Paul, Robert, and Jamie all looked at each like a silent bomb just dropped in the room and Jamie said, "Well that makes things interesting and actually puts some pieces of the puzzle together."

Peter opened up the blinds to let the sun in and handed Angela her clothes. He looked at her and said, "You did great for your first time with me to go to the inner temple. We will make another trip soon, but it will just be you and I in the room. The rest of them were just here for security. Now that you know the way with me, we will revisit soon, because there is a new person who must talk to you that Lilith told me about while you were talking to Joe. You might not ever physically see Joe again, so I hope he told you enough to complete his quest for him." He then leaned closer to her ear so no one could hear what he was whispering and said, "Remember you have something in your pocket. Don't touch it, or acknowledge it, with everyone here. Wait until you get home. It's like a connection to Joe. Like a cellphone, but better."

Angela looked at him directly in his eyes and gave a small nod and then smiled.

Peter helped her with her shirt and pants and handed her shoes to put on, also. Peter then said, "Everyone, please, it's time to get some fresh air and depart the energy in this room. And please remember, you made a pledge and vow not to discuss this secret room attic or what happened here this afternoon." He looked at all of them directly in the eyes and then smiled, "I would hate to make you disappear and not have your bodies found." He smiled and then said, "I am good at killing people, but you are all safe as long as you stay quiet."

They all looked at him with surprise and fright.

Peter laughed, "I am just kidding. Relax, please." He winked at all them. Peter opened the attic staircase that went into the empty office next to the yoga studio and climbed down the staircase first. Then helped everyone down nice and safe. Peter then pulled the cord and the attic stairs folded back up and the cord went back into the ceiling.

Chapter 15: Peter on 18th Street

Robert said, "Peter, you left the light on up there."

Peter pulled out a fob-like device you would use to open and start a car. He clicked it, and everyone heard something hydraulic shift in the ceiling and click. He said, "I have a remote control on the door and it makes sure no one goes up there but me. I also have multiple cameras all around for security. I do not trust anyone." Peter then said, "Robert, in celebration of this rekindled friendship, do you still have that old and run-down cheap ass bar on Main Street? Could we all fit inside there and have some cheap beers or whiskey?"

Robert impatiently said, "It's a high-end whiskey bar with an excellent restaurant inside it, and how dare you…"

Peter said, "I was only razzing you my dear friend, I was only razzing you. It is so nice to see that facial expression again."

Robert smiled, and smiled again, and everyone was laughing at him, "Yes, let's have an early dinner at my place. I'll call the manager and get us a private table put in the library."

Peter said, "A room with a simple bookcase does not define a library." He said this with a smile and knew that Robert was getting razzed too much. He ended the conversation with, "Robert, I only razz my inner circle of friends. If I did not like you, I would not tease you."

Robert smiled, "I know my friend, I know." As he responded he rolled his eyes in jest.

They all walked up to the Jeep and Peter said, "Angela, why don't you walk with me to Robert's place. We need to talk about what happened. It will only be a ten minute walk." Angela looked at him and knew she needed private time with Peter.

Angela said, "I could use the fresh air. Yes, we will walk and meet you all there."

Robert said, "That would be okay. It will give me time to find more books for my library." He stuck his tongue out at Peter, but knew they needed alone time to discuss what they just went through. He started the Jeep and the three of them departed for the short drive to his bar.

As they drove off, Peter said, "Angela, we just need to privately talk about what happened and who to trust. I hope you do not mind?"

Angela said, "Not at all. I need to walk and clear my head and think."

Peter said, "Let's start walking then. I would like to tell you to keep what you heard from Joe a secret from the three of them until you hear his next message. The stone in your pocket will help you reconnect through your mind to him, but you will not see him again in any visions. He gave you a stone that will be like a cell phone to him where he is now. You will need to learn how to create a certain kind of magick circle, set the conditions for security, create communication, and learn how to open your mind to hear him. I can help you with all that if you want to keep moving forward in this process. I have been the teacher to only a few people, but all guided to me by the spirits and gods and goddesses."

Angela said, "Yes, I will not tell anyone what happened and we will keep it between us for now. I would like your help. Joe said that you would help me and he and Lilith both said that I can trust you. Will you tell me how the staff is connected to the Kila?"

Peter smiled, "Of course. And remember it is safe up in my attic office for when you want to start working with it, and you will need to bring the Kila. Wait, I have another idea. Why don't I make an appointment with you at your office and we talk, to start a cover story between us, and then you give it to me from your office to take back to mine. I have certain precautions I can take and nobody would expect one of your clients to walk around with it. You can schedule the session before you meet Nera next week."

Angela said, "How did you know about Nera?"

They had reached Cassenetta's and Peter opened the door for her and said, "She is one of the people that was also guided to me by another goddess."

Angela looked confused at Peter and said, "Nera is the enemy here, I think?"

Peter said, "Yes, she is committed to doing evil, but she is not the true enemy, but rather the pawn for the true enemy. But we shall talk later about Nera. Let's enjoy the dinner with our

Chapter 15: Peter on 18th Street

friends. You can trust me and I gave Lilith and Merc my oath to protect you. I owe them both and this is my payment. Joe was a friend of mine, too, in the present day and in a past life. We were in Tibet together on a sacred journey to find his teacher that had been taken."

Angela took his hand and looked into his eyes, "I trust you. Now let's have dinner."

They walked into Casseneta's and found the library where Robert, Paul, and Jamie were sitting already. Paul and Robert already had wine glasses filled and they were laughing and looked relaxed as Peter and Angela walked in. Peter paused, mock-dramatically before sitting down, "Robert, you added more books. It does look like almost a library."

Robert said, "The last time you were here was when I bought the place, almost thirty years ago."

Peter said, "Has it been that long? Well, pour me a glass of whiskey with the wine and let's see how your chef cooks our dinner."

Everyone smiled and new friendships were started among all of them. As Woodrow, the manager, closed the door to the library to let them have their privacy, he got on his cell phone and texted a number, *Peter and Angela are here in the library*. The reply text back was, *Thank you*.

Chapter 16

The Next Energy Session

Angela woke up with a headache. The last thing she remembered was drinking and eating a fine dinner at Cassenetta's with Peter, Paul, Robert, and Jamie until closing time. The manager had called them all a reliable taxi to take everyone home. She rolled over in her bed and looked around her room and she was still dressed in her clothes from last night, but with a hangover from too much whiskey. She should have known better, but after the session with Peter, it was easier to just drink than to think about what actually happened with her and Joe.

She got up out of bed and walked out of her room, into the smell of coffee and breakfast cooking. She was now totally confused, then she saw Peter cooking and coffee brewing, and a blanket on the couch where he must have slept. Just the other night she spent at Paul's place, but at least she was in her own home this time and a kind man was cooking her brunch again. Life could be so much worse. Kind men cooking breakfast for her was always wonderful.

Angela said, "Good morning."

Peter said, "Good mid-morning to you. It's almost lunch time, but I heard you start to wake up, so I decided to feed you brunch and coffee before we do another energy session this morning."

Angela said, "What? We just did one yesterday."

Peter said, "I know, and doing two sessions in two days is

Chapter 16: The Next Energy Session

not recommended, but I had a dream last night about Lilith and we just need to do another one today. It's critical, you just have to trust me. You need to go back to receive a message."

Angela said, "Could I enjoy my breakfast and coffee first?"

Peter said, "Of course, I have spent all this time cooking we shall enjoy it. I don't do energy sessions until after lunchtime anyway. Pshaw!"

Angela looked amused and bantered back, "Do you even know what that word means? You don't look the type to use slang. You know you being in an older, more refined generation."

Peter said, "Pshaw is an expression of contempt or importance, a word used to express a feeling of disbelief, and my best definition is a word you use when you don't know what else to say. What surprises you more? That I know the word or that I know the definition?"

Angela just smiled and shook her head at him, "How everyone described you is definitively not who you are. It is a great mysterious story, but you are definitely not eccentric or odd. You are highly intellectual, real, and quite magical. There is so much more to you. You are quite amazing, but you are more amusing."

Peter said, "I am many different identities to many people. I am more of a chameleon, I change colors as time goes by. I have been traveling for many centuries."

Angela said, "Centuries? What do you mean by that?"

Peter said, "We will talk about that after our healing session. We need to go back one more time."

Angela grabbed her stomach mock-dramatically, "Lunch and coffee first, naturally."

Peter finished cooking brunch and she could smell the eggs, bacon, and toast; all the wonderful smells. He had her sit at her table and he served her fresh coffee, and eggs benedict, with some extra sides. Peter knew his way around a kitchen and looked like he had been a chef before.

Peter said, "Just help me a little and tell me I cook better than that Robert character. We were competitive in our younger years, especially over the attention of beautiful women."

Angela blushed, having not been referred to as beautiful in many years. She appreciated the compliment and appreciated the food more. They enjoyed conversation and good food and once their brunch was complete and the dishes washed, Angela said, "I guess we should do another energy session?"

Peter smiled and nodded and pulled his long gray hair back into a ponytail, tying it back with a rubber band as a couple stray strands fell into his eyes. He had these beautiful crystal blue eyes. He walked outside and she thought he was leaving, but he opened the back door of his car and pulled out his folded massage table and a large black bag. When he came back inside, he started putting the table together in the middle of her living room.

Peter said, "For this session, we will use shamanic techniques that were used over a thousand years in Asia, and could even be traced back farther in pockets of what is now Mongolia and Tibet. These techniques are more naturalistic and bring in deeper spirits and more divinity. We are not going to the inner temple, but somewhere else. I am a shaman who interacts with the spirit world through altered states of consciousness, and sometimes I go into a trance when I travel with the person. The purpose is to bring in the spiritual world to the physical world for healing and teachings. The shamans were the first healers, religious leaders, magicians, and storytellers."

Angela said, "How long have you been a shaman?"

Peter looked up at as he was starting to pull things out of the black bag. He said, "For a while, and that's the best answer I will tell you now. I will give you a more accurate answer when you are ready."

Angela just said, "Pshaw."

Peter smiled, "Exactly."

Angela said, "Do I need to get in my underwear again?"

Peter smiled and said, "No, not this time."

Angela said, "What about this time?"

"You are fine in the clothes you have on, there is no reason to take off anything. I only request no shoes, but you do not have any shoes on anyway, so should not be an issue. Now get on the table."

Chapter 16: The Next Energy Session

Angela laid down on the table like she had yesterday. He pulled out some sage from his black bag, which he lit and moved the smoke above her body, letting the smoke settle on her and purify her body. He said, "Burning sage is also called smudging and is an ancient spiritual ritual. Many cultures around the world do this. This practice connects with the spirits and enhances intuition. Sage is the most commonly used herb to help cleanse and create a positive environment. White sage is a closed practice for many Native Americans, but this is just regular old sage, so no need to fret." He then pulled out several feathers as he saged over her; an owl and a hawk feather, which helped with the smoke and to bring wisdom and strength to the session. She did not mind the sage at all and it felt like when she was back in the Catholic church as a young girl, smelling the incense during mass. He then pulled out several bowls of various sizes that looked hand-made and said, "Have you ever experienced a sound bath before?"

Angela had heard of sound baths during her sessions with some clients, but had never done one because she had not seen research confirming sound waves could heal a person. But she always let her patients believe that sound could heal them.

Peter placed several sound bowls around the room within range of his arms and he began to play them with a solid sound. He would echo them by running the mallet around the edges that caused a unique sound frequency, which was hard for her to decipher, but the combinations of sound that interacted over her body began to have an effect she did not expect.

Peter said, "Sound baths have been used to heal the body for thousands of years and are a spiritual cleansing music to the soul. This, and sage, and shamanic techniques will awaken your hidden soul inside you, so that we can see who, and where, and what is inside you. Sound clears the clutter and creates harmony in your energy so we can connect. In today's science talk, sound baths are rooted in quantum physics and the sacred geometry. More people should do it, but Western thought still thinks it a new age ideology. I always say that the things that worked over a thousand years ago still work today and should be more open to people's minds."

He continued to work the bowls over her body where the sounds would synchronize at specific parts. Angela was feeling a unique experience and opening and awakening and with the sage and the smells, she wondered what was next. Then Peter said, "I am going to put crystals on parts of your body to help ground the effect." He put a crystal on her throat, and then raised her T-shirt to put a crystal on her sternum, and one above her belly button. He then undid two buttons on her jeans and placed another crystal just below her belly button. Peter said, "I put a specific crystal on your chakras for awakening and to balance your chakras. The word chakra is ancient Indian teaching from the Vedas, which originated somewhere between 1500BC to 500BC. The chakras are energy vortexes that allow and expel energy. The crown chakra is the top of your head and I placed a white clear crystal to clear and raise your vibrations. I put a purple amethyst on your third eye chakra, between your eyes for inner vision, ability to understand, and receive. I put blue lapis lazuli on your throat chakra, to speak the truth and see the truth. I put a green serpentine on your heart chakra, to deal with love and to reassure the way of the mind and the heart. I put a bright yellow tiger eye on your solar plexus chakra, right above your belly button to help with self-confidence, power and moving forward. I also put a bright orange calcite above your pubic bone, to work passion, creativity, and sexuality. Lastly, I placed a small deep red shungite crystal, lower on top of your jeans; you likely can't feel it, but it helps with feeling safe, grounded, and your stability. I bet you did not think you would be getting a lesson on chakras today. I need you to be perfectly be still while I do the sound bowls one more time with the stones on your body. The stones are like having a grounding wire on each part of the chakras that helps carry the sound vibrations into your body for alignment and synchronicity. Please be perfectly still; do not move."

He then pulled out another larger healing bowl and rang it once, which electrified Angela where the crystals were on her body. She felt like it was the gonging of a large door inside her body and something was asking to come out. He rang it again and again, and the tingling sensation was something she had never

Chapter 16: The Next Energy Session

felt before. It was opening something inside, which she did not know. Peter continued to work the large Tibetan singing bowl for a few minutes, and then knowing she was in a complete state of relaxation, he turned on a recording of Tibetan mediation sounds to keep her in that mental and physical state. He started doing energy work. What he did not tell her was this specific approach would have her travel to a place she had never been before. He did not want her to have anxiety, but rather, be able to just let the mind flow free.

* * *

Angela was dreaming and deep in thought and travel. She saw herself on a mountain trail in the snow, and there was a woman with a black cape and hood running down the trail, crying, and she ran right by her as if Angela was invisible. Angela continued to walk up the trail and she could tell there was light coming from the cave and she heard voices. She peered into the cave, not wanting to be noticed, and she noticed a woman who was hurt and a man was tending her wounds and caring for her. There were other people in cave. And then the woman looked like she had passed away and her tattoos had disappeared and…they were transferring to the man with green hands. She could not see his face due to his cloak. Then she saw him pick up a staff from the ground. The staff looked exactly like the one Joe had given her. The man in the cloak turned to look at her with his green face, and immediately she was awake on the table with Peter. A little shaken and scared, but fresh and alert.

Peter was looking at her from above the table, looking exhausted. He said, "Did you see what you needed to see?"

She said, "I saw where the staff came from and a green man."

Peter said, "Good. That was exactly what was supposed to happen."

Chapter 17
Jamie and Angela Connect

Peter did not stay long after the energy session and was soon out of Angela's house. He looked like he was on another quest, like he received a message during the session. He left quickly, and then Angela was all alone in her house, trying to make sense out of all these new experiences. It felt like a mission had been completed. Seeing that man become green and tattooed and hold the same staff now sitting in Peter's office.

As Angela was alone and hearing the quietness, she thought of who she should contact, just to wrap her mind around everything that was going on. She immediately thought of Jamie. She had also been pulled into this chaotic circle of friends, not by choice, but by someone else's design. She texted her, *Jamie, I need to vent, talk, and calm my mind, can I talk this morning with you? Please. /r Angela.*

Within one minute, Jamie responded by text, *Sure, come to my place, I attached my address, welcome now.*

Angela looked at the text and then tried to rationalize what she was doing and what she was in. Then she realized she must trust her intuition and trust herself and Jamie was the one person who could calm her down. She then texted back, *Be there in 10 minutes.*

She got up and made sure she was dressed, then looked at herself in the mirror at her unkempt hair, and then realized it was

Chapter 17: Jamie and Angela Connect

another woman and she would understand. She just put a baseball cap on her head and picked up her keys and left her house.

Within fifteen minutes she drove up to Jamie's condo and knocked on her door. She could hear, "Come in." She opened the door and walked into a dark living room, but she could see Jamie, with only a white T-shirt on, sitting on the floor doing Oracle cards, and drinking tea, "Welcome, my wonderful spiritual friend. How may I help you on this tranquil Saturday morning?'

Angela took off her shoes and walked up next to her. "Jamie, I am so confused with everything going on. How am I to solve it all or analyze it all?"

Jamie took a sip of tea, "My friend, you are not supposed to solve it, you are supposed to experience it; that's what's wrong with your thinking."

Angela sat next to Jamie and made herself comfortable. She took the tea from her hand and took a deep drink of it and said, "My sweet friend, please explain more to me."

Jamie took the tea back and took another drink, "Angela, you are thinking of this from the wrong perspective. You need to just experience it for what it is and not try to make sense of it. You will confuse your brain even more. Just let it be. You do not need to solve the world, just finish Joe's mission and intent."

Angela took the tea back and said, "That's easy for you to say. You have angel blood in your veins, and you don't have a misguided quest from a beloved professor on your shoulders to deal with."

Jamie took the tea back, "Well, I agree with you, but I have no idea what this angel blood does or is good for, so I feel like a spiritual orphan that no one wants." As she said this she put her arm around Angela and handed her tea back for her response.

Angela accepted the tea, "I am afraid. I do not know why, but I am afraid of what might happen. I just have this feeling that something terribly wrong is about to happen and I can't stop it. I just can't explain it, it's just what I feel right now." She handed the empty cup back to Jamie. They both laughed.

Jamie closed her eyes and said, "Angela, things will be okay. I have already seen it. There will be a death, but it will not be yours or mine, and it's not really a death, but a transition. You and I are meant to complete another adventure together soon. We have to combine forces to help each other and someone else in need. My angel blood will protect you because we are spiritual sisters. I have always known that I was different and it is nice to know that I was not crazy, but only a partial angel. That does not mean that I am a freak. That's a good thing."

Angela just listened and smiled at Jamie's freedom in life. Jamie had a simple job, a simple condo, and no attachments. She could just quit and pack her car and depart within 24 hours if her life just needed to change. While Angela had a practice and a career that kept her in her office with appointments, and knowing that her clients helped pay her employee's salary. Having no obligations and full freedom was such a foreign word to her, but one she would like to have someday. She envied Jamie's freedom. She said, "Jamie, what do I have to do to make sure you and your angel blood power protects me?"

Jamie smiled, "Just hang with me today and relax. I am a simple person."

Angela said, "That is easy. Now let's make more tea, please, my sweet angel."

Jamie smiled, winked, and took the empty cup and placed it on her lips, pretending there was more tea, then placed her head on Angela's shoulder and said, "We are sisters until the end. I will give my life to protect you."

Angela touched her head, "Thank you. I hope it never comes to that. When are you going to show me your wings?"

Jamie looked up at Angela, "I do not have any real wings, I just have a large tattoo."

"That is what I meant."

Jamie smiled shyly and took off her shirt in front of Angela, exposing her full skin, turned around and said, "Well, these are my wings. It's just a tattoo, but the angels were so fascinated with the design and even touched the tattoo."

Angela said softly, "May I touch it?"

Jamie said, "Sure, let me lean against you so it is easy." She sat back down on the floor and snuggled next to her, letting her

Chapter 17: Jamie and Angela Connect

move her fingers across her wings just like the angel had. But when Angela touched them, the tattoo moved without Jamie knowing it. Angela would move her fingers, and the wings on her skin would move with the fingers and the wings wanted to fly. Angela assumed it was her some type of majick making her see things.

Jamie said, "What are you doing? It feels like you are digging your nails into my skin?"

Angela said, "I am just barely touching you."

Jamie said, "That's odd. It felt like my shoulders were moving inside myself. Just a weird feeling."

Angela stopped touching her, left her shirt off, and brought a blanket off the couch. They just held each other, lying on the floor, enjoying their new friendship and fondness toward protecting each other. They both snuggled under the blanket entwined together and feel asleep on the floor.

* * *

As they were asleep, Peter walked into Jamie's living room and watched Jamie and Angela asleep on the floor. He smiled at the two and pulled out of his pocket four white crystals. As he held them, they began to glow. He placed them in the four cardinal corners of Jamie's living room. As he placed the fourth crystal along a windowsill, he could visualize the crystal grid that he had created to protect the two asleep on the floor. He smiled and then looked around, curious what her space was like; he noticed an old Scottish Highland soldier print on her wall in full kilt and broadsword. Peter just smiled and grinned at the image. As he was walking out of the living room, he looked back at the two asleep on the floor. He smiled and said, "Blessed be," and quietly departed.

Chapter 18
Nera's Second Visit

After the weekend energy experiences and working with Peter, Angela had to go back to work at the behavioral health clinic. It had been a full weekend and she was still trying to comprehend what had happened, but she knew she needed to work now and be a professional psychiatrist. She had not looked at her Monday schedule before departing on Friday, as was her habit, so she was fully surprised when she saw that Nera was her first client on this morning's schedule. Seeing Nera on her patient list stopped her in her walk and made her collect her thoughts on how she was going to counsel her in the next hour.

Angela poured herself a coffee inside her office and tried to think of a plan of action, because she knew her assistant would signal the start of this first session any minute. She opened up her filing cabinet and pulled out her wrapped Kila and looked at it one more time for some signal. Then she realized Joe had left something in her pocket, which she had completely forgot, and felt good that she had the same jeans on from the other day. She reached into her pocket and there was a solid black crystal, about an inch long, but heavy and dense. She picked it up and closed her eyes and thought of inspiration. She could feel Joe's voice in her head and he was there with her, and all of a sudden she was ready and confident to receive Nera and whatever wrath she tried to bring to her today.

Chapter 18: Nera's Second Visit

The secretary called Angela and said, "Miss Nera is already checked in and ready for her session."

Angela said, "I will be right there to bring her in the office." Angela squeezed the black crystal in her hand and could hear Joe's voice in her head, *I will help you in confronting Nera. You got this.* Angela smiled and put the crystal in her pants pocket again. She stood up and looked at herself in her small mirror near her desk. She smiled and said, "Joe, thank you!"

She walked to her door and opened it and then walked down the hallway. She waved at Nera and held the security door for her so she could come with her. Nera was quite different this morning than her initial counseling meeting. She had no makeup and was plainly dressed, with yoga pants and a simple T-shirt, quite opposite from their first meeting. She seemed in distress and not confident at all.

Angela welcomed her to their next session and had her sit down on the couch in her office. Angela locked the door behind them so they would not be disturbed for the next hour.

Angela sat next to her desk and swiveled her chair to face Nera, "How has the last week been since our last session?"

Nera looked at Angela, who noticed that in addition to no makeup, her eyes had deep circles underneath, "Angela, I have had a horrible week. It's been so terrible I can't sleep and feel like the curse put on me by Paul is getting worse. It's making me so crazy and wanting to do things I should not do."

Angela quickly noticed that she included Paul and the curse again and she said the typical licensed therapist statement, "Nera, please tell me more about Paul and this curse." Angela knew better than to divulge anything about her and Paul's experiences since her last meeting with Nera. She also had a quiet confidence in her voice after meeting spiritually with Joe.

Nera said, "I still have this horrible curse because that bastard Paul would not release me from it. I just don't know what to do. My friend Samael is helping me come up with a plan to turn the tables on Paul. He needs to help me. But Paul is such an honest person."

Angela said, "What do you mean with Samael? Is Paul really

that honest?"

Nera was slightly confused with the change of questions and said, "I thought I talked about Samael in our last session?"

Angela said, "No, you never mentioned Samael. Who is this man and how is he helping you?"

Nera sat in the chair, quiet for a moment, and tried to answer the question. It was much more difficult and complicated than she could quickly answer. Nera said, "Samael has been a friend since I was a child. He was always there when I had bad dreams and was that secret friend that I never told my parents about. He has always been my friend. Only recently did I meet him as a real person. He was there after Paul and Robert completely embarrassed me, when everyone came back from their past lives and spirits in Paul's backyard. That was not the plan. That was not how it was supposed to end. My plan was going to work, until the spirit of Anna showed back up. Paul was going to use the athame against me and free me from the curse and I would have my freedom back, but no, Anna had to ruin it for me. The plan was going to work until Anna showed up. I helped murder her. She had a horrible death, but her spirit had to show up and ruin my plans. Her purity and love for Paul and the others help changed his mind in using the athame against me. I was so close. So that means next time, I must assure no safety spiritual nets are available for Paul, if and when he uses the athame against me to finally free me from my unfair curse. This horrible curse for my actions in the past."

Angela asked, "What do you plan to do to Paul? This time when things go as you plan?"

Nera said calmly, "I plan to kill Paul to assure the curse is released. Samael will help me with this plan, and death would be good for Paul, as it was for Joe."

Angela said, 'What do you mean for Joe? Did you have anything to do with Joe's death?'

Nera said, "Debts are due upon receipt. Joe was due a receipt and could not pay up, so the end result was he had to pay with his life to save the woman he loved. Do you know who he loved?"

Angela said, "No. I do not know who Joe loved that he would

Chapter 18: Nera's Second Visit

sacrifice his life to save?"

Nera smiled at Angela with an evil smile, "You, my dear. He sacrificed his life to protect you."

Angela was confused, shaken, "What do you mean he sacrificed his life to protect me? I do not understand?"

Nera said, "The payment was due and the angel came to take you. He intervened and protected you, and made a deal with an angel to take him instead of you." She giggled, an uncomfortable sound. "Did you not know how much he loved you?"

Angela felt light headed and could feel the blood leaving her face due to the shock of this news, "Please explain more to me. I do not understand? Tell me now! Which angels?"

Nera looked straight at Angela, "The angel was going to take you, because in a past life, your past life, you had made a deal with him and promised they could choose a past life to take as collateral for the deed. So they waited for your life in the present moment. You see, you and Joe were what they call Twin Flames. A twin flame is an intense soul connection, falsely assumed to be the person's other half. No, they are like two spontaneously arising fires, bringing light and transformation at a radical level. Twin flames show each other their insecurities, fears, and shadows. The falsity regarding twin flames is they complete you, but really they are meant to encourage you to be more complete. People lose the goodness of twin flames alighting when they try to fit the narrative toward what they grew up hearing about life and magic, like from TV and books." Nera smiled at Angela and said, "I bet when you met Joe you had an intense sense of attraction and it felt like home, didn't it? You and Joe had lots in common in values, past experiences, and interests, didn't you? Your differences even complemented each other, didn't they? He fully supported you on your full purpose and helped you grow and heal, didn't he? Even now that he has passed away you are still drawn to him spiritually and you know when he is near, don't you? Finally, twin flame relationships are tumultuous, intense, and not smooth, but you keep coming back together. It's like the relationship is divine with the super psychic connection, and being around him made you be better than you ever knew you could."

Angela was having difficulty with everything that Nera was saying because it all felt true, absolutely everything felt true; this thought of Joe being her twin flame made perfect sense. How it felt like there was always this connection between them. She had never heard of the term before in her life, but if it was true, maybe Joe was her twin flame because there was always this immediate connection. As she was getting flustered with Nera's comments, she put her hand in her pocket and touched the crystal that Joe had given her in the inner temple, and she felt immediately calm. She actually smiled back at Nera, like holding a pair of aces while playing poker.

Angela said, "If everything you say is true, then why are you here in my office? Is it to try and manipulate me, or is there another reason why you are here?"

Nera was stunned by the question, because she thought that she had Angela in a vulnerable position emotionally with all her comments, but she was realizing that Angela was stronger than she thought. Nera was trying to think of a knock-out blow to ready Angela to be open for manipulation, but she was having trouble thinking of something. Nera felt like her bluff was exposed by the comments and thought of a statement to deflect by saying, "Does it bother you that Joe sacrificed himself for you?"

Angela said, "I know that Joe loved me and that I loved him, and we were probably twin flames. I have even had contact with him lately and talked with him through Merc and Lilith."

Nera looked up at Angela with anger at that last statement regarding Lilith and Merc. She hissed, "What did you say? You can't talk with Joe, because of where he is. Did you say Lilith and Merc? There is no way you would have known those two people unless they made contact with you at the inner temple. How did you get access to the inner temple? Did Joe introduce you to the inner temple?"

Angela said, "This is your session. Why does my visit bother you? What was Joe to you? Remember, I ask the questions."

"You just made this very personal. Please tell me how you know Lilith and Merc. I have never been invited to the inner temple. I deserve an invitation. How on Earth did you get invited

Chapter 18: Nera's Second Visit

and go? You have nothing important about your bloodline and you have such insignificant past lives. Only little things happened in your past lives, nothing significant or worth noting."

Angela said, "What do you know of my past lives?"

Nera said, "I know quite a bit of your past lives, but none of them have personally affected me, until now. Your life, this current life. You have become significant in my life. I need you do something for me and you will do it, whether you want to or not."

Angela said, "How do you know my past lives? No one has told me details. I only know that I had some past lives with Joe, but he never gave me any details. It really does not matter to me. I know who I am and my purpose. Why do you want to hurt Paul? Please answer me!"

Having the conversation go back to the subject of Paul got Nera confused because she was on a task about accessing the inner temple, and Angela's purpose was to change conversations and inquire about Paul. Angela repeated, "Why do you want to hurt Paul?"

Nera, full hauteur, said "I said that I would kill him, not hurt him."

There was silence between them for a few seconds, as if both of them were at a draw and each contemplating what move to make next. Each of them was thinking fast on what to say, but not to reveal anything to the other. Angela's phone rang into the silence and she said, "Excuse me." She then answered the phone and it was her receptionist. She was now twenty minutes late on her session and her next patient was checked in and waiting. Angela said, "Thank you. We are done with the session. Please tell the next patient that I will be done soon." She hung up the phone and Nera knew the session was over, she was standing up and getting her coat on.

Nera said, "This is not over. I will see you next week, we have lots to talk about."

Angela said with a fake professional smile, "Yes, Nera, we have lots to talk about. Please do not do anything you will regret in the next week without calling me. Here is my business card and my personal cellphone is on the back. Please contact me if you are going to cross any line."

Nera smiled, "I cross the lines all the time, but I will call you if I am in a dark emotional place. I may need your help on something else. Thank you for giving me your cell."

They were both cordial and polite to each other as they exited her office and walked down the hall to the secure door where her next client was waiting. The security door was opened by the receptionist and Nera smiled at Angela and she thanked her, and then gave her a hug as if they were old friends.

As Nera was starting to walk out, the receptionist said, "Paul is waiting in the lobby." Paul had been watching the events of the hallway and waiting for the right time to stand up and walk toward Angela, who was getting hugged by Nera. As the receptionist said the words, Nera started walking toward to the exit. She bumped into Paul and they both looked at each and the mood immediately changed.

Paul, with his dry humor said, "Nera, it is so nice to run into you. How are you doing?"

Nera was irritated, having realized she had been played a fool by Angela. She politely knew people were watching her and there were video cameras recording it, and she said, "Paul, it is so nice to run into you, too. Are you also seeing Dr. Angela in therapy?"

Paul said, "Yes. She has been my therapist for years. so I'm quite good, and you should never underestimate her." He then winked at Nera, which upset her and she said, "I better get going. I have another appointment."

Paul then said, "Tell Samael hi for me. I know he is waiting in your car for you."

Nera's face went red and it was all she could do to hold it together, because inside she wanted to hurt Paul right there in the lobby. but she could not. And how the hell did Paul know about Samael? She was frustrated, and talking to herself as she left the building, and Paul was waving at her through the glass doors. She opened her car door, got into her running car, and slammed the door.

Samael just smiled at her and said, "Did you send Paul my regards?"

Chapter 18: Nera's Second Visit

Nera was pissed off, "Screw you. What was that all about?'

Samael said, "Well, Paul knocked on the window while you were in there with Dr. Angela and we had an inquiring conversation about certain things. You can't kill him, I forbid it. He is too useful. He might help us."

"Fuck you. I have been waiting to kill him ever since what happened a couple months ago. I don't care what you say."

Samael said, "If you kill him, you will have the curse three-fold, and it will follow you in future lives. I forbid it. You will not hurt him. Now Angela is an option."

Nera smiled, "Thank you for giving me some crumbs off the table."

"Anytime, that's what I do."

As Paul was waving at Nera through the glass doors, Angela said, "That is enough Paul. Let's go back to my office. I will have to cut you short to get back on schedule since Nera ran twenty minutes over.

Paul replied, "Sure. Let's go talk. I always look forward to our sessions. They help me so much. Plus, I need to talk to you about the conversation I had with Samael. We made a gentlemen's agreement, let me fill you in."

Angela said, "You know the way to my office. Let's go and get the latest scoop on your deal with an evil man. This seems to be a trend for you recently." As they walked into her office, Angela received a text on her phone. She looked at it and it read:

Angela, thank you so much for the session. I greatly appreciate it. Paul told Samael that I could use the Kila. Thank you. Love, Nera,

Angela said, "Ok Paul, what the hell is this about letting Nera use the Kila which I am protecting and no one is supposed to know I have it? You are so in the doghouse with me."

Paul said, "Trust me, I have a plan."

Angela said, "That is what I am worrying about, Paul. I know you." She gave him a funny scowl in which he just gave her a funny face back. Angela said, "You are a mess."

Paul said, "I know. I have a plan though."

Angela sat in her normal chair and Paul sat on the couch.

But this was not their usual session due to the events with Nera right before him, and Paul being somewhat instigating as Nera departed. Angela just said, "Talk to me. What is your plan and why did you bargain the Kila? It's not yours to bargain with."

Paul sat back in his chair and said, "Well, the three angels need someone to try and kill Lilith, if possible, and they are going to convince Nera to do it."

Angela said, "What? That does not make any sense. Why would they want that? What is the point?"

Paul said, "It came to me in a dream. Samael told me if I knew where the Kila was, it could be the tool to do it, and Nera would be the person."

Angela said, "The Kila holds the souls of demons. Would we not be letting Nera release the demons that are trapped in the blade?"

Paul looked sheepish, "I had not thought of that. I totally missed that. That would be worse than anything."

Angela just looked at Paul with a dumbfounded look and said, "Well, yea, Paul. What were you thinking when you were bargaining the Kila to the one person we do not want to possess it? Did you have a senior moment or something?"

Paul looked back at Angela. "We can't let Nera come close to that blade at all. That would be too dangerous."

Angela leaned back in her chair with agreement, "So what are you going to do now, my glorious thought-provoking hero?"

Paul smiled, "That's why I had another Kila hand made from my dream." He reached into his blazer and pulled out a Kila which was handmade and looked authentic and close to the one she had. He even handed it to Angela to inspect its quality.

Angela said, "How did you know what it looked like? You have never seen the Kila."

Paul said, "I had it made from the visual of my dream. I thought the team from Tibet did a marvelous job in just a few days. There are simple characteristics that all Kilas have and they knew what I was talking about regarding colors and size."

Angela stood up and went to her filing cabinet. She opened the drawer, looked into the back, and reached for the package of

Chapter 18: Nera's Second Visit

cloth that secured the Kila that Joe had left her. She pulled out the cloth with the twine wrapped around it, brought it to her desk, and slowly opened it to reveal the authentic Kila that Joe had left her, and compared it to the fake one. Angela picked it up and handed it to Paul to feel, and touch, and look at. They looked similar, and if no one has ever seen the original Kila, then this switch might work.

Angela sighed, "So tell me what your plan is again?"

"I have not thought it all the way through, but have the big things down. I know Nera would like to hurt me, but Samael will not let her because we agreed on that in our discussion. Samael can't kill Lilith because they are spiritually connected and bonded, but then he would also spend a great deal of eternity in the underworld. So he needs a patsy and that is where Nera will come in. If Nera uses the Kila to kill Lilith when she is in human form on Earth, then the three angels have accomplished what they want and to get even on how they all first met. Nera will just get betrayed by who she thinks is her only ally and friend. But I am not worried about her destiny or future. I am loyal to Lilith. The key here is for Nera to not use the magical Kila, but the other one, the fake one. Then nothing will happen, I think. I know it sounds like a far-out plan, but we also have a secret weapon, who's name is Jamie. She has special angel blood. Robert and I did some research and believe that Senoy had an affair with Jamie's biological mother, which is a forbidden affair with humans when they were both in human form, visiting. Gods and angels are not supposed to have affairs or sexual contact with humans, because they could give them special blood that gives them powers, which then God can't control due to self-will or self-determination and that stuff. Apparently after that little Pandora joke, some new rules got implemented."

Angela said, "Paul, I already know that Jamie has angel blood inside her. That is not new."

Paul said, "Okay, well, then you must already know that Jamie was only twelve years old when her mother died, and her stepfather had left years before, and she only found out lately about the angel thing when the three angels visited her in her apartment a week ago."

Angela smiled and said, "I did not know those details, thank you. But does Nera know any of this? Does she know about Jamie?"

Paul said, "Not that I know of."

Angela then said, "So you want Nera to try and kill Lilith with the fake Kila, and so, why do we need Jamie to help in some way?"

Paul said, "Jamie is our protection against Nera and Samael once she and Samael find out that we did not give her the real Kila. They will not be able to release any demons to help them. Nera will be even more upset than the last time we had a final situation with the athame."

Angela sat back in her chair thinking over the plan and Paul's rationale and realized it could possibly work, but she had only one last comment, "What will Jamie do to protect us?"

Paul said, "I do not know. I only know that having Jamie with us will assure that no one will harm us, and Lilith will not be hurt, either. And Samael is blood, so the only person who could harm us is Nera, and Jamie will protect us from her. Jamie does not know it."

Angela smiled and for once since her work day started, relaxed, "Okay, now that we have that all settled, let's have our normal session about something else in your life that is not spiritually trying to hurt you or me. Maybe we can talk about your boring professor position or something?"

Paul laughed, "Okay, we shall talk about the boring things." They started talking like they normally did about the mundane life as a professor he had and the time passed peacefully.

Angela mused out loud to herself as they hit a long pause, natural in the wind down of a session, "I guess I will keep the Kila secure in my office, since you will give Nera the fake one."

Paul said, "We will need to give it to Peter for safe keeping soon. He will know what to do with it. Plus it belongs on the staff that you brought back. They are a pair."

Angela said, "What do you mean they are a pair?"

Paul said, "Well, there is an ancient story that a man of green

Chapter 18: Nera's Second Visit

was given the staff by an angel, and a goddess gave him a knife, to be used together to defeat his enemies that outnumbered him 50 to 1. If Joe gave it to you, it is now connected to you, because he was the last keeper of the ancient staff."

Angela looked confused, "How did I just find out about this crucial information since I carried it back through the inner temple with Peter? Why didn't Peter tell me, or you, or Robert?"

Paul looked amused, "We all thought that Peter would have told you the story when you walked to the bar alone. What did you talk about then?"

Angela then immediately remembered that no one knew that she met with Peter the following day and did another energy session. And she promised Peter she would not divulge. So, she said, "We talked about Joe, and Lilith, and Merc."

"Well, we all assumed he told you about the staff and how important it is."

Angela was then thinking on why Peter did not tell her. He maybe did not think about telling her, or he intentionally did not tell her. She would need to find out his motives on the staff. Their session time was over and Paul knew the drill that it was time for him to depart her office. She pointed to the clock, and like normal, they both got up at the same time and gave each other a hug before they opened the door, and then were all professional as they walked down the hall. As Angela opened up the security door, she said, "Don't forget to reschedule our visit with Lena."

Paul had not thought of that, and as soon as he walked outside the building he looked at his cellphone and texted Lena to see if she had any available slots this week so they could get their session back.

Angela smiled on how quickly Paul was diverted with shiny things. She closed the security door and walked back to her office where she had left her door open, which was odd and something she never did. She looked inside to see if anyone was there, but her office was empty. She had left the Kila on her desk, uncovered, and the blade was glowing and the room was cold. Angela felt a chill down her back and all of a sudden, her door slammed closed.

Chapter 19
Kilas and Angel Depart

As they returned from the Green Man back to Kilas's ship, Angel nodded and gave her a quick kiss on the lips and left immediately to prepare. Kilas called Craig and Greg over and gave them specific directions to get the ship refueled and ready to depart within two hours. They started to ask reasons for the quick departure, but knew it was no use and when given orders they executed them. They began to run diagnostics on the ship and ordered fuel from the ground support droids. The process to depart in two hours was beginning. Kilas was now only worried if Angel could make it back to her in time, but she trusted her gut, which told her that Angel would keep her promise.

    Kilas secured the athame back in its leather and secured it in her safe on her ship. She was having challenges on what was happening and why, and trying to rationalize this illogical chain of events in her life. She always liked to be so in control of things, and this was too fast for her. This was risky, but it felt so right. It was a leap of faith, which she had lost many years ago. She felt love again, and joy, which she thought she would never feel again because she had been running away from this for many years. The connection with Angel was immediate and trusting, and to travel with her to the Green Man validated her feeling toward Angel and did not discourage it. The Green Man was some mysterious entity that she had been searching for to help her explain herself, but she

Chapter 19: Kilas and Angel Depart

never thought it would be a green man like she was also green. She could not wrap her head around the idea of portals, but it was real, and she had a witness to vouch for her.

As Kilas was getting the ship ready to depart, Angel went to her quarters and packed quietly, to not cause any attention. She looked around her room, which was barren and did not have hardly anything in it, and she filled up her backpack with everything that had meaning and was going to leave the rest. As she was strapping everything together on her backpack, Kobar walked in and said, "Looks like you are about to depart."

Angel said, "I was about to come and talk to you."

"Sure you were. It looks like you are about to jump out of here with someone?"

Angel said, "Yes, there is a bigger prize to tell you about and you must sit down."

Kobar, interested now, sat down and said, "Tell me everything."

Angel said, "I made a connection with the woman Kilas, and she knows where another treasure is, but it's not on this planet. It's the big ticket one you have been looking for. It's from another portal." She let the word portal have its effect on Kobar that she knew it would. She could see the glint of greed hardening his eyes.

Kobar said, "A portal to another dimension?"

Angel said, "Yes, I even witnessed it with Kilas. It's in an artifact which she did not tell you. She was fully honest with the other artifact, which will make you rich on the scrolls, but I want to explore this portal again with her. Guess who we met on the other side?"

Kobar said, "You and Kilas portaled to another dimension and met another person?"

Angel said, "Yes we did. We met the Green Man?"

Kobar said, "The fabled and mythical Green Man?"

Angel took his hands and looked straight into his eyes and said, "Yes, I talked with the Green Man."

Kobar stood up, "I must have this artifact immediately."

Angel said, "No, you can't have it yet, because the Green Man said if we returned we could go into another portal, and I have to learn what that is. You can't interrupt my plans. This could bring in a bundle of portal keys, which then you could have control, if you let me do my job. You must trust me in this. Let me go and gain her trust more and I will bring in the prize, like I always do. This one will be the biggest, but we can't stop the events that have been predicted so far. I have to go with Kilas to a destination and we will portal again and find out where the other portals are. Once I return, we shall share the prize and you will have to release me from my bargain from your service."

Kobar said, "I believe you, but I could easily stop her from taking off and take the artifact and make you both do what I say under my control."

Angel said, "You could, but we would not be following the guidance from the Green Man, and then he would never show the other portal, and you would never gain anything except a worthless piece of iron. You must let the events happen as foretold."

Kobar said, "You play a convincing card today, and with our history we have shared, I will believe you. But I need insurance. I need to know you will return."

Angel turned around and raised her hair over her bar code and said, "You already have a tracker on me, so you will know where we are going and when we have portaled to another dimension. You will know everything about where we are all the time. Is that enough insurance to appease you?"

Kobar laughed, "I forgot we had a tracker inserted into you. Well yes, okay, that will give me my insurance that you will come back, and that we may slowly be following you."

"If you follow us, please keep a distance greater than the radar systems so that Kilas will not be suspicious. Deal?"

"Deal!" They shook hands, which meant it was a pact and a sworn deal.

Angel said, "Now, let me go with no trouble from the guards. Let me keep my bargain with you and we might make the biggest prize yet, okay? Make sure everyone of your controllers let us depart the sector."

Kobar said, "Yes, it shall be done. We shall let you depart

Chapter 19: Kilas and Angel Depart

carefree, but my follow ship will be departing fifteen minutes after you depart, to start."

Angel said, "That is fine, but keep a long distance. You have a tracker, so no need to follow close, keep your distance at all costs. Our plan needs to work. I need to go back and meet the Green Man again. Don't screw this up, Kobar!"

Kobar said, "I give you my word…I give you my word."

Angel said, "Good. Now it's time for me to meet Kilas and we need to depart soon. The Green Man wanted us to depart within two hours from returning. I will keep you posted."

Angel picked up her bag, looked at her watch, and waved. She walked out of the room and the security force detail looked at Kobar. He nodded yes to them to let her go. He sat down in Angel's chair, thinking about the riches and opportunities he could seek if she returned with the secrets of the portal which so many key leaders were looking for. He could be important quickly in this region to a much higher level. Of all the people in his world, he knew he could trust Angel because he had raised her as an orphan when she was abandoned as a teenager. He was the only father figure she ever had, and that was not saying much.

Kobar pulled out a cigar from his pocket and lit it while sitting in the chair. He kept telling himself that this payoff will be good and he could trust Angel. She was like the daughter he never had. He knew when she was passionate about something that it was usually right, and he needed to trust her.

Angel was walking down the corridor to Kilas's ship and kept looking at her watch, knowing that her time was running short and that she might be left, so she started running. As she came near the hangar, she could hear the engines running and she was in a dead sprint because she was afraid that Kilas might leave her. But as soon as she had the ship in view, she saw Kilas at the end on the ramp waiting for her, and she ran to her and hugged her. She whispered in her ear, "Thank you for not leaving me."

Kilas kissed her on the cheek, "You still had two minutes left, you are early. Welcome to my ship. Are you ready for an adventure?"

Angel grabbed her hand and they both walked in as the

ramp door was rising up and closing. They were giddy and Kilas walked her into the cockpit and formally introduced her to her humanoids, Craig and Greg, who were piloting the ship off the planet. As Kilas and Angel were about to depart the cockpit, Craig said, "Where is our destination? You did not inform us."

Kilas looked at both of them, "I want you to find the farthest planet that is inhabitable, but so far away that no one will disturb us. The more desolate the better. We will spend a day there in isolation to make sure no one is following us. Do you understand?"

Craig said, "Understood. My calculations say that we could reach a far moon of Ashton in about four hours. They only have a small colony of one hundred people on it, mining for resources. We could land on the opposite side. The air is not habitable, but we could use oxygen masks if we wanted to explore the surface."

Kilas said, "That is perfect. I will be in the main galley. Let me know when we are ten minutes out from landing."

Craig said, "Affirmative."

* * *

As Kilas and Angel were waiting for the ten-minute notification, they were sitting in the galley looking at each other with anticipation. They had the athame on the table, opened up from its cloth covering, just lying there in the center of the table. They held hands across from each other, waiting to touch the athame together once they were given the notice. Kilas said, "Are you sure you are ready for this?"

Angel said, "I have been ready for this moment my whole life. I always knew that I would meet you and that this moment would come that would change my life forever."

Kilas smiled back at her, "I feel the same way."

Craig got on the intercom and said, "Kilas, it looks like we have a ship following us. What do you want me to do?"

Angel said, "It must be Kobar. He has a tracker on me and is changing our deal."

Kilas said, "What deal—what are you talking about?"

Angel took a knife from her boot and said, "Kilas, do you

Chapter 19: Kilas and Angel Depart

love me? I need you to cut the tracker out of my neck right now. Do you love me? I had to make a deal with Kobar to let me leave and I lied to him and told him he could track me. But he promised to stay a long distance away and I was going to tell you later once we transported to see the Green Man, but we do not have time. You must cut it out of me right now. I love you and I trust you."

Kilas did not know what to say or do, and then Angel put the knife in her hand and turned around. She moved her hair so that Kilas could see the small scar on the barcode where the bump in her skin showed where the tracker was. She was shaking and held the knife without knowing how to cut the skin. There was a voice behind her that said, "I can do it if you want me too." Kilas looked behind her and it was Craig looking at her and he said, "Kilas, I can cut the tracker from Angel's neck. I have been programmed with basic surgeon skills, so it would be less dangerous to Angel than if you did it. You just have to give me the knife and I recommend to use a scalpel instead for a precision incision and allow better stitches."

Kilas handed Craig the knife from her shaking hands and he took the knife calmly and put it down. He picked up the scalpel and told Angel to lie down on the table facedown and Craig moved her hair out of the way. Craig said, "Angel, I will cut a small incision and pull out the tracker. I recommend we put the tracker on an escape pod and send it in another direction so the tracking ship will follow the tracker and not us. Once the tracker is out, I will burn the incision to heal it and close the incision. It should take less than three minutes. Kilas, please get the escape pod ready and as we enter the new atmosphere of the upcoming planet. We can bounce the escape pod off the atmosphere and send it off into deeper space so we have true isolation."

Kilas stood, paralyzed. Craig gestured with the scalpel, "Kilas, go and get the pod ready. Once I cut the tracker out, we need to put it on the pod and send it immediately away so the ship following will pursue the pod and the tracker and give us time to truly escape."

Kilas nodded and looked at Angel, and Angel said, "I will be fine. That is a great plan from Craig. Now get the pod ready and let Craig cut the tracker out of me. Now go."

As Kilas departed to get the pod ready, Craig took the scalpel toward Angel's neck and said, "This will sting a little." He quickly cut at the skin and within seconds had the small tracker out and he was cauterizing the wound to heal it quickly. He even put a small bandage on it to keep it sterile.

Craig said, "Angel we are done and you should not have an infection. Do you have any other tracker inserted into your body? I can check if you want?"

Angel said, "I do not think so, but please check. They might have put another inside me without me knowing."

Craig picked up a small scanner and started to go over the rest of Angel's body, looking for any other trackers. He came up with another spot on her ankle. He said, "You have a much older tracker in your ankle. Would you like me to remove that one, too?"

Angel said, "Yes. I want that tracker removed immediately."

Craig repositioned her ankle and then said, "This might hurt more. This one is embedded into your bone and looks like they put it into your ankle many years ago."

Angel was remembering when she had ankle surgery, but that was when she was a teenager, many years ago. She remembered that Kobar had paid for the medical procedure so that her ankle would improve. Kobar had implanted a tracker in her when she was only fourteen years old. She had a severe emotional reaction to a person who was the closest thing to a father figure that she had, who had betrayed her trust by putting a tracker inside when she was a teen. Angel said to Craig, "Get that freaking tracker out of my ankle immediately and then we can send both trackers on the escape pod and I can be freed from Kobar forever."

Craig said, "Would you like to be sedated because this might hurt some?"

Angel said, "No, just make the cut and tear that tracker out of my ankle and send the pod to the other side of the galaxy. I am good with the pain."

Craig said, "I will respect your request." He immediately opened up her ankle and Angel cried with full tears, feeling the

Chapter 19: Kilas and Angel Depart

full pain of the cutting on the skin. Craig could feel that Angel was in pain and then said, "Give me fifteen more seconds and it will be complete."

Angel said, "Thank you." She was also crying at the same time with the excruciating pain.

Kilas walked in and looked upset, "Craig, what are you doing?"

Craig said, "I am removing the second tracker from Angel's body as she requested. I would recommend you comfort her immediately, because it is quite painful right now."

Kilas went to Angel and looked into her eyes, "How are you feeling?"

Angel said, "Craig found a second tracker in my body from over a decade ago and I requested he take that one out also. I assume they are both implanted by Kobar. Just look at me and hold my hand. The pain is terrible." As Angel was saying this, tears rolled down her face and she grimaced in pain and gripped Kilas's hand as strong as possible.

Kilas did as she was instructed and held Angel's hand. She looked into her eyes and comforted her with her words. Soon the extraction was complete.

Craig said, "This is going to hurt because I am going to burn the opening to cauterize the tissue and prevent any infection. Kilas, please hold both of her hands. She might pass out from the pain because she refused any anesthesia."

Kilas held her hands tight and watched the pain in Angels' eyes as her skin was being burned to seal the wound, just like Craig had mentioned, Angel passed out from the pain, in Kilas's arms.

Craig said, "Kilas, I have injected some pain killers into Angel which will assist her with the pain for the next one or two hours. What I need you to do is comfort her when she awakens and let her know everything went as planned. I will send both trackers on the escape pod that you readied and send them across the galaxy so they may not track her anymore. She is free now. Please let her know when she awakes."

Kilas said, "I will. Craig, thank you for doing this for her."

Craig said, "I would rather not have any trackers on our ship for protection of ourselves. I will now put the trackers on the escape pod and eject them with your final permission."

"Please."

Craig took the bowl holding both trackers, which were covered with Angel's blood, and walked out to the escape pod. After loading it with the trackers, he entered a grid in the galaxy that would make the escape pod travel for weeks. When Kobar finally tracked it down, they would be twice as far away from the people looking for them. With a few more buttons on the keypad, Craig sent the escape pod away from their ship. Craig then walked back into the galley where Angel had been lying on the table, but now she was sitting up with Kilas's help. Angel looked like she was still in some pain and Craig said, "The painkillers will have an effect for at least a couple of hours. Kilas, I will help you take her to her room and I want you to be by her side for the next couple of hours." Craig said, "I will continue to pilot the ship to the farthest desolate planet in this sector, as originally requested."

Kilas agreed and Craig helped Angel off the table and put her arms around her. Together they took her to Kilas's cabin room and laid her down on her bed and put a blanket over her. Kilas laid next to her so she could comfort her. Kilas kissed her on the cheek and the both of them fell asleep on the bed, while Craig and Greg piloted the ship to the farthest planet.

* * *

After two hours of flight, Craig walked to Kilas's cabin and knocked on the door. Kilas walked to the door and met Craig in the hallway, "What is it?"

"We have found a more desolate planet with no name and no colonization on in; it is a perfect planet to land on for a few days and let things settle."

Kilas said, "Thank you, Craig. And also, thank you for helping Angel."

Craig looked back at Kilas, "You care about Angel, which means we shall also care for her and protect her as needed. She is

Chapter 19: Kilas and Angel Depart

a part of our small family."

Kilas smiled, "I agree. I give you permission to find a safe landing spot and land the ship on the lone planet. I fully trust your expertise in piloting."

"Of course you trust my piloting, what a silly comment. Where would we be without Greg and Craig's piloting?"

Kilas said, "Craig, are you learning sarcasm?"

Craig said, "Yes. Sarcasm is quite enjoyable and amusing, but most important, if received well by the person, the fun is made out, too. There is a trust factor in this protocol."

Kilas smiled, "Craig, keep it up. I like it."

Craig smiled and left their room and went to land the ship on the new planet.

Chapter 20

Important Questions to Ask

After Angela was done for the day, she texted Paul and asked if they could meet at Casseneta's. Within a minute, Paul texted her back to *meet at the library at 7pm*. Angela smiled as she got in her car. She turned on her sports car and looked in her rearview mirror and saw Peter sitting in her backseat. She could hear her voice get shrill with stress, "What the hell are you doing and how did you get in my car?"

Peter smiled and said, "Those are not important questions to ask right now. What I need you to do is go back into your office and get the Kila before the security guard leaves. Just tell him you forgot something and put it in your purse and return back to your car."

Angela said, "You expect me to do what you say after you nearly scared the crap out of me?"

Peter said, "I don't smell anything, so you actually did not. So go back into your office and get the Kila, now." He smiled and tilted his head to the right in a sarcastic way. She was mad and upset but knew to trust Peter, so she left the car running and went back inside. She opened the filing cabinet and put the cloth-wrapped Kila in her purse and walked back out. She thanked the guard again for letting her back into her office. Now Peter was sitting in her front passenger seat, looking at her. She sat in her car and pulled out the wrapping that held the Kila and handed it

Chapter 20: Important Questions to Ask

to Peter. She put on her seatbelt and said, "Where do you want to go?"

Peter said, "I hear there is a gathering at Casseneta's tonight. We should go there before everyone shows up."

Angela frowned, "How did you know about tonight?"

Peter said, "Stop asking questions that are irrelevant and just drive. You are so simple."

Angela was pissed and upset and frustrated and had lots of intellectual questions to ask Peter, but he was just some omnipotent person who, like knew, everything that was going on. She kept thinking how he knew about the meeting tonight when they just thought of it minutes ago. There was something about Peter that was definitively not normal, but great to be next to right now.

Angela said, "Could I stop by my place to change clothes before we go to Casseneta's? I hate wearing work clothes to social meetings."

Peter said, "That is fine. Plus, I have been waiting to return where you live anyway. That should solve some of the questions I have about you."

Angela said, "What questions?"

Peter said, "Just drive. Don't worry about such simple questions."

Angela just rolled her eyes as exaggeratedly as she could, but quite unable to achieve full affect since she was driving. Within fifteen minutes they were pulling up to a wonderful house, with a three-car drive, in a luxurious neighborhood. The garage door went up and she parked her sports car next to a vintage 1970 Jaguar convertible and a Harley Davidson motorcycle. They both got out of the car and Peter said, "The questions have been answered. You do own a classic and motorcycle."

Angela looked at him and said, "I thought the questions had more depth than that, like spiritually or metaphysical. Not something simple about a sports car and a motorcycle."

"Why would you think all my questions are deep and metaphysical? I merely had a vision of speed and you wearing a helmet while we were walking from the inner temple, and this has solved that for me. It is that simple. I thought it would be an older motorcycle."

Angela smiled and shook her head, "Peter, why are you so mysterious and calm all at the same time? I am going to change clothes quickly. Please make yourself comfortable."

Peter walked in the living room and said, 'Thank you, I will just take a look around. I can make an assessment of someone by how they decorate their house and what artifacts are publicly displayed."

Angela did not even close her door as she was undressing and changing because Peter was definitely not interested in her, but in artifacts and other things. She quickly took off her business clothes and searched for some comfortable clothes. She was looking for her favorite yoga T-shirt, but could not find it. Then she knew it was in her hamper, so she smiled and dug in her hamper and found it. It was her lucky T-shirt, and she smelled it and it passed the test, so she put it on. But then realized she forgot her bra. She just smiled and said to herself 'meh.' It did not matter with the crowd she was hanging with tonight and she would have a leather jacket on, so it would not matter. She was intending to ride her Harley to the bar and have Peter hang on to her for fun. She was going to be in control of the drive. She looked at herself in the mirror and approved her look, and then walked out of her room to see Peter looking at her bar. What was he doing?

Peter said, "You can identify a person by the kind of booze they have in their bar."

Angela said, "So, what kind of person am I?" She was hoping for a quick sarcastic answer, but that was not going to happen.

Peter said, "You like to be highly educated and distinguished, you like the hard work you have put into your career, you have loved and lost and loved again, but you wait for a man that treats you like an equal and not a subordinate. You wait for a man who loves jazz and spontaneity, you wait for your equal, intellectually and emotionally, in your desire and capacity to be adventurous. You are still waiting for true love."

Angela stared at Peter and felt sad because everything he has said was true. All of it, every single word. She was waiting for

Chapter 20: Important Questions to Ask

someone to fit her standards. She was almost forty and had still not found it. She felt a shot into her stomach. How the hell did he know so much just by looking at a liquor cabinet? That was improbable and just not practical. Who really is Peter?

He walked over to Angela and hugged her and kissed her on the cheek, "I am ready to ride your Harley and be the backseat bitch."

Angela said, "How did you know we were going to ride my Harley?"

Peter said, "I can tell by your jeans and your outfit, and you have on a leather jacket. No one drives their car around wearing a leather jacket anymore. It's not the 1950s, but that was a fun time. Plus, I can't read your mind, that would be illogical, no one really reads minds. It does not work that way."

Angela looked confused and what he said about her outfit was true, and his last comment about reading her mind was made in jest. But there's no way that could be true. She looked back at him and smiled. "Well, I have a surprise for you anyway. I have another motorcycle in my shed that I needed to warm up and it has a sidecar. You will need some goggles to wear." Angela said, "Follow me." She walked out her back porch to a separate garage and she touched a key panel which started to raise the door for the garage, and right in front of them was a vintage motorcycle from WWII.

Angela was about to tell him what it was when Peter said, "It's an Indian Model 340 B with an air-cooled V-twin sidecar from 1941. This had a 1206cc huge engine, and is capable of 30 horsepower at 4,000 rpm. During the war, this was a wonderful bike, and the sidecar could mount a machine gun."

Angela was dumbfounded, as she was hoping to brag about her vintage motorcycle that took her over a decade to refurbish. He said almost everything to perfection about her baby. He was either one of the smartest men in the world, or there was something about him that made him quite unique. He walked over to it and touched the cycle like it was an old friend. He looked at the engine and the side car and was talking to himself, almost crying, reminiscing about something.

Angela said, "Peter are you okay? It feels like you are familiar with this type of bike."

Peter said, "I did many missions with this bike. You have done an exceptional job with refurbishing the original engine, and you have the correct leather seat. And the front is refurbished, not original, but looks just like it. I would be honored to ride in your sidecar. There is always plenty of leg room in these. Please do not go over 30 miles an hour in a left turn—the side car wheel can come off the ground slightly."

Angela just smiled and thought the only way for him to have known that about this motorcycle was if he had driven one a lot, because that is not in any owner's manual and has to just be learned by hours on the bike. Angela asked, "What kind of missions? I did not know you served?"

Peter was sitting in the sidecar and knew exactly where everything was and was touching the steel frame. "I did combat missions in multiple wars." He did not elaborate.

Angela handed him his goggles and watched him put them on before she mounted the Indian. She cranked it up and watched Peter smile as if he was riding it like a boy on his first big wheel or something. She just smiled to herself and was happy to bring some joy to him because he was always so serious and stoic. He most definitively had an old soul. He was not from this time for sure, his mannerisms were classic. She cranked up the engine well and slowly drove the Indian out of the garage, clicked the garage door down with her fob, and they drove slowly down her driveway to the street, and began the slow evening cruise to Casseneta's.

The weather was crisp and cool, but not too cold. She looked at Peter and he was smiling for sure, and enjoying the view and the ride. She was happy to put a little joy into her new mysterious friend. Her initial thought about riding the Indian with a man in the sidecar was the typical gender struggle, and a man riding a sidecar while a petite woman drove, this was the common thing with men she had tried to date over the years. Her status and position were always a hang-up and she just wanted to be an equal and not a subordinate. Peter took riding in the sidecar

Chapter 20: Important Questions to Ask

with ease and class, and was not at all thinking of gender roles, but just full appreciation on the engines and the history of the bike. He was like no man she had ever met. Within about fifteen minutes they arrived in front of Casseneta's and she parked in the motorcycle in front. Paul, Robert, and Jamie were talking in front and watched them drive up.

Robert pointed at Angela and was surprised to see Peter. Angela pointed at Paul and was surprised to see Jamie and Robert. There was the usually hellos and greetings and slowly everyone walked inside the front door.

Peter said, "I think I left something in the side car." He walked out alone while the rest of them were going into the library. Peter did not leave anything in the sidecar, but wanted to look around to see if anyone was following them. He knew someone was looking at him from somewhere, but he could not find the source or person. He shook his head and then walked back inside to join the group.

* * *

Robert had a table brought into the library so they could have dinner while they talked about the most recent events and how to sort them out. Robert said, "I ordered you what you had last time when you were here, if no one minds, so we can enjoy the time." The food arrived shortly with several bottles of wine. The manager, Woodrow, gave Robert a thumbs up and made sure everyone was good, and then he closed the doors and secured them so no one could disturb them.

As he was walking back to the bar, he texted someone, *They are all back in the library*. Within ten seconds, there was a quick text reply back *Thank you*.

* * *

Robert took hold of the conversation, "Peter, what should be done with Nera?"

Peter said slowly, "That's not the problem. The problem is

Samael and his motives." He took a sip of wine and smiled. "Let's look at this from another perspective. Remember what happened last time with the athame? It was a portal to another dimension and time, and had access to places. It could control time. Paul was instructed, by probably an Archangel to be identified later, to hide it and secure it from Nera, but we do not know what her final objective was to find and receive the athame, except she wanted the curse to be taken away from a past life when she murdered Paul. Well several times in fact. It seems her pastime is to keep hurting Paul." He pointed to Paul because it seems he always died in regards to Nera. He chuckled, "Paul, you just don't have any luck with Nera." He continued, "Let me continue. Robert, you assisted Paul in his backyard, and all the spirits of the past lives of the knights joined in where time from the present and current joined together, and you played both for a short time. That was a crossing of time into time. Now Paul, you did not hurt Nera, which is what she wanted, to get rid of the curse, so she still has it, which is terrible on her right now. It is driving her mad. Now, Angela my dear, is now in the middle of this, too, because she has the Kila and I have her staff secure, and together those two pieces joined can't be defeated. Is everyone caught up to where I am going so far?"

They all were eating and listening and nodded their heads for him to continue.

Peter continued, "The new character now, that is mysterious, is Jamie here." Everyone looked over to her and she blushed slightly. "She has been brought into this equation to assist the three angels in their quest, which is clear, but not clear. Jamie has angelic blood in her, and the only reason to bring that up is there is something that she will have to do for them, because they are forbidden, and that is the question here. Though she is untrained in the mystic arts, she has great power and magical potential. Her presence here means the most. But the key fact is, Nera does not know about Jamie, which is our advantage, and Samael and the angels hate each other due to Lilith, but business is business and they work together. Nera is just a pawn for Samael. She is capable of being dangerous, but someone else is helping her, which we do

Chapter 20: Important Questions to Ask

not know, and I can't feel who it is. There is a goddess involved inside Nera from a long past life who still resides, but I can't see in my visions."

Paul interrupted, "Peter, a couple months ago, I was a doing a circle with Nera and we had gotten drunk, here exactly, and we did a spiritual circle at her condo. And during the circle, a spirit spoke out of her, and talked to me and told me to be afraid of Nera, and that she was not to be trusted. Then when Nera awoke, she was frightened that a goddess spoke to me, and I was quick on my feet and told her there was no message But there was."

Peter looked at Paul and asked, "Did the messenger identify herself?"

Paul said, "She said her name was Diana."

Peter looked down and looked quite sad. Robert looked the same way. Jamie and Angela glanced at each other, equal in their lack of knowledge.

Paul said, "Does Diana mean anything to you two? We have the right to know."

Peter looked at Robert to explain and he took over the answer. Robert knew that Peter was too close to this one.

Robert took a drink of wine preparing himself to explain and said, "Diana was a Roman goddess, she was identified as the goddess of the hunt and wild animals. Later in history, she was Luna, the goddess of the moon. She is most famous for being the fertility goddess and was one of the few gods with no children. Women have worshiped Diana who were trying get pregnant, and were about to give birth and wish for an easy birth process. In folklore and myth, Diana traveled in a trinity with *Egeria* the water nymph and *Virvius* the woodland god. Diana has also been named many other names; the Queen of the Open Sky, a sun goddess, a moon goddess, the Lady of the Beasts, and also been called the goddess of common lower-class people and slaves."

"Diana was the child of Jupiter and Latona, and her twin brother was Apollo. What makes this unique is that in the current Paganism, Wicca, and Witchcraft they say Diana had a daughter, *Aradia*, who most famously became the Queen of the Witches. Diana has become one of the strongest and most independent female goddesses. Diana is famous for disliking men, guarding her chastity, and more important, was extremely vengeful."

"In historic and classic paintings, she is always a young beautiful goddess, clad in a tunic and boots, always carrying a bow and set of arrows. She usually has animals in her paintings, like dogs or deer, who accompany her on the hunt."

Robert added to the explanation, "The Diana festival is always celebrated on August 13th. The archetype of Diana is the first child of nature. She prefers to be in nature, is sensitive to nature, loves to be solitary in nature, loves to be with animals more than people, and due to being in the woods, she is physically fit. The goddess Diana inspires young women today to continue to aspire to change, to continue to look forward, explore and redefine themselves."

Robert had to take a long sip of wine, "There is more that I must discuss now. There was also a violent cult almost 2,500 years ago on the shores of Lake Nemi, about 30 miles from Rome, where Diana's highest priest must kill his predecessor to take over. The shores of the lake was where this cult religious rite was. They killed in the honor of *Diana Nemorensis,* 'Diana of Nemi' or 'Diana of the Woods'—this is an Italian version of the goddess Artemis. The site of the cliffs on the lake were noted as Diana's mirror. If you were the Diana temple high priest, you were called *rex nemorensis* or "king of the sacred grove", because there was also a large oak tree that grew which was absolutely forbidden to break a branch off. Only a runaway slave was allowed to break a branch, thus earning the right to challenge the high priest to a challenge to death. If the slave won and killed the high priest, then they were the next *rex nemorensis*." Robert smiled and snickered, "It's a little like the Garden of Eden and David and Goliath put together."

Robert drank some more wine, "This cult lasted up until the Imperial Age and Emperor Caligula was angered by a priest that had been in power too long and ordered him to be killed. Later, around 200 A.D., the actual fight for priesthood became symbolic, and not literal, and then the cult of Diana started to fade. It was almost completely gone with the rise of Christianity.

Chapter 20: Important Questions to Ask

Then it merged—historically unproven with no evidence except folklore—into the cult of the Virgin Mary. With the introduction of Christianity, Mary had become their new Diana symbol."

Peter then said, "Let me add a few more things. On August 13th the Romans would always have a weeklong celebration to pray for a good harvest and keep the storms away that might hurt the crops. What you must also know is, August 15th is now the Catholic feast day of Mary's ascension into heaven, which technically, and secretly remembers Diana. Thousands of women in antiquity would flock to Nemi to offer thanks and pray for her trust for the next year, and implore her continued help. Years later, worship for Diana also arrived in Rome, to Avetine Hill, where they would flock to her shrine to conduct a ritual hair washing, and help with pregnancy and childbirth. At this point, the Romans identified this following and made Diana a trinity of sorts, by calling her Luna the moon goddess, Hekate the underworld deity of magic, and as the goddess hunter Diana."

Peter looked at Paul, Angela, and Jamie and they looked like students in class. He said, "I hope Robert and I did not bore you with our short knowledge of Diana."

Angela said, "Well let's bring all this back around, I hate to be the psychiatrist in this equation. So why would Diana be aligned with Nera? Or how, or why, would that be if Diana spoke to Paul through her during their last circle?"

Peter said, "Thank you for asking that. There is one more thing that I might say to answer your question. I assume Nera is in a witch coven based on Dianic Witchcraft. This type of witchcraft is female-centered in its orientation to goddess energy, ritual, and traditions. These types of Dianic witches only honor women goddesses, mainly Diana, and this brings us back around to a person called Charles Leland, who wrote a book *Aradia*, which talks about the importance of womanhood, magic, and healing. These witch covens practice magic and meditation on healing themselves from men's actions, and celebrating their feminism and their sacred feminine. These covens are female-only and celebrate woman's body, and are usually naked when they do these rituals. Dianic witches are the only witches who condone spells and hexes against people, and especially men, because they do not believe in the term 'no harm'. They highly encourage violence against men. This type of witchcraft is where many women come for overcoming trauma and raise awareness about violence toward women. Dianic witches pride themselves on lesbian and bisexual female members; men are forbidden to join. It is where you will find all the so-called radical feminists."

He stopped to get another sip of wine and continued, "That's why *Aradia* is important right now. It is also called *The Gospel of the Witches* that claims that ancient Diana and Herodias cults are linked to ancient mysteries of an all-women coven. This book claims that Aradia was sent to Earth to establish witchcraft and to teach it to witches. This book was published in 1889 and has been scrutinized and disputed for over one-hundred years. What you may not have connected is that Diana and Lucifer conjoined to create Aradia. The claims are that this is the oldest religion. This gospel is unproven, but is agreed upon to be pre-Christian. It's been written that Diana was the first creation and is divided among the light and dark. She becomes the light and Lucifer becomes the dark. Lucifer's name means "light bearer" and Aradia is destined to become the messiah of the witches. She actually lives in heaven at first. Then Diana, against all of heaven, sends her to earth to teach witchcraft. Her mission is to teach poisoning and malevolent acts against oppressors.

He paused, looking solemn. "Since Paul heard Diana come through Nera during a sacred circle oriented toward women, but he was a man, Diana in her compassion, talked with Paul to warn him about the harmful intentions of Nera, in which she kind of broke her followers' creed. You see, Diana is believed to still love men, and though some men need to be oppressed, there are some men who no harm should go to because there are good men in the world."

"Nera is highly likely to be in a Dianic coven. We need to send someone to try and get into this coven to find out what Nera is up to. Someone needs to befriend Nera at these meetings and they might find out anything that we may not know. The person must also be a woman." At this time Paul, Peter, and Robert all

Chapter 20: Important Questions to Ask

looked at Angela and Jamie, who were of course, the only women at the table.

Jamie and Angela both looked at each other and laughed and smiled. Jamie said, "Since I have angelic blood, it might help me to get into this coven, so I volunteer for this quest. I have even loved a woman once, or maybe twice, or maybe three times." She laughed and Angela smiled at her.

Angela blushed and looked down and her hands. She looked back up and said, "I should go with you to try and get into this coven. We could go as a couple." She winked at Jamie. Angela said, "Psychologically, it would better to go as a couple to prove to them that we are together. And it's much more easy to deny a lone person than two. Trust me on this. This is what I do all day."

Peter said, "That sounds like a perfect plan, even though there are not perfect plans. But with them both trying to get in together, it could work well. I have a good feeling about it. Now we just have to contact Lena and find the gatekeeper to the local Dianic coven."

Robert said, "If they brought the Kila with them, it would help them get in quicker."

Paul said, "Oh that, well I forgot to tell you. I made a deal with Samael this afternoon."

Peter said, "Paul, please tell me you did not make a deal with Samael."

Paul drank some more wine with a smile, "I did make a deal with Samael that Nera could use the Kila to try and hurt someone, but I have a plan, and was going to give Nera a fake Kila, and not the real one that has trapped demons in it."

Robert said, "Did a mortar hit you too close while we were in Kirkuk? Why on earth would you do that? That's stupid."

Angela said, "I supported his decision and he explained it to me. I am responsible for it, it's my mission for Joe. But we will not give her the real one, because Paul had a replica made that looks just like the real one."

Robert and Peter exchanged a wry smile and Peter said, "The decision with the Kila belongs to you. Joe gave his life to save you. We trust your decision. You will know what to do with the real Kila when you need to, just rely on your intuition because Joe is always with you."

Paul said, "My plan will work. I thought most of it through, but with Angela and Jamie trying to get into Nera's coven just makes my plan even better."

Angela and Jamie threw some bread rolls at Paul and both said, "Yea, right. Pshaw."

Everyone laughed. Paul just raised his hands in surrender. The conversations about Nera and all the goddesses had formally ended, and now they were just chatting about types of bourbon, whiskey, and wines. The manager opened the doors to the library and informed them that they were closed for the evening. The kitchen was closed and the bar was trying to close out. Robert said, "Please let the staff go and close the kitchen. I will lock the front door and turn on the security system when we call it a night."

Woodrow thanked Robert and let the staff know that they could all go home and the owner, Robert, would close up. As the group continued to finish their last drinks, all the lights went out except for the library.

Robert poured the last bit of wine from their third bottle among friends, and he said, "Once we are all done with our last glass we should go. I can call a taxi for everyone so they get home safe. There is no need for anyone to drive home drunk."

Angela remembered she rode her Harley and said, "I am not leaving my motorcycle outside your bar for someone to steal parts from or steal it. I shall drive home. Peter, I want you to go back with me for my security, if you do not mind."

Peter bowed, "My dear, it would be an honor to defend your integrity if required. I am ready to depart whenever you are."

Angela saluted back, "I am ready."

Peter said, "To this wonderful fellowship, we shall be departing. Thank you for the lovely discussion and fine food and wonderful drink."

Angela and Peter started to get their coats on and the rest decided it was time to depart, too. Everyone said their goodbyes and started walking toward the front doors. Robert said, "I called

Chapter 20: Important Questions to Ask

a cab for the rest of us to take us home. We will stay outside and wait for the taxi." Everyone was outside watching Angela and Peter put on their helmets and hop on the Harley with the sidecar. The temperature had dropped and Paul said, "You two stay warm." Angela cranked the Harley and put on her gloves, and Peter just smiled and made a peace symbol with his two fingers. They slowly departed and started to drive down the street toward her house. Angela was driving well for drinking so much and Peter was enjoying the cold air on his face. They pulled into Angela's driveway and they noticed her garage door was up and the lights were on, which was odd. They pulled the Harley into the back garage and got off and Angela said, "I swore I locked everything when we departed."

Peter said, "You did. Who else has a key?"

Angela said, "No one."

They walked through the back door and realized someone had been in her house looking for something, and the place had been searched thoroughly. Angela realized she had brought the Kila to dinner and reached in her pocket, but it was not there. She did not know where it went and rushed into her office to look for it. She quickly looked in her briefcase and could not find the Kila. She began to panic. She came back to Peter, who was standing in the living room. She said, "The Kila is gone. I thought I took it to dinner, but don't have it now. Someone might have taken it."

Peter smiled and said, "No, it is not lost." He put his hand into his jacket and pulled out the Kila that was still wrapped in cloth.

Angela asked, "When do you pick it up? How did you do that?"

Peter said, "I picked it up while we were at dinner. I wanted to personally secure it. I had a hunch someone might try this. It's very amateurish to do this this way, no class in leaving a mess. The best way to search a home is to not leave any trace so the owners are not suspicious."

Angela walked over to Peter and grabbed the Kila and unwrapped it to assure herself. She said, "Thank you."

Peter said, "Let's lock up the place. You are staying with me tonight for your safety, but I will drive the Harley and you will sit in the sidecar. I want you to grab a to-go bag to last forty-eight hours. Go pack now and I will look around your place for any evidence on who did this."

Peter looked around and found that someone had placed a listening device and several cameras in the house. He knew they were not from Angela, and he knew he was being listened to. He did not remove them because that's the last thing you want to do. But since he knew he was being watched and listened too, he walked into Angela's room and told her to be silent. He grabbed a picture off the wall and grabbed a piece of paper and a pencil and started writing on it so she could see what he was writing. He wrote, *Keep talking normally, but your house is bugged and someone is listening. Hurry up and pack and we will depart.* He nodded at her and she started to cry and he shook his head to stay calm. He whispered to her to keep packing, but hurry.

He walked back into the living room and kept looking around. He knew he would need to bring his specialized equipment to fix the bug problem, but right now he wanted the people who were listening to have nothing to report the rest of the night.

Angela had her bag ready and Peter whispered, "Lock all the doors, but leave the lights on and secure your house with your security system." She did as they walked out the back door, back into the garage, and to the Harley that was still warm from their last drive. Paul took the helmet and hopped on the cycle and turned it on quickly, as if he had hundreds of hours driving, and Angela hopped in the sidecar with her bag. She looked up at him and gave the thumbs up and he slowly pulled the Harley outside the garage. Angela took the remote and closed and secured her garage, and then they slowly pulled down the driveway and down the street and out of the secluded neighborhood. Angela assumed they would go his office on 18th Street, but he was heading out of the city on a country road that was desolate. They must have been ten miles outside of town when he pulled up to what looked like an abandoned house. He took the gravel road next to it and kept driving into the woods until they came to a beautiful house that looked like a ski lodge. He pulled the motorcycle into the grass and kept driving up a trail to a barn, and he then stopped, but let

Chapter 20: Important Questions to Ask

the Harley go to idle. He got off and opened the barn, and then he got back on the Harley and drove it in his barn and then turned off the motor. It was a simple pole shed with tools, a riding lawn mower, and a tractor safely stored in it. Angela said, "Where are we?"

Peter said, "This is my home. I wanted to keep your motorcycle out of sight in case someone is using satellites to find photos of your movements. But the bug on your cycle, I ensured fell off as soon as we departed your house."

As they were walking out of the barn, he turned on a heater to mask any heat signature that the motorcycle still had. It was dark as they were walking together up the gravel driveway. Angela said, "It's a beautiful house."

Peter said, "Thank you. Hardly anyone knows that I live here and I keep it pretty secluded. I do not get out much." They walked up the side and up the deck, and Angela was impressed by the view. The motion detection lights came on as they walked closer to the house. Peter said, "I have a pretty good security system and everything is motion detected, and also heat detected, so I know when there is someone here who should not be. And there is only one way out or in by vehicle to my property. It makes it pretty safe. Plus, I have short circuit TV cameras watching most of the property. I live here alone. Almost no one knows that I live here. For all my business activities and the university, I always use a PO box at the main post office. I never have any packages arrive here and I have no friends who I invite here. You are the first person to visit me in almost five years. I like my seclusion."

Angela was looking at the deck and the view, and then they walked into his home. She entered a great room with a tall sloping ceiling that looked like a ski lodge, with windows everywhere to see nature. It was a beautiful room.

Peter said, "I found this jewel almost fifteen years ago and offered them cash at asking price. I fell in love with the place as soon as I saw it." He continued to show her other rooms, and she was amazed by his complexity of bookshelves that were in almost every room, and he was such an outdoors person with big windows in every room.

Peter said, "Your room is downstairs. Beware of my guard dog." They walked downstairs and he walked to the right and said, "Good evening, Luke." He lowered down to pet an older black Labrador who was so cute, but full of gray hair on his muzzle and paws. "This is Luke and he is fifteen years old. He lives down here because he can't walk upstairs any more, but he has been a wonderful companion throughout the years. He will like your company for a couple days."

Angela said, "A couple of days?"

Peter said, "It is Friday night and there are people watching your house, so you can't go back tomorrow and we need to see who is watching your house. Then you need a buffer day, so stay until Sunday. This is a wonderful weekend cottage. I have lots of acres to walk and hundreds of books."

He walked to her room and turned on the light, "You can stay here in this room. You have your own bathroom over here and a small kitchen right there. That reminds me, we need to secure the Kila." He pulled it out of his coat and walked into another room, which looked like a storage room, except there was a steel door along the wall with a keycode access. Peter walked over to the door and punched in his key code numbers on the key pad and the cylinders of the heavy door lock clicked and shifted the door slightly open due to its weight.

He said, "I need to show you one more room. I have this thing for privacy, so I dug into the hill behind the house and built a secure bunker. It's got five feet of concrete surrounding the walls. This could take a direct explosion and survive. You know, if someone wanted to drop a bomb on my house and I have a few seconds to get here, I will survive. It's wonderful life insurance."

He had computers all along one side of the room and the other side was filled with weapons. There were all types of weapons; from rifles, shotguns, handguns, spears, daggers, and multiple swords.

Angela said, "What are all these weapons?"

Peter said, "I have collected them throughout the years. I pretty much used every one of them. I have been in quite a few wars."

Chapter 20: Important Questions to Ask

Angela pointed to a broadsword, "What war did you use that one in?"

Peter said, "The Battle of Glen Fruid in 1603. I fought for the Clan Gregor." He then took the Kila and put it in a case with a secure lock on it and put it on his desk. He turned around and looked at Angela and said, "What?"

Angela crossed her arms and said, "If you were fighting in 1603, then you are over 300 years old."

Peter said, "Oh that, that was from a past life, okay? It's actually a movie prop from a movie. I could not be that old." He then walked out of the bunker and helped Angela out and he locked the door behind them. He said, "The Kila is well secured. No one can get in there unless they kill me and Luke, my dog." They both looked at the sleeping dog and laughed.

Angela wanted to know more information, "What movie is that broadsword from? Why do you own an authentic Scottish broadsword? Thank you for securing the Kila."

Peter said, "You ask too many questions."

Angela said, "I am a psychiatrist, it's a good habit."

Peter said, "Let's talk about it tomorrow. I promise you can analyze me all day while you enjoy the woods, and relax, and we find out who is watching your house. Okay?"

Angela said, "Deal. I am tired."

Peter said, "I will be up in my great room with the fire, reading or writing until 1 or 2am. So if you can't sleep, that is where you can find me."

Angela said, "Thank you, Peter. I appreciate you helping me now and offering your home to me to stay at."

Peter said, "I am your protector. I will protect you fully in this life."

Angela said, "With that said, let me get some sleep. We will talk in the morning."

"Luke will protect you, too." They both looked at the Labrador one more time, that was snoring loudly on his dog bed.

Angela said, "I will be fine. Thank you and good night."

Peter walked upstairs and headed to his bar to pour a late drink and to read a little bit. He went to his bookshelf and took out an older antique book and brought it to his chair. He turned on his deskside lamp and put the book on his lap. It was about the Battle of Glen Fruin. He started to open it to a few sketches of the warriors and came upon a certain page of a Scottish Warrior.

* * *

Peter had fallen asleep in his chair, reading all night, but his watch went off at 5:30 in the morning because he always watched the sunrise from his front porch. His front porch was oriented east, and his house was laid out in cardinal directions, with windows to let the sun and moon enter his house during certain special moons. The architect had built this house and used old druid ways to align with the moon and the stars, and the windows were also aligned to allow light and moonlight. It was astronomically aligned. That was the main reason he bought the house; he knew immediately who built the house, but the architect who built the house had a heart attack at forty-two and only got to live in it for a few months. Peter knew he got a gold mine in this natural, metaphysical, and spiritual sanctuary.

He had only the kitchen light on and hummed a little to himself as his coffee was finishing. He took his coffee out on his porch and watched the oranges streaking the sky that started on the ridgeline, and he was just watching the beauty of the sunrise. This was his morning ritual; he would watch and meditate and simply enjoy life. As the oranges and reds and yellows were slowly filling the sky before the sun appeared, he heard something in his house and he looked toward his front door and Angela was walking out with a cup of coffee.

Angela said, "I would like to have coffee and enjoy the sunrise with you, if you don't mind?"

Peter said, "Not at all. The sunrises are beautiful from my porch. Please enjoy the view with me. I am glad you found the coffee."

Angela said, "The coffee was easy. Walking over your sleeping Labrador in the hallway was the challenge."

Peter smiled, "He is a good dog. He has been with me for

Chapter 20: Important Questions to Ask

fifteen years. He was my therapy dog and got me through some hard times. He is an old soul like me."

Angela sat in the chair next to Peter and watched the steam come off her coffee in the cold morning air and said, "Peter, am I going to be okay? I am scared about everything with Nera. I feel like I am going to be okay, but another part of my mind tells me that someone could be harmed. I am having trouble dealing with all this. All I want to do is complete what Joe wanted me to do with the Kila. That's the most important thing for me right now."

Peter looked over at Angela, "We will complete your task for Joe, I promise you. You will be safe; I promise and give you my oath."

Angela put her feet up in her chair and wrapped her arms around her legs and drank a sip of coffee, "I trust you."

Peter said, "You can."

Angela said, "I need to tell you one more thing about me. I am a witch."

"I know. You have always been a witch throughout time. We have always made a good pair throughout history; this time will also be a wonderful partnership. This is just the next chapter in the novel. I already knew that information and I trust you, too."

Chapter 21

Jamie and Angela

As Peter and Angela were enjoying the sunrise with their coffees, Jamie had awoken in her house with a frightening dream. She dreamt that their Dianic coven deception plan did not fool Nera at all and Nera, with the help of Samael, turned on them all with a severe vengeance. She woke up with a cold chill and knew she had to text Angela: *Angela, can we talk now?* She was wondering about the early morning hour as she sent the text.

Angela was still enjoying the sunrise when she responded, *Of course how about right now?* Peter suggested she visit, so Angela gave Jamie directions. Jamie decided to drive there, straight away, to talk about her dream to both of them before they started this masquerade to try to get into Nera's Dianic coven.

Within a half hour of Angela texting, Jamie was cautiously and slowing driving up the long driveway to Peter's estate. Angela and Peter were watching her slowing come up the driveway, in hesitation, not knowing what was at the end of the driveway. As she finally turned the corner and saw the house in the woods, Angela and Peter waved at her from the front porch and they could see her smile. As she saw them wave, there was an instant look of relief on her face as she pulled near the driveway.

Jamie got out of her car and waved at them with celebration that she found the place. The first thing she said was, "I have driven by this property so many times, I never knew there was a

Chapter 21: Jamie and Angela

house on this hill. Wow, what a freaking view you have."

Peter bowed slightly, "Thank you. Would you like some coffee?"

Jamie said, "I would love some. We need to talk about my dream and how Angela and I are going to join Nera's coven."

Angela ran up to Jamie and gave her a hug, "Come up on the deck and sit with us. Peter will get you the coffee. Let's talk."

Angela and Jamie held hands as they walked up the steps to the balcony and Jamie said, "What an awesome view, wow, so cool." She sat down in Peter's chair and Angela sat down next to her. Jamie was about to start talking when Peter walked from the house to the porch and handed a cup of coffee to Jamie. She said, "Thank you. Now I have to share this dream with you."

Peter sat down on the extra chair he pulled out and he and Angela sat waiting for the rest of the story. "My dream was very vivid. I had this dream that you and I quickly got into Nera's coven and she was happy that we turned the tables. She liked that you were already a practicing witch. We were in conversations all the time with Nera and instantly became quick friends, and she was like our escort. Since you were already a witch, Nera focused on my education as a possible future member. Everything was going well, and you, Robert, and Paul, were all watching us and staying informed. Then there was this one night of celebrations on a roof, and Angela got to sit in the circle because she was already a witch, and I sat outside the circle because I was in training. They started chanting to start a ceremony and a handsome older man came into the circle and started to dance slowly, like welcoming spirits, Then he stopped all of a sudden and said, 'We have a true witch in our midst. We have a descendant of their ancient blood in our presence. It's an amazing night.' He started to look around at everyone and I kept my face down, not to look at him, and then he walked over to me and touch my face to look at him and he said, 'What is your name child?' I said, 'My name is Jamie.' He smiled and said, 'What is your true name?'

"I repeated, my name is Jamie, again, but he did not believe me. He said, 'I know your ancient name, but I shall not repeat it in front of everyone. You can't be here. You are forbidden to be here. It is not your time yet'. He grabbed me and picked me up and then there was this big flash of light and I fell down. I woke up in a cold sweat in my bed and I thought I should immediately text you so maybe you might figure out what happened?"

Angela and Peter were listening to the dream and then Peter got up from his chair and walked into the house with his coffee. Jamie asked, "Angela, what do you think it means? Are we walking into a trap?"

Peter came back into the porch carrying a small pouch. He sat back down and looked at Jamie. He said, "Jamie, anytime you spend time with Nera, you must wear this." He handed her a black pouch and Jamie took it and opened it and poured the contents in her hand. It was a necklace with a large blue stone, with an etching on that looked Jewish or Sanskrit with three words on it.

Peter said, "I give you a holy amulet, with the three angels' names on it. And with this amulet you can't be hurt by Nera or anyone else. The amulet will protect you while you wear it."

Jamie put it on now to make sure it fit, "Peter it is beautiful, but what does it mean?"

"Any amulet, especially lapis lazuli, with the three angels' names inscribed on it, whom are the ones who came to bring Lilith back to heaven, and who have talked to you in person, shall be worn and be protected from all demons in the realms, and especially Samael and any others that seek and might harm you. The spiritual beings who take temporary human form will not be able to smell your angel blood immediately, so you must be careful; if you wear that it, it is like an invisible cloak, and no one from the spirit realm can seek you out. It's like a force field of energy keeping you safe. It's one of the oldest promises made in negotiation among the gods."

Jamie felt the amulet around her neck and immediately felt different. She said, "Thank you, Peter. How did you have this and how do you know this?"

Peter said, "That is for another time to discuss. What else about the dream do you remember? What did the man look like?"

Jamie leaned back in the chair and took a sip of coffee and then said, "I did not get a good look at the man in my dream. He

Chapter 21: Jamie and Angela

just had this energy about him, it is just hard to explain."

Angela said, "Peter, who could this be?"

Peter said, "I do not know yet, but we will figure it out."

Jamie asked, "What does this amulet mean with Samael?"

Peter said, "You are protected with that amulet. Just make sure you wear it whenever you and Angela go or do any work with Nera's coven. It will protect you. No one, not even Samael, can hurt you with the amulet around your neck. Really, you should have it on all the time. You and Angela still must join the coven to find out more about Nera's intent."

Angela asked Peter, "How do we find Nera's coven and how on earth can we get into the coven without help?"

Peter said, "Lena will help find the coven and we will go visit her this morning. You two will finish the reading with me like you were supposed to a couple days ago. Lena is so looking forward to meeting with you both again today. Let's have some breakfast and head over to Lena's."

Angela and Jamie asked, "Do you know Lena?"

Peter said, "I was the one who taught Lena to be a psychic, very long ago."

Angela and Jamie both looked at each in amazement with this new information.

They all went inside the house with their coffees, following the thought of breakfast to its natural conclusion.

* * *

After breakfast at Peter's, he led them to his garage and everyone looked at his old 1980 Landcruiser that looked like a combat vehicle, with a winch and cattle guard on the front grill, an extra tire strapped on top, extreme all terrain wheels, and extra gasoline tanks on the side. It looked like something you would see on a safari in Africa and even had the extended exhaust that ran along the side of the vehicle.

He said, "I know it looks rough and a little old, but it is the safest vehicle to ride in if anyone is trying to follow or chase us. It can go anywhere. It also has personal add-ons that I put on myself to make it more entertaining."

Angela and Jamie laughed and Jamie called "shotgun" and hopped in the front seat. She then saw the interior and all the display screens and looked funny at Peter and asked, "What are all these screens for?"

Peter just smiled, "Don't touch. Just watch." He turned on his truck and several of the screens looked out of a comic book movie, and not a car demonstration. He said, "I have cameras attached to every corner of the truck to include heat signatures and a radar weather system, and other fun systems. You never know what you will run into when you drive with me."

Jamie smiled and looked back at Angela and moved her mouth saying "what the hell" in silence but they both smiled.

Angela also said, "Do you also have crystals for protection, wooden stakes for vampires and silver bullets?" She said, "just kidding" and then Peter hit a button and a compartment opened up next to her with a large caliber pistol, silver bullets, a wooden stake, and a clear box of crystals. She just shook her head and said, "I will never doubt you again."

Peter said, "My dear, I have lived long, full, and adventurous."

Angela just smiled and thought to herself, if she needed a protector, she knew that Peter would fully protect her. She was still trying to figure out who he truly was and what the true story was, because he was so damn mysterious and never divulged too much about anything in his life. But he always referred to lives instead of life, so she may be thinking too much in his exact word use or he meant exactly what he said and was just seeing if anyone caught the word choice. Since she was a psychiatrist, she was highly trained in the choice of words. She knew she would eventually find out more about Peter, but right now they were heading to Lena's to get a reading and find a way to join Nera's coven. For once in a long time, she felt safe with these new friends. She had never relied on anyone in a long time, but she knew this new group of friends were special and would always have her back. It was a new feeling, but she liked the feeling as they continued to drive.

Within a few minutes they were downtown and pulled up

Chapter 21: Jamie and Angela

next Lena's antique shop, where she worked in the back of the store with her table. They all got out of the truck and watched Peter use his fob to lock his beast vehicle, and there were five different sounds, like turning off a computer Angela and Jamie simply smiled and shook their heads. Peter opened the door and let them walk in the store. They knew the way to Lena's table in the back. The store clerk knew they were coming and asked if they needed any coffee or tea and they said, "No, thank you."

Lena looked up from her table and waved hello, and gestured for them to come to her table. She resumed shuffling her cards as they walked up and said, "Angela and Jamie, it is so nice to meet you again, I think I can help you with what you need." Then she got up from the table and walked over to Peter and gave him a hug and they whispered at each other, then they both smiled and hugged again like old friends. Jamie had not seen Lena ever get up from around the table and they both could feel that Lena and Peter were close.

Peter said, "Lena, I want you to talk to Jamie and Angela without me. I will be walking next door to the book store to pick up several antique books they are saving for me. It just feels right that this needs to be between the three of you for this session. You know how I am about things. I think this will be best in making spiritual decisions. They need you to help them see the situation clearly enough to feel confident in their decisions about how to navigate the dangers."

Lena said, "I fully agree. Enjoy the book store. Check the metaphysical section, you might find a green hard covered enlightened book that you have been looking for."

Peter smiled and said, "Thank you." He walked out of the antique store and departed down the street.

Lena said, "Angela and Jamie, we need to do a special reading this morning. I do sense that Angela is a witch with significant training. Naturally, still needing more training, especially more psychic development." Lena smiled at Angela and winked.

Angela said, "How did you know that? I have never told anyone."

Lena said, "I am a psychic. Plus, your spirit guide told me

when you walked in and I can also feel it. I can feel your unique energy and feel that you have not practiced in a while, but you are still believing in Joe, right?"

Angela said, "Yes. Do you know Joe?"

Lena just smiled and said, "He is here with us, suggesting you hold that stone in your hands during our chat."

Angela had forgotten about that. She reached down to her coat pocket and pulled it out into her hand and looked at the glowing stone and showed it to Lena.

Lena said, "That is a sign that he is here with us. He is your protector."

Angela looked at the glowing stone, half-whispering, "I think I can feel him?"

Lena said, "He is right next to you. You can talk with him through your mind. Jamie and I will chat with the cards and you can sit back and watch. Jamie are you ready for the cards this morning?"

Jamie said, "Yes. Maybe it will help me with the angels and my dream last night."

Lena was laying out the cards in a circle with no emotions as yet, and then placed the last card in the middle. Lena said, "I know about the three angels. You and I would be best served to start classes immediately so you can control your unique magic and power, given how little awareness you have, and how quickly events and forces are pressing in. The dream you had last night was a possible premonition, but Peter is correct. If you wear that amulet, you are fully protected and no one can hurt you. So, remember to wear it most of the time, you never know when you will need it."

"I will not take it off." Jamie smiled and touched the amulet.

Lena looked at the cards. She touched all the cards sporadically and kept going back several cards. Lena looked like she was talking to someone, but there was no one there. Lena nodded in agreement, paused, then said, "Jamie, the cards are exceptional this morning and I have never seen this combination in many years. You have potential to use your power for good. You will use it soon and you will be tested, but you will choose wisely. The

Chapter 21: Jamie and Angela

challenges will surprise you and some things do not mean what they seem. Be careful who you trust. You will find love soon, but you must be careful, it is not what you think. Jamie, do you know who your biological father was?"

Jamie said, "I never met my biological father. My mother never talked about him at all, whom I am assuming was the angel. My mother died when I was eighteen. She played golf like three times a week and drove her golf cart more than her Cadillac. She is a hoot, but she has never asked or told me about my biological father. I stopped asking when I was eighteen."

Lena said, "We will explore your father more later at another session. I recommend monthly sessions for the next couple of months so we can identify the forces that are conflicting around you." Lena touched the seven of swords, "There will be a stressful event coming into your life soon, or it might have already arrived. But you are stronger than you think you are and just trust your intuition, trust your power. Don't doubt yourself at all, just close your eyes and feel and do. Promise me that you will do that, just close your eyes, focus and just release the energy. You will surprise yourself, but let it happen. Trust your heart, trust your intuition, it will lead you in the right direction."

Jamie looked at Lena, "I feel like something is awakening in me which I can't explain. It feels warm inside and feels right. I am not scared, but just don't know what will happen. It's like this energy inside me that has been idle too long."

Lena said, "Exactly, that is what it is supposed to feel like. You are on the right track. Do you have any sage in your house?"

Jamie said, "Nope. No sage."

Lena said, "I want you to buy some sage on your way out and I want you to light it and walk through your house with it lit. Take it to every room. If you have any questions, just call me and I can walk it through with you as you do it. I also want you to buy some crystals and put them out during the next full moon to charge. Make sure you clean them with water, or bury them before the full moon, so they are cleansed. The moon will energize them. And I want you to place at least four crystals in the cardinal headings of your home for protection. I also want you to find an essential oil for you to be more able to remember your dreams and to relax. During your dreams, you might experience a thing called astral traveling, which will feel like dreaming, but it means you are traveling astrally and visiting other places and other people. This dreaming is positive. Keep your amulet on your night stand, it will still protect you even on your night stand. I also want you to write in a journal for just a few minutes every morning so you can reflect on your dreams. Just write them down, or anything you remember, and I want you to bring the journal the during our next session to discuss. You have a wonderful potential; the cards are positive and the only thing I will emphasize is that you keep seeing me and we work on your psychic development. We don't want you to be seduced by the other side. You have power that is about to be brought to you."

Lena started putting the cards back into a pile and looked up at Jamie and asked, "Are you okay?"

Jamie started to cry slightly and said, "Thank you. I now know that I have a higher purpose. I now know that I am not crazy. I trust you and will follow your guidance. Could we meet in two weeks? That is what my intuition tells me to ask you."

Lena said, "That would be great. Same time, same place."

Angela, who had looked preoccupied during the reading, said, "I had a conversation with Joe in my mind. Is that possible?"

Jamie and Lena both looked at each other in surprise and Lena said, "That is possible, and expected, he is right next to you. What did you two talk about during the reading?" Lena was putting her cards away as she asked.

Angela said, "We talked in my mind if that is possible and he told me things I need to do to help Jamie to fulfill her destiny, and getting into Nera's coven is one of them. He told me what to do with the Kila when the time comes, but I am not allowed to tell anyone. Does that make any sense at all?'

Lena smiled warmly and endearingly and said, "It makes perfect sense, no explaining is needed for me. Now since we have both of your attention, you need to get into Nera's coven, is that correct?"

Angela and Jamie said yes at the same time.

Chapter 21: Jamie and Angela

Lena said, "Well, I am also a part of the coven that Nera attends, but I have not attended in several years. I could go to the next meeting, next week, and just bring you two with me as my personal guests. Angela, since you are already a witch, it is easy to bring you. But since Jamie is not a witch yet, she will have to prove she has a right to attend. We will have to prepare you for their test that they might give you. If the current leader of the coven does not approve you, you are unable to attend. Do you both realize this is an all-female coven that prefers women's rights to their bodies, and prefers lesbianism to honor the sacred feminine body."

Angela said, "Peter and Robert both told us about this unique coven."

Lena smiled, "Well, for a male point of view that is fine, but let me tell you from a person in the coven. You will be tested, each of you. If you claim you are lesbians you must prove it, and if you claim you are not, then you must prove it. There are sometimes sexual interactions in some of the ceremonies which you must be prepared for. We should meet in a couple days to talk about the coven, but not now. Jamie and you have had quite a bit of metaphysical stimuli during our sessions today and I think you are at capacity. I want you both to come here alone in three days and meet me at 6pm. Okay, remember our business is not over until you get accepted into the coven. See me in three days. Do not forget. I will be here right at 6pm. I want you to walk in those doors exactly at 6pm, not earlier and no later, timeliness will be important. Okay, now both of you give me a hug." She stood up though it looked like it pained her, and she gave them both a hug, and walked them to the front entrance of the store. As they said their goodbyes and she closed the door, they both noticed that Lena flipped the sign from open to closed and she locked the door to the store behind them.

Jamie and Angela both looked at each other, fatigued and slightly dazed. Peter was waiting for them outside with two coffees, knowing what they both needed.

Angela said, "How did you know?"

Peter said, "I drink coffee, so I might know some unique

coffee things."

Jamie said, "That's a funny quote, but does not really fit you, whatever you are."

Peter said, "What do you think I am?"

Angela chimed in and said, "You are definitely not what you seem to be and all full of surprises. You find me some good Scottish whiskey, I might tell you some more, but right now that is all you get."

Peter said, "Well, the objective of today is to meet Lena and finish what was interrupted a couple days ago, which we have done. The rest of the afternoon is really up to you two. What would you like to do?"

Jamie said, "We could go to my small apartment and finish our coffees and talk about everything?"

Peter frowned a little bit and said, "Okay."

Jamie said, "That's perfect." She grabbed Angela's hand and kissed her on the cheek and said, "Peter, take us to my condo about three miles from here and make it pronto."

Peter said, "Sure, everyone put their hands and feet inside the vehicle for safety and we shall arrive there in a few minutes." He also added, "Please do not touch any buttons without permission, you do not know what will happen."

They looked at Peter. Angela said, "Peter, please tell me that you do not have an ejection seat like Batman or James Bond?"

Peter smiled, "It's not quite an ejection seat."

Jamie said, "Well, stop chatting. Let's go to my place." As Jamie was smiling she received a text on her phone from Lena.

Lena texted her, *Change. You and Angela need to meet me at my shop tomorrow at 9pm. We have been invited to the coven. Wear the amulet. Bring a journal to write in. See you then.*

Chapter 22

Inkeri (A Female Viking 876 AD)

Inkeri stood in the cold, watching the sunrise over the snow and the northern sea near her cottage. Her long blond hair flowed in the sharp cold wind off the sea. Almost every morning she took a short walk along the cliffs in pre-dawn colors to watch the sunrise over the coastal waters. The wind was bitterly cold and frosted her eyebrows and hair, but she did not mind, she loved the cold, it was a part of her soul. There was no place else she would rather be than in the cold. She lived near a village on the shore. It was an austere barren frozen land, but her cottage was warm and dug into the earthen hillside, so it was always warm in the winter with her stone fireplace and chimney. She looked back at her cottage and could see her footprints in the frozen ice.

The winters were harsh and prevented most invaders from going this far north; no riches in this small settlement, just some livestock and a few families. They were in one of the most remote areas of the northern region. Food was scarce and everyone hustled to grow and gather all the food they could during summer. Because the winters were difficult in food storages, everyone waited for spring to hurry up, so they could plant more food.

There were other villages like this one along the coast, each about a half-day walk along the coast from the other. The villages would call troops together when there was an enemy approaching or they needed to show a defiant force to keep strange groups from drifting up north. These villages were all related and they all supported each other, but all liked their solitude and their cold environments.

As Inkeri took in the beauty of the sunrise, her dog barked at her, signaling that he was hungry. He had white fur, with blue eyes, and his head was bigger than hers. She yelled out "Kai, hush up, I will be right in to feed you." The huge dog smiled and barked again and wagged his tail. She laughed at her dog. She lived alone in the cottage. She had not married, by choice, because she wanted to find love, and not just a mate. She wanted an intellectual equal and not just another guy. With those personal standards, she knew why she was still single. She always felt her standards were too high, but it was okay and she was content with her relationship decisions.

As she walked back to her home, there were several standing stones near her place with ruin markers, telling history of the place to make sure the history was not forgotten. The ruins were their written alphabet. The markers said that the property was protected by the goddesses and to be within good intentions.

As she was walking back, she saw a sea vessel coming into view. Hopefully the battle was good and they did not lose many men, but she knew reality; there would always be the dead as part of the equation. The sail they used would identify if they were out on war. She remembered her experiences on the vessels when she was younger. She enjoyed the hard work, the adventure, but at a certain age she was encouraged not to go out to sea anymore, but to focus on house duties.

She knew that she would be needed when the ship got to shore and so hurried back to her home to feed her dog and then eat some food for herself. She knew it would be a long day. She made some hot tea, one of the simple pleasures here in the cold. She also had two cats that lived in her cottage, mainly to curb any mice in the house, but also to equally annoy her dog. She had simple handmade furniture which she mostly made herself. She was a highly independent warrior woman. She changed clothes and put warmer boots on and her layered fur clothing to help her stay warm, as she would need to walk to the village to assist the

Chapter 22: Inkeri (A Female Viking 876 AD)

vessel. One of her duties in the village was to take care of the fallen, and prepare the boat for burning the dead bodies to allow their souls to go to Valhalla.

As she approached the dock with several other women, there were two men wrapped in cloth being carried out. The cold had stopped the decomposition of the bodies, which were not fully frozen yet.

She and the other women went right into working on the burial ceremony, and the men were pulling out the Viking small boat to put the bodies on and to push out into the water. She was the youngest of the group of women, but they all accepted her due to her work ethic and that she was what they called an 'Old Soul', in which she had wisdom beyond her years. The women all cleaned up the bodies and were well versed in their tasks and making sure the bodies were ready for the spirit world. They cleaned up the marks of war, and sewed up wounds, and made the bodies presentable, and dressed the dead men in the best clothes for their final appearance. The men got the boat ready, filled with wood and twigs so the fire would burn hot and fast. The archer was notified and knew he would have to make the shot to the boats in one shot, or lose his reputation.

Inkeri was a kind and gracious woman. Everyone in the village trusted her and always wished her the best, but on days like this, she worked with full dignity and honors to these fallen soldiers. The women always knew she would set high standards in which they all respected her for it. They just adored her for her graciousness. In this small village, everyone cared and looked after everyone like a large extended family.

The villagers knew that she had loved once, because the man she intended to marry died on a battlefield several years ago, and after that she had not been interested again in love. Everyone was devastated when they brought his body back and how she would react, but she wanted to prepare the body like all the fallen warriors of the village, and she did her duty and held her emotions. The women were so surprised that she did not cry, but assumed she cried in her cottage that night after all the ceremonies. She always kept a brave face. Always.

The ceremony began at twilight. The vessel berthed on the shoreline, adorned bodies at rest in the center, as was proper to move their souls to the next world. The entire village gathered around the vessels. Chants were sung, the ritual songs were also sung, the boats were pushed out into the water. As the boats got distance from the shore, the archer lit his arrow and took aim. Everyone was watching as he pulled his strings taunt and released the flaming arrow to the boat and, as always, was a perfect hit. The wood and the branches lined the boat so it would catch on fire more quickly, and within a short amount of time, the small vessel was full of flames and engulfing the bodies with fire, sending their souls to Valhalla.

During the ceremonies the chieftain had notified that there would be another raid in two days, so the men would need their rest, and they would need two replacements for the lost men.

As Inkeri was departing and walking to her cottage, a group of men were loading the ship with swords and lances, and dried food and meats. As she was noticing the men, there was a young man along the wall of the building, crying, frightened, and nervous. Inkeri walked over to the young man and asked what was wrong, "Young man, are you okay?"

The young man looked at her with fear in his eyes, "In two days the soldiers are taking me to replace the fallen ones. I have never been to war and I feel like I will not have enough courage."

Inkeri said, "Young man, what is your name?"

He stood up tall and said, "My name is Erich. I am only sixteen." He was looking for courage inside himself.

Inkeri was kind to the young man, she knew he just needed the right words to believe in himself to be brave. Erich was quite young and disheveled, and she could tell he adored her gentle and kinds words. She said, "I see that you are brave inside. I want you to promise me to be brave. You do know everyone else is also anxious and afraid every time they go out onto the sea, but they don't show it." She touched his hand and he looked at her blue eyes and found his courage. When Inkeri looked into his eyes she could immediately tell that he was an old soul himself. She put her hand into her pocket, and pulled out a white stone, and put it

Chapter 22: Inkeri (A Female Viking 876 AD)

in his hand. "Erich, I have been carrying this special stone on me for many years and it has given me courage through the years. Now I want you to carry it into the battle, and once you return, I want you to give it back to me. I trust your courage."

Erich looked at the stone in his hands, "I promise to bring it back, and I will make you proud of my courage."

Inkeri said, "Be courageous for you and for the village, but I am one of the villagers you are protecting in battle. Protect me."

He smiled and she could tell he was being filled internally with more courage than what he had before.

* * *

A couple of days later, when it was time for the men to go onto the ship, she watched with the other woman to encourage victory. She saw Erich. He stood brave and strong among the other men. He walked up to her and said, "Thank you and I promise to be brave for you."

She smiled and hugged him and also kissed him on the cheek, "You're courageous; now fight like a warrior and please come back."

Erich smiled, "I promise to come back, and I will be brave first." He winked at her on his way to the ship.

As the fleet departed, there were mainly just women, elderly men and young children in the village left. That evening most of the women gathered in the community building for a communal meal; all talking tales and wishing the warriors well in their future battle.

All of a sudden, three bearded men from the next village came into the building; they seemed drunk, looking for trouble, aware this village's men were gone to fight.

The elder women stood their ground. The drunk villagers came asking for free food and sex and coins, but all the women refused. These women were proud and strong northern women.

Inkeri walked up to the men and asked them politely, "Please leave us. Our brave men are off battling again, while you are being drunk tonight."

One of the drunk men said, "Stupid woman, you are not scaring me."

Inkeria said one more time, "Please depart and head back to your village. Go back to your own village, before you embarrass yourself."

The three drunk men just laughed again.

Inkeri quickly pulled a dagger out of her dress and drove it into the man's hand that was at her table. Her dagger had such force that the tip went through the bone and wood, and completely went through the drunk man's hand. The drunk man screamed, but could not move his hand away because the blade was holding his hand to the table, and he screamed again at Inkeri. With his other hand, he took a swing at Inkeri and she blocked the blow and wrapped his extra arm behind him, where it was severely painful. She held the arm in a way that she could dislocate his shoulder quickly if she just shifted her weight slightly. She then drove his head onto the table and broke his nose. He could not move and was helpless and bloodied by what Inkeri was doing to him. He was now at her needs.

The other two men started to pull their daggers out when they realized every woman in the building had either a sword, or a bow and arrow, aimed at them. There must have been almost thirty women ready to harm them. These were true Northern Viking women. The leader of the group, who was helpless and bleeding said, "Enough! We are not wanted here and shall leave."

Inkeri quickly pulled her dagger out of his hand and he screamed again. She then pointed her dagger toward his neck and released his other arm, "Get out of here and do not return, or I will not be so nice as I was this time. You have not pissed me off yet. You should see me when I get mad. This is just flirting."

"Someday, we will meet again and it will not end this way."

Inkeri gave a playful wink and saucy dip of her hips. Threat emanated from her. "I look forward to that day, and next time you shall lose a part of your body."

The drunk men departed the building and the women all laughed, because even though they all had daggers and bows, they had not used them in years. They all knew how to use it, but

Chapter 22: Inkeri (A Female Viking 876 AD)

it had been a while. They were all proud of Inkeri and her bravery, and with that she had become their leader, though she was still so young.

At the end of the evening and all the women talking about their bravery, she finally went back to her cottage. Her dog and cats greeted her at the door like they had been waiting for her all day, and not just a couple hours. She lit a candle and pulled out a bag of crystals and rocks, and laid them on a table with the candle and said a prayer to her goddess. She then pulled out some liquid of lavender, and put it on her hands for healing, and just breathed the aroma to calm down from all the events that had piled on top of one another in a short space of days.

* * *

A few days went by, the first outbound group arrived by boat to the village; they had been defeated, but fought well. The other ship arrived, and the men who needed medical assistance were attended by certain women, and Inkeri was one of the key ones. As she was sewing up open wounds, and mending broken fingers and cuts and bruises, she heard about the bravery of Erich and how he saved quite a few of them, but was mortally wounded and probably would not make it through the night. She had not seen him yet because his ship had not arrived.

She was immediately concerned and felt the weight of inspiring him to be courageous. The last ship of the afternoon finally arrived; Erich was being carried off ship by some men.

She asked about him from the men who were carrying him and they said he only had a few hours left and may not make it through the night. The wound was now infected and spreading, and his skin was turning yellow and losing color. Erich was so pale and void of color in his skin.

She insisted to the men on seeing him and thinking of what type of wounds it was Erich had, and the men told her that he did not have any family, so she also insisted on bringing him to her cottage to care for his medical needs. They followed her directions and carried him into her house. Another older and experienced woman had followed them and looked over the combat wounds and could smell the infection, and warned her that she might be wasting her time, he was not going to make it through the night.

She liked a challenge and she decided she would do her best to see what she could do. She cut his ragged clothes off, cleaned his wounds, and covered him in clean linens. She started to re-clean the wounds and more thoroughly look at the infections, and it looked like he was stabbed and slashed in the right leg. His hand was severely cut open, with a couple fingers broken, and she noticed blood was seeping from his back. She noticed a wound on his neck, and when she turned him over she saw a small birthmark smeared with blood on his left shoulder. The other woman consoled Inkeri saying, "He will not make it much longer." After she left, Inkeri knew there was one last hope that she could attempt; she had not done spirit talking or spells with the goddesses since she was an early teen.

She went into her bedroom and found a small bag. The pouch had her sacred rocks and stones from her secret hiding place. This was her grandmother's old religion in which she was taught as a young girl, handed down from generation to generation by women. These traditions came from a faraway cold island from the north. Her grandmother would always say she had a spiritual gift and one day she would use her power; she only thought she was kidding, but over the years her grandmother had taught her much about nature, herbs, and spirit talking. She was a quick learner and it came to her in in her dreams, also.

She worked on Erich for another hour with the old magick, with the stones, crystals, and herbs to try and save him, and when his eyes did open finally, she asked, "How do you feel? Is there any pain?"

Erich, haltingly said, "I feel no pain. I feel proud. I am proud. More than I have felt in years." He gasped for air and continued. "I feel the best in years. I did my duty and helped my kinsmen in battle. I fought a valiant fight and I am ready to depart my life with courage." He then said, "I will meet you in another lifetime, in another place, I promise. Please take care of her, please. Promise me."

Chapter 22: Inkeri (A Female Viking 876 AD)

She was confused and did not know who 'her' was but said, "Of course I will. I promise."

He smiled, closed his eyes, and he had passed away. And with his last breath she could tell he was proud, courageous, and also happy in his last moments. He had had an honorable death.

Inkeri teared up a little; her ever-present reaction to witnessing actual death.

She went over to the water pail and started to clean his body one last time, which is the normal ritual before the ceremony for the dead. There was a small knock on her door and several of the older women had come to her house to check in on her and Erich.

One woman said, "Well, that is a problem, because who is going to take care of his puppy?" As she said that, a small shy winter-white puppy, with one blue eye and one brown eye, slowly walked into the cabin and started crying for her master.

Inkeri looked at the sad puppy as she walked toward her, and leaned down and looked at her with those beautiful unique eyes. Inkeri melted with the sight of this adorable puppy. One of the women said, "I guess we will ask one of the men to find her a home. That dog is going to be huge once she grows."

As Inkeri knelt down and looked at the dog's eyes, the puppy tilted its head back to her and smiled. It was instant love. "I would not mind keeping Erich's puppy. He had asked me to take care of her and I did not know who 'her' was until now." She picked up the puppy and said, "Yes, I will keep it if okay." The women all nodded and smiled.

* * *

As the alarm was going off in her house, Jamie woke up feeling happy after having an incredible dream about the cold and a puppy. She did not dream much, but kept a journal by her bed and immediately started to write down the events of her dream so she could analyze them later when she was more awake. She knew if she did not immediately write them down, they would be gone. She received this advice often from therapists, and now Lena a couple weeks ago, once her ability to have vivid dreams started coming back. She kept having the series of dreams of a woman in the snow. She sat up in bed and flipped her side light on and tried to write as fast as she could, because in less than ten minutes everything would fade. These dreams had only started coming back to her a few weeks ago and coincided with the angels visit. And with the latest events Paul was having, she could not see any connection yet, but that did not mean there was not one.

Chapter 23

Inkeri's Fight

Inkeri looked at the female puppy with two different eye colors and felt an instant affection. The puppy had such sad eyes, like it knew its master had died. The women and men had taken Erich's body from her home and were preparing it for the last ceremony. Inkeri cleaned the table of blood and continued on to cleaning blood from the floor; she found a stone that must had dropped out of Erich's pocket. It was the stone that she had given him to be brave before he departed for the battle. It was the stone that he promised he would return to her on his way back. She had forgotten about it while she was tending to his wounds and now that she found it, she started to cry again, knowing that he kept his promise to her to return it to her. The small puppy came to her as she was on the floor, wanting attention, because her larger dog had not decided yet on this new family addition and her two cats did not want any part in dealing with a new puppy. She could feel the contempt in her cats, but her dog needed to be the better dog, instead of not liking this orphaned puppy.

She picked up the stone and cleaned it off and put it in her wooden box with the rest of her sacred stones and crystals. She closed the box and knew that Erich had fulfilled his promise. She was getting ready for bed after such a long day and put on her night gown. She let her cats on her bed with the new puppy, and her bigger dog would lay by her bed, protecting her throughout the night. She would sleep well tonight with so much good energy in her bed. The only thing she was missing was a man to love her. She had loved men, but it had not worked out yet; she still had faith that it would.

Her new puppy cuddled next to her, which annoyed her two mature cats, and the older dog just snored on the floor. When they awoke in the morning, all the animals seem to be on her bed trying to get her attention, but it was her new puppy that stayed asleep the longest, still under her covers and snoring softly after such a long first day in her home.

She awoke to her new puppy stretching and slightly scratchy her arms. She got out of bed slowly with the light coming through the windows, and walked into the kitchen. She found the food for the cats just returning from their pre-dawn prowl, and also her large dog who needed to go outside to smell the morning air and dew on the ground and take care of business. She fed them all, her animal family, and then remembered her new addition, her new puppy that was still asleep on the bed. She woke her up like a small child and brought her into the kitchen with the rest of the animals and made food for her new puppy, in which she happily ate and drank.

She walked out into her front porch to watch the sunrise and enjoy the morning cold and the frost on the grass. Her cats were, of course, going to have nothing to do with outside now that the sun was up and stayed in her cottage. Her large dog loved to do a post-breakfast romp and her new puppy was venturing, ever slowly, outside into the cold and the wet dew on the grass. She slowly and clumsily walked out into the grass. Her older dog just smelled her and looked back at Inkeri with some contempt, but she could tell that the older dog would like the entertainment and mild amusement of the puppy. It was the patriarch style of male dogs to take care of the puppy and raise it. Inkeri smiled at her simple life and enjoyed the moment of the sunrise with the cold air and the entertainment of her animals. She would head into town soon and see what she needed to do for Erich's final ceremony tonight. Since she worked on Erich for hours, the other women had taken his dead body and excused her from her normal duties

Chapter 23: Inkeri's Fight

on preparing the fallen soldier for its final voyage. She knew the ceremony would be in the evening and the village would come out to celebrate his life. She knew she did all should could do for him, and nature, and God called him.

She finished her morning ritual chores and enjoyed her land by walking her dog and new puppy around so she could smell the scents of home and mark the territory. The puppy stayed along her ankles, somewhat scared of her older dog still, but it was such a cute dog. She had spirit and spunk, and even one time gave this tiny cute bark back to her older dog who looked amused and somewhat proud of her.

As the day became relaxed and the waiting until the dusk ceremony was to start, her small animal family all came inside her house and chilled by the fire place and rested. Inkeri even snuggled in her blanket and soon everyone enjoying an afternoon nap.

There was a knock on the door and her dog barked, and Inkeri got up and checked on the door and it was the women from the village, coming to get her for the ceremony. She quickly apologized and that she just woke up from a nap, and one of them said, "My dear, you were up almost all night with that boy, keeping him alive. You deserve your nap." Inkeri did not feel guilty anymore in the comment about resting and deserving an extra-long nap.

Inkeri got ready quickly and met the women outside. They all walked from her house together. It was their tradition to arrive in solidarity as a group, because there was always one of the dead every time that affected one of the women, but together they could keep them strong by standing with them. They approached the shoreline and the village people had all gathered and the sun was setting along the water. The torches were lit to let everyone see. The bodies were each wrapped up and each body had its own makeshift vessel that they should be free to travel. There were only three fallen men during this last conflict, and Erich's vessel was on the left side. The leaders of the village spoke words and everyone was proud that these men fought for their village and that their names should never be forgotten. As soon the speeches were over, the archers lit their arrows and the vessels were pushed out into the water. Within moments, the archers pulled back on their bows and launched the three arrows. Each hit their targets, and soon the vessels and the bodies were engulfed in flames and their souls would be released for their next journey. As the last of the flames ended, the villagers all started to head to their homes.

Inkeri started to head to her home, also, but alone this time. As she was walking, she heard a voice in head tell her *Do not go home. The enemy are setting a trap for you.* Inkeri did not know what to think of voice in her head, or maybe she was just having a talk to herself and there was something she forgot to do before she should go home, but the voice said, *Inkeri, this is Erich. I am with you now, to protect you. Do not go home. You are in danger.*

Inkeri stopped in her tracks. She knew she was close to home and knew the way, but felt there was something different going on, and nature was too quiet right now. There was something in the air, a different scene. Maybe her voice was right. Then she remembered the name Erich. She thought in her mind, how did Erich send her a message? He was supposed to have traveled to be renewed. The voice said, *This is Erich. I choose to stay as a spirit and protect you and to be brave again. I have not done enough here to go honorably into the next step.*

Inkeri thought to herself that Erich had made the wrong choice, but as she walked closer to her home she could hear horses, and men walking in her house and talking. She now knew Erich was warning her and she now believed the voice. She was perfectly still and just listened to the voices and the tried to decipher what they were saying.

One of the men yelled, "She will be back soon. Everyone, now takes your places in the woods. That woman will see her death tonight after we have some fun. No woman that puts a knife through my hand will live to tell the tale. Take her alive. She should be by herself. Now go into the woods and wait and I will be inside the house. Bring her to me once you get her." As he was talking to his men, Inkeri's large dog came into view and started barking and growling at the men, knowing they were no good, and the puppy was behind him. The man said, "Kill that dog now

Chapter 23: Inkeri's Fight

so that she is not warned." There were two arrows that went into the large dog and another man ran up to it and drove a knife into the dog's stomach to put it out of its misery. The last acts of the dog was to protect the puppy. The man who killed the dog then picked up the small puppy that was barking softly and yelping with pain. He said, "What do I do with the puppy?" The man on the porch said, "Break the puppy's neck, so that you shut it up." The man then broke the puppy's neck and threw it on top of the large dying dog. The men were now walking into the woods waiting for Inkeri.

Inkeri saw it all and there was no compassion in her heart now. There was death and revenge to these pathetic men who would kill her family. For these men, death was not enough. They needed to suffer. She felt hatred in her heart, something she had not felt in many years. She wanted to make them die in their own blood like they did to her loyal dog, who was still gasping for air as he was dying. Inkeri was looking back into her life, her hidden life, when she was a much different woman. There were times, when she was younger, where she did things she regretted. Well, she regretted she did them, but they needed to be done. A long time ago, she had men when she was younger and emotional. She had hunted them down, but they all deserved what they got. She remembered the ways to be silent, to make weapons, to kill quietly, to stab a man where they are paralyzed and can't scream and die slowly. She was trying to remember all the ways in which she had put aside. The sight of what she saw turned her back into the way she used to be. She was going to kill each of them. She would take her time with the one in charge, and no one kills her family and gets away with it. Inkeri slowly walked farther away, knowing she had to collect her thoughts and make some makeshift tools that would kill these worthless men. The voice in her head came back and said, *would you like me to help you?*

Inkeri, in her mind, said, *Yes, please. It is a noble thing. How can you help?*

Erich said, *I will bring help. I can take my spirit into an animal and bring help. I will not be long.*

Inkeri said, inside her mind, *I will take any help you can provide*. Inkeri pulled out her knife and found some small branches from fallen down trees and started to sharpen them to make stakes. She made about ten of them and had only counted five men total. She knew where to drive the stakes in the throat and lower back area to severely hurt the men. She knew that if she used two at a time she could take them down quickly with no noise. She put mud on her face and hands, and took off her cumbersome dress so she could maneuver quickly. She caked the mud on her skin so the torch light would not reflect her skin if she was close. She knew how to hide and she would be silent. She knew the woods and she knew her trees, and she made an intention for the wind to start blowing to make more noise in the forest so that she would not be heard. She called upon the goddesses to help her.

She then remembered when she was a young girl and she would worship the goddesses, and sometimes they would help her, but she had forgotten the way. She squeezed her eyes shut and said in her mind, *To the goddesses who I have worshipped, I know that I have not been good about remembering you, but this point in my life I worship you, all the goddesses, to help this one woman against five men who do not deserve to live any more. Help me and I will be dedicated to you.* She bowed her head and sent the intention. She had doubt she would have any help, but during these times in life is when you need the goddesses the most.

As she thought she was truly on her own, the winds slightly moved the trees and it felt like a storm was brewing. Inkeri doubted it was her, but she was not going to turn down any natural assistance. The winds came up and made noise among the trees. As Inkeri was looking for the first man, she could not hear her steps on the ground and thanked the wind for helping her. Inkeri was walking quietly and she heard a stick crack behind her. She quickly turned around and raised a stake and saw a large artic wolf with two colored eyes, one was blue and one was green. Inkeri was frightened because the wolf was huge and strong, but the wolf stood there and looked at Inkeri and then sat down and bowed his head to her. Inkeri was frightened, but the animal

Chapter 23: Inkeri's Fight

looked up from the wolf's eyes and she felt comfort. There was a voice in her head, *I have come to assist you. We will communicate through our minds. I will do what you say. Erich is bringing more help. I am the first. I am Vul.*

Inkeri was shaking with the size of the animal, but the eyes calmed her down. She moved her hand toward the top of his head to touch him and the wolf allowed it, and with the touch she could feel his duty to her. He tilted his head so Inkeri could touch his ears and scratch them. Inkeri looked at the wolf again and sent a message, *Be quiet, follow orders. We kill them one at a time.* Vul looked at Inkeri and nodded his head. Inkeri felt more confident, and the wind was blowing, and she now had this large wolf helping her. She wondered what other help she might need.

She slowly walked to the first man, who was just slightly by the road and would be the first to spot her if she was walking normally. She noticed he was standing there looking bored and ready for anything. She was within a few feet of him when she signaled the wolf to walk down the road to him to get his attention. Vul walked out slowly onto the road and made small noises on the trail, and as the man was looking at the sounds, Inkeri came from behind him and drove two stakes across each side of his neck that punctured through immediately. The man grabbed his throat, but there was nothing he could do. And since the throat had two stakes in it, he could not make any noise. The body collapsed silently and blood poured down the chest. Inkeri looked at the eyes of the man who was realizing death was coming soon, and could see the fright in his eyes. Inkeri then ripped out the two stakes, which collapsed the throat all together and tore the blood vessels apart, which would quicken death. The man lay slumped in the woods, dying in his own blood. Inkeri felt no remorse. The wolf came up and nodded his head.

Inkeri sent a mental message to the Vul, *Where is our next prey?*

The wolf turned around and started to walk in a new direction to scent out the next man. The wind kept blowing, like a storm was coming, and their footsteps were hidden in the sound. Vul slowed his walk and sniffed in the air. He sat on the ground on his back legs and pointed with his nose the direction of the next man. As she walked past the wolf she could see the man, more alert than the first man, but still not holding any weapons in the ready position. Inkeri felt a chill in the air. A night fog was forming around them which gave them more cover, but she could still see the man standing next to the tree. Inkeri pulled out two stakes again to do the same technique that worked on the first man, but as she drove the stake into the man's neck, he moved slightly and she cut his throat, but not too deeply. She fell on the ground next to him, not allowing the second stake to touch his neck. Inkeri was on the ground, scared and motionless, because she missed. She could see the man, who pulled out his sword, about to drive it into Inkeri, when the wolf dove at him with full force. The wolf struck his jaws through the man's throat instantly, which caused the body to drop immediately, and was only shaking due to nerves that were trying to function. Then the wolf turned its head widely and ripped the head from the body, which caused immediate death. The wolf's mouth still had the head in his jaws and looked at Inkeri. It then dropped the head, and telling her through his mind, *See, I can do this as good as you*. Vul licked the blood off his mouth, enjoying the kill a little too much.

Inkeri said, "Good, Vul. Where is the next one?"

Vul smelled again to try and find the scent and slowly started to walk to the other side of the woods, slowly. The wind was continuing and the fog was getting thicker as they walked.

Vul stopped again and Inkeri could see that there were two men hiding behind the bushes, with their weapons fully poised. Inkeri looked back at Vul to tell him about the two men. Then she noticed there were two people standing on each side of Vul, a man and a woman. They were wearing much different clothes than anything that she had ever seen before. They looked so different, but still attractive, but stern; she was a beautiful woman full of confidence. Without speaking, they communicated with Inkeri through their minds. The woman said, *We are friends with Vul, and Erich sent us to help. Let us take care of the two men. We have not killed in such a long time. You would be doing us such a favor and lovely opportunity. It would do our souls so much good.*

Chapter 23: Inkeri's Fight

Bad and horrible men are always so much fun to destroy.

They both were unarmed, but were smiling, anticipating enjoyment, Vul just laid down and watched, and Inkeri stepped aside and welcomed their help. The man and the woman did not reveal their names, but were absolutely not from the north region, but Inkeri was not going to ask questions. Inkeri just sat on the ground next Vul and watched them walk toward the two men. The fog seemed to separate where they walked. They seemed to control it. They both looked at each other, and within seconds were ripping the two men apart, silently and swiftly. They both seemed to cleave their opponents heads off with no weapons, but shear strength, and then cut the men in half. They walked back to Inkeri and Vul with blood dripping from their arms, as if they had dipped them into blood to the bicep. And there was blood on their faces that they were cleaning off, as if they had eaten a chunk of the men, like some beast would.

The man and the woman pulled out thin cloths and were wiping each other's face, to be polite, and then check for blood on each other's faces. Like two cats would do, cleaning each other. But neither cared about the blood dripping from their arms and hands.

The woman now talked with her voice, "Thank you so much for letting us do that to these horrible men. We so enjoyed it. There is only one left in your cottage. You and Vul can handle him." She walked up to Vul and petted him and whispered something in the wolf's ear that took emotion in him. She took the man's hand and started to walk back into the woods and said, "Inkeri, remember the man inside must be killed with style. Not too quick. With quite a bit of torture, take your time. Thank you, again."

The wind blew hard suddenly and Inkeri covered her eyes and then looked back at where two people were, and they had vanished, there was no sign of them. Inkeri thought if they were real, but she did not take much effort and appreciated that they helped her. It was now time for her and Vul to take care of the last one.

As Inkeri and Vul walked out of the woods and toward the cottage, they could see the bodies of her two dogs. Her older dog had suffered greatly, and the poor puppy that Erich had given her had been killed by the men. The two dogs lay there on the ground, side by side, thinking of each other at their last breaths. Inkeria had ice in her veins now, and Vul was growling slowly.

Inkeri turned the knob on her front door to enter her cottage and meet the last man, to settle her score. He was sitting in her chair, poking the fire and he said, "Did you bring me the bitch?"

Inkeri calmly said, "No, this bitch killed all your men and is here to kill you."

The man got up from the chair, and pulled out his sword and dagger, and turned around to Inkeri and the wolf that was walking behind her. The man was upset and frustrated, and then looked at the wolf and was startled and, somewhat, scared. The man then smiled and said, "You are no match for me, even with that dog next to you. You do not know who I am?" He pulled off his jacket and black wings came out of his back. And then his skin turned dark and his eyes turned red. He then said, "You can't kill me, you do not have the power."

Vul growled and Inkeri took another step toward him. Then he moved his hand and Vul was thrown to wall and Inkeri was pulled up in the air, suspended. He walked over the fire and pulled out the poker and said, "I think I shall some fun with both of you."

There was a knock on the door and the man looked confused. Who would be knocking on the door at this time of night? Well, he shall include them in his little game tonight, too. Inkeri was still suspended and having a tough time breathing, and Vul was in pain after being forced to the wall with the man's magick.

The man walked over to the door and as he slightly opened it, the wind took over and blew him to the ground, with some fog that entered the cottage. The mysterious man and woman walked into the cabin, that helped Inkeri with two of the men. They walked right into the cottage as if they owned the place, and with a point of their fingers, released Inkeri from the magical suspension and released the power against Vul.

The man had been flown to the floor and was now upset. He forced his black wings full outward, and as his back faced the people he said, "You visitors are both going to pay dearly for

Chapter 23: Inkeri's Fight

interrupting me." Then he turned around and was shocked in who he saw.

The mysterious man said, "I am surprised you would break the rules, my old friend. We are here to put balance in the situation."

The mysterious woman said, "You should not be down here hurting innocent people and causing harm to animals." The woman touched Vul on his head, giving him strength.

The man said, "You two can't be here, it is forbidden. You just can't. How and why are you here? It's not possible."

The mysterious man said, "Well, this young woman helped a brave man go into battle and he died. And tonight he was supposed to move his soul to a higher place, but instead, he stayed in this world to protect Inkeri. He called the gods and goddesses for help, to help this brave woman. So we were the ones who volunteered, with special permission, to come here. And we find you here. Of all the people, you are here. How delightful. You know you will lose your wings for this. Too bad, my friend."

The woman said, "I have a message to give you."

The man with black wings was upset and started walking over to the woman. The man stopped him with the power from his hand, and the man was vividly upset and pissed off. Then the woman walked over and put her finger on the winged man's forehead. The pain was terrible, as the man dropped to his knees and tried to catch his breath.

The woman said, "Inkeri, you may do what you are destined to do to this evil person." Inkeri pulled out the blade from her cloth and the blade was glowing. Vul was growling loudly and the man on the ground on his knees just laughed, "You stupid woman. They can't hurt an immortal."

She smiled and said, "Your wings are gone, so now you are mortal and can bleed and die."

His smile went to fright as he looked behind him to see that his black wings had been clipped by her magic. He said, "No, you can't do that. How did you do that? That's impossible."

Inkeri and Vul came closer to the now mortal man. The woman was walking out the door and smiled back and said, "Don't ever mess with a scorned woman again."

Inkeri drove her blade into his heart and Vul attacked his throat. The man screamed and the two strange people walked outside, not to see the rest. The man was going to die a well-deserved death, as a true human and bleed to death, slowly. Inkeri drove the knife deep into his heart and Vul had nearly devoured his neck and taken his head off. While the man had become mortal and did not know how to defend himself, but now only knew how to die a slow death.

The strange man looked back with approval and they both walked outside under the stars. "You, my dear friend, Lilith, I always love doing adventures with you." He took her hand and kissed it.

She smiled, "You are not so bad either, Merc."

Merc said, "Should we correct an evil action?"

Lilith asked, "What do you mean?"

Merc pointed to the two dogs. "You know we could make things right again."

Lilith said, "You are the expert in this area. I like your idea, go ahead."

Merc went over to Inkeri's large dog and new puppy. He bent down on his knees and put a hand on each of them and slowly closed his eyes. He turned his head to the left and to the right, looking like he was struggling with something. As he was touching each of the animals, their wounds seem to be healing, the blood was disappearing, and the open wounds were sealing up. His hands were glowing. Suddenly, both animals opened their eyes and looked at him. The puppy barked slightly, and the big dog rolled on all fours.

As this was happening, Inkeri and Vul walked outside the cottage and were witnessing the miracle. Inkeri had tears in her eyes and Vul sat waiting patiently. Merc let go of his hands on both dogs and got up and looked at Inkeri, "I thought I should undo an evil act. They deserve to live and to be with you. Someday, I might come back here looking for a favor, but enjoy your dogs until they die of old age." He nodded to the wolf. "It's nice to see you again, Vul."

Inkeri said, "Thank you for saving my life. And thank you for

Chapter 23: Inkeri's Fight

bringing my family back to life. I will be in your debt."

Lilith said, "Merc, it's time to go. Inkeri, please keep up your honorable work and if you ever need us again, I put a crystal in your pocket that you can use to call us when you need us. Vul, always nice to see you again. Take care of this cottage and don't let any harm come to Inkeri. It is time for us to go."

Inkeri looked back inside, but the body was gone, and she guessed Lilith and Merc had magically cleaned it up. She then hugged her large dog and her new puppy walked up to her feet and looked at her. She picked up the puppy that she thought was lost and petted her large dog on the forehead. Then Vul, the giant wolf, walked over to both dogs and licked them on their nose, communicating with them both, and they were respectful. Inkeri looked toward the path for Lilith and Merc, and they had disappeared. And then she looked and saw Vul's tail walking into the woods, and it was just her and her family again. She hugged them both deeply, with tears running down her face. She then remembered what the woman said about a crystal in her pocket and she felt for it with her hand and could feel it in her pocket. She then knew everything was going to be ok.

* * *

Jamie awoke from her dream in a cold sweat and breathing heavily. She felt like it was so real in her dream. She looked at her hands and feet, but they were clean. She sat up on the side of her bed and was wondering why these dreams were occurring to her. She wanted to cry, but there was no reason, because the dreams, even though they were traumatic, they turned out as they were supposed to. Where good wins over evil.

She looked over at her Australian Shepherd, who was snoring of course, next to her bed and she said to herself, "If anyone hurt my dog, I would surely hurt them worse." Her dog woke up and looked at her. Then rolled back over, wanting to go back to sleep, because it was not time to go in the backyard to do one's business yet. Jamie smiled and tucked her feet under her covers and went back to sleep.

Chapter 24

Lilith and Merc Revisit

Lilith was sitting in her favorite American organic restaurant in Kansas City, at a table in the back room for more privacy. The owner, Jane, was like family and Lilith always came here when she visited the Midwest. She was waiting on Merc for dinner, but he was running late, as always, and so she just enjoyed the lovely glass of red, the 110-year-old building, the vibe, and the blue bird paintings on the wall from some young and inspiring artist.

Merc finally showed up with another long-winded story on why a god can't come to dinner on time, with saving the world again and again. Lilith lounged back in her chair, utterly comfortable in her own boredom with his meandering

Merc said, "Dinner is on me since I am late."

Lilith said, "Of course, my sweet dear, you get to pay again for dinner, because frankly, you are always late. But we did have fun yesterday, didn't we?"

Merc said, "Well, we did save that little world, whether you believe me, or not."

Lilith just drank her wine and smiled, "So, have you heard about Nera and Samael?"

Merc said, "No, but catch me up on Nera and the famous fallen angel, Samael that is the topic of discussion." He then said, "You know, on social media, they like worship that asshole. They should all know him for real and know he is an asshole, but a

Chapter 24: Lilith and Merc Revisit

great guy to get drunk with."

Lilith said, "I don't watch or pay attention to silly programmed information operations of social media. It is just another way to falsely influence less minded people to believe in something false, in which they must believe him, or be criticized for thinking with some actual logic and reasonable premises. It is not worth my time. Social media is just drip-feeding misinformation to the people to believe in a false hope of nothing changes. Political parties have not changed in 2,000 years. You should know that."

The owner of the restaurant stepped over and said, "Lilith, it is so nice that you visited us today."

Lilith got up from her chair and hugged the owner, "Jane, it is always nice to see and visit your wonderful restaurant."

Jane said, "Who is your handsome company?"

Lilith said, "Jane, this is Merc. But he is what I call the always late for dinner guy because he is always saving the world."

Merc shook Jane's hand and said, "Really, I could come to dinner on time, but then what would Lilith complain about me about."

Jane smiled, "Well, you two have a wonderful dinner and I will pull out my best bottle for you both; and Merc, it is always good manners as a man to show up before your date, or exactly on time. It is a character flaw, so maybe if you can save the world, you can improve in timeliness in the next couple of years." Jane left their table and talked with their waiter. Lilith smiled ear to ear on Jane's last comments and Merc just shook his head.

Merc smiled when a complimentary bottle of wine came to their table and their waiter poured them two glasses. Merc took a small drink and said, "That's a good wine," then he looked at the label on the bottle and there was traditional looking Hermes figure with winged sandals on, and he shook his head again. Jane came by to ask about the wine, "How did you like the wine? It's from Lilith's new vineyard, if you did not know."

Merc was looking at the label and then looking at Lilith and said, "Really, you put me on the cover of your wine bottles."

Lilith smiled.

Jane then looked at the label, "The image looks much more

fit than you, and I would assume since the person has wings on their feet, they could get to dinner on time."

Lilith said, "Jane, thank you for the comment. I do like how our latest batch of wine came in and was produced."

Jane smiled in agreement, "I will check on your dinners."

Merc said, "Do you just think of ways to tease, razz, and harass me? Am I just here to amuse you?"

Lilith replied, "Yes, you are for that reason and we have good intellectual discussions. Cheers." She put her glass of wine in the air to receive a toast from Merc back, in which he politely did with a smile and grin.

Merc toasted his glass with hers and said, "It is great wine."

Lilith said, "Of course it is. Now let's talk about Nera."

Merc said, "Well, what is she up to now? I also assume Samael is using her again like a puppet?"

Lilith shook her head, "They are plotting to kill us."

Merc almost spit up his wine, "You are kidding, right? That would not be smart of Nera, and I don't how she could do it. And she would have to go through me first. You know I love you very much and would not let anything happen to you. Samael would also get into trouble. Wait, is he still in love with you? I bet Samael never got over you."

"That was a long time ago, when I was much more emotional and younger. We had a fling and other things, some children. Some people still think he is Lucifer and not Louis. People just don't do their historic or religious history, or they trust the Catholic church's version, which always has an agenda to it."

Merc said, "Well, doesn't everyone of intellect know that Lucifer was a fallen cherub, and one of the highest angels in heaven. He was one of the most bright and beautiful among the cherubs, and when he fell from heaven. he was one of the most powerful among the Satans. Which means adversaries and not what most people think."

Lilith said, "Correct. And then Samael was high in the heavenly creatures and the Seraphim, he has twelve wings when he is not in disguise, he is the ultimate accuser, seducer, and destroyer. He is really the Angel of Death, who enjoys taking the

Chapter 24: Lilith and Merc Revisit

souls from men. He still resides in the 7th heaven, but also the chief angel in the 5th heaven. He is still the commander of angels and the chief of Satans. He loved me a long time ago. He was the one who revenged me in the Garden and helped trick Adam to mate with an angel of prostitution. I so miss Naamah. She was a good friend back in the day."

Merc then said, "Samael was nowhere near the high character of Lucifer, I mean Louis, and was always an angel in dark nature. He was always a primal angel who God created to execute his will at any cost. But due to his nature, Samael is still regarded as good and evil."

Lilith agreed and said, "Right. Lucifer is a fallen famous angel, and Samael is less ambiguous and less famous. Lucifer was truly not evil, while Samael was clearly of evil nature. Lucifer aimed to be the best and most powerful cherubim and to be the highest of all angels, but his vanity was his downfall. While Samael wanted to be the new God and wanted to overthrow God from heaven, all he wanted to do was destroy faith in the hearts of the humans. He is truly evil, spiteful, and treacherous."

Merc said, "I never understood why G had Lucifer punished more than Samael. I mean, Lucifer was banished, who was just too vain and was sent to hell, while evil Samael got to stay in 7th heaven. That shit never made sense to me."

Lilith said, "Me, neither. This dinner was wonderful. Oh my God, I must compliment the chef."

Merc said, "Yes, this food is divine."

Lilith focused on enjoying the food and then paused, "Samael is putting up Nera to try and kill me for revenge, you know."

Merc said, "That was what I assumed, but he will fail. I have seen it. Someone will be wounded and someone will die in this process, but you will not be hurt at all. In regards to our discussion, my assumption regarding Louis and Samael is that G redeemed Samael for being treacherous and hateful, because at the end of the day, they are equal to those who hate. But Louis was vain, so he closed his mind and thinks he is superior to everyone, and of course he can never be redeemed."

"Stop ruining my dinner with the topic of Louis and Samael,

please."

Merc said, "Well, my sweet dear, you brought it up to begin with."

Lilith looked at Merc and gave him the middle finger to express her true feelings.

Merc said, "Lilith, now that is so impolite and improper of you. I am so shocked."

Lilith gave him two middle fingers which almost made him spit up his wine while he was trying to drink it.

They both laughed and continued to enjoy their dinner.

Merc said while eating, "I would not worry about Nera trying to kill without the athame. But if she had the Kila, that might be an issue. Sameal so much wants that Kila."

Lilith said, "I am not worried about the athame anymore, but the Kila is with Peter now in his house."

Merc said, "Peter! Well, I guess they finally found 18th Street. Remember it took Nera nearly a month to find Peter's place once we gave her the advice and way more hints than we gave Angela. Peter was supposed to live a true solitary life. He is immortal and can't die. He does not need any attention to himself. He could compromise his true identity. Since we sent them looking for him, I guess it's our fault, but it is all by design."

Lilith said, "Well, it seems Paul, Robert, Jamie, and Angela helped find Peter and he is fully into this scenario equation helping Jamie and Angela."

Merc shook his head, "That's just great, Peter is now really involved. He usually does not actually help. That changes the scenario on certain things. You can't trust Peter fully, he has friends on both sides. You know what he did in the 1400s. He can't be trusted."

Lilith said, "I know, but remember all the things you have done in your past. And you do not need to remind me what happened, I was there, too."

"You know, we forgot about the three angels, because they are up to no good, too."

Lilith looked at Merc, "Thank you for bringing them up. We have not been tracking those mischievous ones who have

Chapter 24: Lilith and Merc Revisit

an agenda which we are not aware of. I sure hope they are not in collusion with Samael, because that would cause unwanted troubles."

Merc looked down at his meal, "What if the three are working with Samael? I think we would have to bring in some more help to keep things in order."

Lilith smiled as she finished her dinner, "Yes, we might need to bring in the big guy. We shall see what happens next. Loyalty goes so far these days. Humans are so easily swayed by magick, and trinkets, and shiny things. We shall think about who needs to assist, you know how I hate asking for help."

Merc smiled, "Yes, of all the things I know about you, is that you absolutely never like asking for help, until you absolutely need it."

The waiter came to their table and asked them if they needed dessert and they both were full from dinner.

"Jane has paid for your dinner tonight, but had to depart before saying goodnight, and leaves you this message, 'Please dine more often, green is a wonderful color to have around in the spring, it has such special and wonderful powers". The waiter smiled as Merc and Lilith knew exactly what Jane was referring to. They both got up from the table and Merc did leave a large tip for the waiter, who did an excellent job. They walked out of the bistro, arm in arm, and Lilith put her head on Merc's shoulder, "That was a wonderful dinner, thank you. We should make a journey into the woods tonight."

Merc said, "You read my mind."

They walked out into the street and along the quiet dark sidewalk and disappeared into the night.

Chapter 25

The Coven

All the shops along the street were closed, but there were quite a few parked cars in the street. Jamie was wearing the amulet. Jamie and Angela both held journals as they crossed the street and walked, exactly at 9pm, into Lena's store. The door was unlocked and most of the light were turned off, but as soon as they walked in Lena was waiting for them and said, "Are you ready to be together and attend a coven meeting?"

Jamie and Angela both nodded their heads and said, "Yes."

"I need you to both hold hands as we walk, in which is a sign that you are together, and you must show public affection to each, and not afraid to show it to them. You need to be convincing that you are together."

Jamie and Angela both held hands tight and were nervous of the unknown that they were about to go into, like a sheep into a lion's den kind of feeling. Lena had them follow her to the back of the building where there was an old elevator that looked condemned. But she punched the number three and the light came on. The elevator coming from the third floor sounded like it was on its last leg. The elevator arrived from the third floor and opened up its doors, and there was a woman in a black robe standing there and said, "Lena, it's been a long time, but please explain who is with you and if they can pass the test."

Lena said, "As a founding member of this Dianic coven, I use

Chapter 25: The Coven

my privilege to bring these two women with me tonight, to open their awareness to our coven and to be possible future initiates to our family. I have received pre-approval already from the council, if you want to check."

"That will not be necessary, I can feel that you are telling the truth. Welcome all of you to the Dianic coven. Please enter the elevator. Tonight, we have a ceremony and also have a guest speaker from the other side."

Lena, Angela, and Jamie entered the elevator. The woman touched the number three and the doors closed, and the ancient elevator moved to the third floor, shaking and wobbling along the way. Once reaching the third floor, the doors opened to a dimly lit room with women in black, red, and white robes. They were chatting among each other as Lena, Angela, and Jamie walked into the room. A woman came up to Lena, "Lena, here is your robe. We should have had it dry-cleaned, but it has been several years since your last attendance. We are honored with your presence tonight."

Lena put on her robe and said, "Who is the guest speaker?"

The woman said, "Our guest speaker is a representative from Samael's spirit. We are conjuring the spirit tonight."

Lena said, "Well, may I get new robes for my guests."

The woman said, "Lena, of course, I will get robes for your guests immediately." She looked at the corner and gave the signal for two other woman, who immediately arrived with two brown robes for Lena's guests. Lena said, "Please put these on and the color brown is for new initiates and beginners, before you ask any questions." Angela and Jamie quickly put on their robes to look like they belonged. Lena told them in a quiet voice, "I want you to remain holding hands tonight and promise to stay by each other's side if we get separated."

Angela and Jamie both nodded and held hands after they put on their robes.

Lena said, "Now follow me and we shall introduce you to the leaders." Lena walked into the crowd, searching for certain people to find in the groups, and she turned left and found a woman sitting alone in the corner, with a white robe and a glass of red wine, reading a large book. Lena walked up to her and said, "My friend Sara, I have returned, and I have brought you two possible new initiates who have special abilities that could bring more power to the coven."

Sara looked up and smiled at Lena and closed the book. She said, "Lena, it has been too long. You look so good. And it is always a pleasure for you to attend our meetings. Who have you brought to us?'

Lena had Angela and Jamie stand next to her and introduced, "Sara, this is Jamie, who has been visited by our three angels who are our friends, and she has angel blood in her veins. She can be powerful within the coven when properly trained. She will need to be initiated properly, but could be a great advantage."

Sara said, "Lena, you have brought me a great prize. I can feel her angel blood already."

Lena said, "Sara, I expect the utmost confidentiality among your women. I do not want the other women to know about her potential because there could be jealousy."

Sara said, "Lena, I fully agree. No one will know about her special abilities, I give you my word."

Lena then said, "I would also like you to meet Angela. She is a doctor, but has also been selected to travel to the inner temple with Lilith and Merc."

Sara stopped and looked at Lena, "How is that possible without divine help? My dear, please come here and let me touch your hands. Come now, do not be shy."

Angela walked to Sara and held out her hands; Sara took both of her hands and closed her eyes. Within a moment, she looked back up at Angela and said, "Angela, you are already a witch, a solitary witch, and you are powerful though you do not know enough about spells and other advantages. We must change your colors immediately to purple because you are not an initiate, for sure. You are most definitively an advanced solo practitioner." She looked at the woman by the robes and signed one robe and gave the signal for purple, and within a minute the woman came back with a purple robe for Angela and the other robe was taken away.

Chapter 25: The Coven

As they were finishing their discussion a woman came up to them wearing a red robe, and as she got closer, pulled her hood down, and it was Nera. Angela and Jamie looked at her with caution and immediately Sara said, "Nera, I want you to be the formal escort to Jamie and Angela. No harm shall come to them tonight, do you understand?"

Nera said, "It will be my pleasure. And I already know Angela, but have never been introduced to Jamie."

Jamie said, "Hello, my name is Jamie. Angela's my girlfriend."

Nera looked amused and then frustrated, and looked at them holding each other's hands tightly and could feel their fondness toward each other. Nera then said, "It is a pleasure to meet you." She did not reach out her hand to shake her hand.

There was a loud bell. Sara stood up in her white robe and said, "Well, I guess I should say a few words before the ceremonial ritual starts. Excuse me, Lena, but it's time to go to work."

Lena said, "Of course, we can talk afterward."

Sara walked by Angela and Jamie and said, "Please meet me after the ceremony for a private conversation on your future in our coven. I would so much like both of you to join." She touched both of them on the cheek and smiled, "We shall have a wonderful future together once you join, it will be so delightful." She then started to walk to the center of the room, to a pentagram painted on the floor.

Lena walked up to Jamie and Angela, "I want you to stand in the back and just listen. Keep your eyes on the ceremony, but look down if someone is trying to look at you. There is quite a bit of curious women who are looking at you both right now, especially when Sara immediately upgraded Angela's robe. There are women here who have waited years for Sara to promote them, and seeing her do that has caused an uproar among the younger ones. One last thing, Nera is your escort, so be careful. Do not let anyone see what you're wearing around your neck. It will cause more trouble for us tonight. Now go stand away from the circle, and be safe, and watch. I have to stand with Sara as a founding member."

Lena walked toward the front, and Angela and Jamie still

held hands and walked toward the back. As they turned around to face the center, Nera was next to them. "You two have to stand with me up front, I insist. It's my duties as your escort tonight, now come on." She grabbed both of their hands and pulled them among the crowd to the front of the circle and broke up their hands and stood between them and held each of their hands.

Lena looked at them with Nera with caution, but winked at them to tell them it will be okay.

Sara rang another bell to start the formal part and everyone was completely silent. She walked into the center of the pentagram. "Tonight, we as a coven will call the spirit of Samael to talk with us, and I want everyone to have full intention when he arrives. He is powerful, and if we are lucky, we might have an appearance by Diana." Everyone smiled with full anticipation on the news. Sara put her hands up for focused silence. "It is now time to chant, and sing, and dance." With the last words she bowed to everyone and raised her hands up high.

Immediately everyone held hands in circles and Jamie and Angela were still holding Nera's hands and now holding the hands of the women next to them, also. All the women started singing a song, movement started in a circle and all the women were holding hands and moving together in unison. Sara and Lena started lighting candles on the pentagram and started to chant. The lights were dimmed, so the only lights were from the multiple candles being lit around the room. Angela and Jamie kept dancing in a circle, and between the darkness and smoke in the room it was having an effect on them. There was a loud gong and everyone stopped and looked at Sara. She then had everyone chant and face the south, the east, the west, and the north. Then there was complete silence. Everyone kept holding hands and then the room got cold.

There was a mist in the air and a figure stood in the middle of the pentagram. A male figure, in a black robe, stood next to Sara. The male figure whispered to Sara and she smiled back at him. He did not have any shoes on and slowly started to walk around in a circle, looking at all the women. "I am so happy to be here among my followers. I am so thankful you all could attend tonight for

Chapter 25: The Coven

this special ceremony. I feel unsettled tonight, because I can feel there is someone here who wants to hurt this coven, someone who does not belong with you, someone new." He started to walk around again. He said, "For those who do not know me, my name is Samael. I am the all-powerful Archangel of Death. I am sure you all think of the Grim Reaper, but I did not bring that costume tonight. My purpose is to seduce humanity into evil, and this coven is against men and how men have killed, tortured, and oppressed women."

He paused, as if getting a message and was quiet for a few seconds. There was not a sound in the room. He closed his eyes, "I am needing to do evil tonight. The opportunity is here in this room and I can't just let it go." He walks over to Nera, who looks at him directly while holding the hands of Angela and Jamie. She looks at Jamie and she signals for Samael that she is the one. Samael says, "I need to take one of you with me tonight, but this one is special, and I can feel her powers inside her. Jamie looks up at Samael with fright in her eyes. Lena looks concerned about these events and Angela is fully scared on what might happen.

Samael takes Jamie's hand away from Nera and says, "My love, you need to go with me tonight to a place that calls you. I have not come here to take your life, but to bargain with your life for something that I need. You, my sweet, will help me get my Kila back. I can feel that someone here knows where it is and my intuition tells me it is you."

Angela was motionless, trying not to think about the Kila so he would not get any signals from her. She looked at Lena, who looked calm, and she nodded back to Angela to stay calm.

Samael looked at Sara, "I have a demand tonight. I am going to take this one with me, but I will bring her back tomorrow, and will give her back if I can get the Kila that was taken from me. I can feel it, but can't see it. If Sara brings me the Kila tomorrow, then this woman will not be harmed. But if you do not, than I shall be the Angel of Death to her. Sara, do you understand?"

Sara stood strong and said, "We will find the Kila and bring it to you tomorrow so you will release the innocent girl. I do not know where it is, but we will find it."

Samael looked angry, "I shall also take this loyal one of yours named Nera. She will go with me to hold Jamie. Nera is quite loyal to me and my purposes."

Nera smiled and kept a hand on Jamie and walked her to him. The three of them were standing in the middle of the pentagram and the mist returned, and the coldness returned, and soon the mist covered the three and they disappeared in front of everyone.

As everyone started talking in the room, there was a woman in the corner, in a cloak, with her hood on covering most of her face. The woman was going to make an appearance, and now was vividly upset with Samael's actions and how he knowingly took an innocent woman with him. He was abusing his powers and was fully upsetting her. She kept her silence and her identity unknown and pulled out her cell phone and was texting someone with the comment, *It's Diana, we need to meet tonight about Samael.* Within seconds there was a response, *Come tonight to my house, you know the way.* Then Diana texted, *Thanks.*

Diana quickly departed out of the room down the back staircase to not be identified or seen.

Sara went to Lena and asked, "Lena, what Kila is he talking about?"

Lena first walked up to Angela and grabbed her hand and assured that she was okay, and then walked her back to Sara. Lena then said, "Angela is the owner of the Kila that Samael is seeking, and we shall bring it here tomorrow night for Jamie." She looked at Angela, who still looked in shock, and assured her that she will be okay.

Sara said, "I would like you to lead the coven tomorrow night because it seems you know more about this Kila than I do. Is that okay?"

Lena said, "I do not mind leading the coven tomorrow night, but prefer we do it on the roof, if acceptable."

Sara said, "I do not mind that at all. We shall all return tomorrow night on the roof."

Sara assured all the candles were blown out, and before she let everyone go she reminded them they all needed to return tomorrow night.

Chapter 25: The Coven

Lena looked at Angela, "Did Jamie still have the amulet on when she departed tonight?"

"Yes, she still had it on."

Lena said, "That is wonderful news. Peter can find out where they went."

Angela said, "How would Peter find out?"

Lena said, "The amulet is also a tracker. Peter knows all the tricks. It is a spiritual protector, but there is also a chip in it that is a tracker. Let's head down to the main floor and text Peter."

Sara came to Lena and fully apologized for what had happened.

Lena smiled, "Sara, there is no worries. We shall get Jamie back. Remember that she has angel blood inside her, she is well protected. But Samael does not know that."

Sara smiled, "I forgot about that. He will be so mad when he finds out."

"You know the three angels, and especially Senoy, are going to be quite upset too with Samael taking her, but that is what I am counting on. I even think Louis might get involved."

Sara said, "Now that I would love to witness. They hate each other. Bringing in Louis could change everything."

Lena said, "We shall see it all tomorrow night. Now let's close up shop here and make sure everyone gets home safe."

Chapter 26

Kilas Travels

Craig and Greg piloted the aircraft to the far side of the planet. Angel and Kilas were both looking at the blade on the table and were ready to touch it and go back to the Green Man.

Kilas looked at Angel, "Should we wait until they land, or just do it now?"

"Let's do it now."

Kilas then set her intercom to Craig and Greg, "I want you to find a safe place on the planet to land, and then I want you to remain in the cockpit in case we have to depart immediately. Keep the engines on idle for at least sixty minutes."

Craig got on the intercom, "Affirmative. We shall land soon and then wait on idle for sixty minutes for further directions."

Kilas said, "That should keep them in the cockpit as we travel to the Green Man and prevent them from interrupting us, like they did to me on the first visit."

Angel smiled and took Kilas's hand and said, "Are you ready?"

Kilas said, "Yes, let's do it." As they held hands, they grabbed the blade at the same time and immediately transported outside the Green Man's cottage. The sun had almost finished setting and they could barely see, but candlelight beckoned from the cottage. They continued to hold hands as they walked up to the front door. They heard voices inside. Kilas knocked on the door.

Chapter 26: Kilas Travels

A man opened the door wearing jeans, tennis shoes, and a T-shirt and said, "Good evening, Kilas and Angel. I am so glad that you could join us tonight with Jack." The man opened the door and invited the two women inside where the Green Man was sitting at the table with a strange woman. The Green Man waved Kilas and Angel into his cottage and pointed for them to sit at the table.

The Green Man said, "Kilas and Angel, welcome to my cottage, again. It is so nice to see you. Tonight I have special guests. This is Lilith, and the man who opened the door was Merc. They are friends of mine. We were having a discussion of facts and Lilith was correcting some of my facts and assumptions about the three winged strangers. First, would you like some tea or wine?"

Angel and Kilas both said, "Wine."

Kilas said, "Is Jack your real name?"

The Green Man said, "Some people have referred to me as 'Jack of the Green', so for my true friends, I let them call me Jack."

Kilas said, "Thank you, Jack..."

Lilith said, "Merc, since you are already up, please bring some cups, and a bottle of wine."

Merc gave her a frown and rolled his eyes, but did as directed and brought back several wooden cups and a bottle of wine. Merc put the cups on the table and poured the wine and gave Lilith, Jack, Angel, and Kilas a cup. He then looked at Lilith for approval and she merely smiled back with a thank you smile.

Jack continued, "Those three angels wanted me to help them. To have you two go back through another portal and bring someone the athame. We will not go into detail, but they wanted both of you to bring back the athame, so a woman could use it to try and kill Lilith who is sitting next to you. When she visits, like she is now, she is vulnerable to certain weapons, and that is one. Those three angels convinced me that Lilith had killed and tortured my teacher."

Kilas and Angel just nodded and took drinks of the wine.

Lilith said, "My dear Jack, let me explain the rest." She looked at Kilas and Angel, "I was close friends with his teacher and she was poisoned by an angel called Samael, otherwise known as the Grim Reaper, or Angel of Death. She contacted me by spirit and I came to her need. There was a special cave in the high mountains that used to have healing waters, and that is where we went. The travel was slow because she was suffering severely from the poisoning. She insisted we keep traveling to the top of the mountain, even if it was killing her. Well, Jack heard that a strange woman had taken his teacher and he pursued us. We had reached the cave that had the healing waters, but it was too late and her weakness was too far. She told me to depart because she knew of the anger that Jack had in his heart, and that he might hurt, or try and kill me. She demanded that I leave her there for Jack to find.

"As Jack and his companions reached the cave they saw me walking down the hill. His teacher made him promise not to pursue and just to be with her as she died, because she wanted to transfer her magick and tattoos that held the magick to him so he could use it for good in the future."

Kilas and Angel both continued to watch Lilith and both took another drink of wine, trying to comprehend it all. Lilith also took a taste of wine.

"I loved his teacher and would never hurt her. The three angels were showing visions to Jack so that he would influence you two to portal to another time and deliver the athame. The point I was making to Jack before you two arrived is that is exactly what I want you two to do, also."

Kilas looked confused and dumbfounded, "I thought the angels were lying. So why should we help them? And the last thing we want to do is hurt you."

Lilith said, "Everyone in this room knows the truth. But the angels do not know that we know the truth, so we need to play the script as they wrote it, so they do not see our hand that we are playing. We need to play the bluff and not let the angels know that in the end we will deceive them, or things might turn out different than anyone expected."

Merc said, "We need to look like we are on their side, but in

Chapter 26: Kilas Travels

the end, we shall let the chips fall where they may. So, we will need you to bring the athame here and then we will help you to portal to yet another time. All three of us will swear to protect you on this quest, and will give our lives to save yours, but we need you both to do what the angels requested. Do you think you can do it?"

Kilas and Angel both looked at each other, trying to comprehend everything that they just heard, and then looked into each other's eyes and smiled and Angel said, "Yes, we can do it."

Merc said, "Excellent. Now I need you two to hold hands right now, because in another time, you are both holding each other's hands, and also holding the athame. We need to bring the athame to this time, so I am going to touch each of your arms and help you bring it to this time. Are you ready?"

They both nodded. Then Merc touched each of their arms, and within a few seconds, the athame was sitting on the Green Man's table with both of their hands holding onto it. The blade was glowing again and certain inscriptions appeared on the steel.

Lilith said, "Excellent work, as always, Merc."

Merc let go of their arms and merely said, "It is just what I do. You should never doubt my skills."

Kilas said, "Now that the athame is here, what do we do next? Why is it glowing?"

Jack said, "It is glowing because we have three angels about to knock on my door. They can feel the athame has returned. They want to continue with our deal to have the athame travel back in time, so that when Lilith and Merc return in human form, the blade could kill them. Remember, they omitted some of the truth in their vision and explanation to me, so I would like to handle this first with them as a courtesy. I want to find out their motive." Jack stood up and looked stern as he walked over to the door, awaiting the knock, right as he reached the door.

He opened the door to see the three angels in their typical black suits and sunglasses, trying to look intimidating, but Jack was not at all intimidated.

Senoy said, "We could feel the presence of the athame. Are the young ladies with you as well?"

Jack said, "Yes, the blade and the two brave women, Kilas and Angel, are here under my protection, but the situation has changed a little since our last visit."

Senoy said, "You agreed to help bring back the blade, so we could send Kilas and Angel back into the portal, so that you, or they, could kill Lilith for us. You agreed. Do not trifle with us Jack."

Jack started to get frustrated, and some of his tattoos were glowing, and he calmly said, "You said that Lilith killed my teacher. You did not tell the whole truth in the images you showed. You left out Samael."

Senoy was mad, "I did not leave out any information. Lilith did kill your teacher and you will help me kill her once and for all. You lie. I am telling you the truth. If you do not believe, ask Lilith."

"I did and she is here."

As he said the last words, Senoy looked embarrassed and paler, and then Lilith walked next to Jack, and Merc walked on his other side at the doorway. The other two angels took a step back. Lilith said, "My beautiful Senoy, what are you trying to do in having me killed?"

She walked out next to him and he took a step back. She said, "Why do you want me killed? You know that would only make the heartbreak worse than what it is. Plus, Merc, my wonderful dear friend, would not allow it, and he and a few others would defend their god-lives to protect me. So, what I need to know is, why do you want me killed? Or is all you want is to hurt me? Tell me—I deserve to know, because you keep telling false rumors and facts about events that you know the truth on for the purpose of deception, and betrayal, and revenge. So, what is it?"

She walked up to him where he could feel her energy and her smell that drove him crazy. "Senoy, you know we could always rekindle what we had, but it takes you being honest right now, right here, for me to reconsider it." She got closer and whispered into his ear, "You remember how much fun we have had; I am much better with age and experience. So, what shall it be? By the way, guess who helped you three to become saints in church?

Chapter 26: Kilas Travels

That was my doing, not anyone else's."

Senoy smiled and looked down to the ground and then looked up and said, "Samael wanted the athame to return to a person called Nera. It seems Nera is a pawn for him, and she gave a blood oath to serve him because he was the only one who promised to help her get rid of the curse. Samael wanted the athame more than anything, and knew we could travel here because we are not monitored. We were the ones who helped Kilas find the blade, and we were the ones who helped the portal find Jack for them. It is all about bringing back the blade."

Merc walked out of the door, "That explains the athame, but work on the emotions of Jack about his teacher to have him be deceived? You are angels for god sakes."

Senoy said, "We knew that Jack loved his solitude, and the only way to bring him out of it was his teacher's death, which he still feels deeply. It was our only trigger point that we knew to invoke an emotion and have him boiling with anger to help us."

Jack said, "That was low, even for you three…but the truth will set you free. Still, going back in time with the athame though, there are events that are about to happen with the assumption that your plan is going on as scheduled. I will escort Kilas and Angel to the former owner of the blade. I believe his name is Paul. But it will not be used to hurt Lilith, but might be used to hurt someone else. The visions are clear and then are blurred, but we still must go back. One thing I must know, did Samael ever tell you three why he poisoned my teacher?"

Senoy said, "He only said that it was her time, because he had originally come for you, but she made a deal that she would sacrifice herself for you. It is the same story that happened in the time the ladies will travel to, with a Joe and a woman named Angela. Samael had come for her, but Joe made a deal. That's the more current mess the three of us are involved in right now. The poison was the same he used on your teacher, that he used on Joe, and a smaller version of what he used in Salem. It's all from a certain type of mushrooms, and mixing with a rye and weed. It becomes a hallucinogen drug, and too much can cause a slow or instant death, or just cause extraordinary hallucinations. It all depends on the amount."

Merc said, "We must continue to act out this script that has been written by Samael so that we see what the truth of his motivations are. I expect you three will not say anything, because I would come looking for you with anger in my heart. Shall we do the sacred handshake to create this promise?" He extended out his hand to Senoy, who reached his hand out to Lilith, ignoring Merc. He smiled, and she smiled, too.

Senoy, solemn, "I swear not to divulge the conversation that we have just completed, and I still love you."

Lilith took his hand tenderly and softly said, "I swear, too."

Merc said, "Well, now that is complete, we will take the group to the inner temple to get any last minute assistance, and then we shall return the athame to Paul and see what happens. Senoy, by the way, a few hours ago, Samael kidnapped your so-called daughter, Jamie."

Senoy said, "What? When did that happen? How dare he!" The other angels were taken back and looked into each other eyes, like their minds were talking to each other. Their faces went from stern to upset. Senoy said, "She is innocent in all of this and has no idea of her power or strength. He is trying to manipulate her, I am sure. We will put a stop to that."

Lilith said, "They are all meeting in the place you know about tonight, in the coven in which you are familiar. Let things happen as Samael thinks they will, so we can finally put an end to it all. He promised to return Jamie tonight in exchange for the Kila. Let this happen and we shall help you protect Jamie tonight, and Samael will get what is due to him."

Senoy looked at the other two angels who agreed on Lilith's terms before saying, "Okay, we have a bargain. But Jamie shall not be harmed, or there will be revenge and death tonight."

Merc said, "We will all help you protect Jamie. We must protect the child."

Senoy said, "Yes, she is with child. We must go. We will be near the events tonight, but not show ourselves until the proper time. You will feel us near. Now we must go and prepare." They pulled their wings out and departed.

Chapter 26: Kilas Travels

Lilith said, "Now that is settled. It is time that we all go to the inner temple together. Make sure the athame is secure. Kilas, you will need to hold on to it, since you are now its new rightful owner."

Jack said, "I have never been. Am I allowed to go?"

Merc said, "Yes, you are allowed, I approve it, and so does Lilith."

Angel said, "What is the inner temple?"

Lilith said, "It is much easier to show you than to explain to you. I think now is the best time as ever to depart, if okay with you, Merc?"

Merc, Lilith, and Jack all stood up and held hands and waved for Kilas and Angel to join them to make a circle. Merc said, "Lilith, do you want to make the chant, or shall I?"

Lilith said, "I shall make the chant to assure we get to the right place. You can't get yourself on time to a simple dinner."

Merc said, "I love you, too."

Lilith smiled back and started chanting words that sounded strange to Angel and Kilas—all of a sudden they were near a cabin on a lake and it was looking like spring. They had been transported again. Lilith let go of their hands and said, "Now follow me to the inner temple and we shall enjoy the company and see who is, also, attending."

They led the group to the small trail to the back patio of a wonderful cabin facing a large mountain lake. Jack, Angel, and Kilas followed the two to the back patio, but no one was there and the firepits were cold.

Merc said, "No one here, which worries me. It feels like there is a gathering that we were not invited to. I propose that we walk through the woods and bring the athame back to Paul."

Lilith said, "I agree. Let's continue walking through the great tree over there, where there is a portal which will take us to the place that we seek. Everyone, please stay close to each other as we walk. Don't want to lose anyone."

Chapter 27

Samael's Actions

Samael stood with Jamie and Nera just inside a cave with a small creek running through it. The ceilings were high, like a cathedral, and the artwork was amazing. It truly looked like a Catholic church that Jamie had attended as a child, except underground and in a cave. There was even a large cross cut out, by the alter, of rock. Samael grunted, "Keep following me, you two."

Jamie was walking behind Samael and Nera was behind her, also looking up into the ceiling, which looked like she had never been there, either. Jamie said, "Why are you kidnapping me?"

Samael stopped, "I did not kidnap you. You showed up to that party. I am only using you as barter to get the artifact that I desire and need."

Jamie said, "That sounds like kidnapping to me."

Samael just said, "Please shut up. I know what I am doing"

Nera sneered, "Yea, please shut up."

Jamie said, "You know angels should not kidnap humans. It could get them into trouble."

Samael stopped, looked frustrated, and looked right at Jamie, "For being a human, you have way too much courage against this angel, or you are the stupidest woman I ever met."

Jamie laughed, "I have been called many names, but I am definitively not stupid."

Samael looked up, "Let's keep going to my residence, where

Chapter 27: Samael's Actions

we will all be more comfortable until we depart tomorrow night, back to coven."

They continued to walk into another cave and then came to a normal, modern living room, with a kitchen, and dining room table, and normal amenities. Jamie and Nera were both fully surprised by the instant change of surroundings.

Samael said, "This is where I live. What, are you surprised? I do live normally. This is where you will be staying tonight and then we will depart tomorrow night, together, back to the coven to finally settle some scores." As he was talking, he closed the door to the cave with a steel door, and locked it with an electronic cipher lock.

Jamie said, "I don't think you need to lock the door for me. I will not be trying to escape."

Samael said, "It's not keeping you from escaping. That door keeps entities, enemies, angels, and demons from finding us and getting into here. Want any food before we turn in for the night?"

Jamie said, "I am not really hungry."

Nera said, "I am starving."

Samael opened up the refrigerator and brought out things to make simple sandwiches on the table, and he and Nera worked on sandwiches. He found some chips and sodas to add. Jamie just looked puzzled at the two of them, almost looking domestic in the most absurd place in an ancient cave.

Samael said, "I am going to watch some TV." He hit a button and this huge flat screen TV came out of the wall, and was almost 100 inches long. He sat on his couch, with his sandwich and drink, and started to flip channels with Nera.

Samael said, "Jamie, what is your story? There was really no reason that I picked you. You were just the woman standing next to Nera, so I grabbed you, that's all. I am not going to hurt you or anything. So tomorrow night, just look really scared so I can keep my scary image."

Nera said, "I can put a few bruises on her if you want?"

Samael said, "Absolutely not, Nera. Crap, is that all you do—think about hurting people? You are so sadistic."

Nera looked pouty and scorned, "Samael, I just want this

curse taken away from me, its driving me crazy. It's a horrible chain around my neck. I am sorry I did horrible things in past lives, my soul is dark as hell most of the time. I am so freaking sorry that I killed Paul like four times in our past lives. Well, not really, because he really pissed me off. This curse just sucks."

Jamie was just watching the two, who looked like a married couple arguing about life choices, while eating their dinner on the couch.

Nera said, "What's so funny?"

Jamie said, "Nothing. You two look, and sound, like a married couple."

Nera and Samael just looked at each other in an odd way and he said, "Yea, no, I don't see that happening. I am an angel and she is a mortal with a freaking curse. It's like some sexual transmitted disease thing."

Nera threw food at him and he just laughed.

Jamie said, "Now where do I get to go to sleep?"

Samael said, "That door right over there is my guest room. It's a simple room and bed. I do not have many visitors here, so might be a little dusty."

Jamie said, "If you don't mind, I'm going to bed. Thank you for being such a kind kidnapper tonight. You are actually quite kind, in a weird way."

Samael said, "You are very welcome, but tomorrow has not happened yet. I can be unkind very quickly."

Jamie said, "Thank you, for now then, and we shall see what happens tomorrow." As she was walking into the room she could overhear the discussion between them, about how to get rid of Nera's curse, and other stuff. Jamie was tired and confused. She looked at the simple room, with a rock carved wall on two sides and framed walls on the other two. Well, it did smell like the jail cell she spent a night in while drunk in Oklahoma City, but she remembered her jail did not have a king size bed. She took off her clothes, crawled into bed and immediately fell asleep.

As she was dreaming, she felt a presence vision from Senoy, who told her to be safe and that she would not be harmed. He and his brothers would help her get away from Samael tomorrow

Chapter 27: Samael's Actions

night. Senoy told her to concentrate on her wings, because they would be growing soon. She did not know what he was talking about. Her dream felt so real, but afterward she fell back into a deep sleep.

What felt like a few hours, was actually twelve hours later, when there was a knock on her door. The door opened with Nera saying dinner was ready, and she turned on the light. As she turned on the light, Nera said, "Oh my God," and left the room, but the light was left on.

Jamie sat up in bed and had slept naked, and only assumed that was what was wrong with Nera. Nera stood up and stretched out her arms and rotated her shoulders around, but something was scratching her and she thought it might have been dusty sheets. She looked over her shoulder and saw feathers and freaked out. *What the hell* was rushing through her mind. Then Nera and Samael rushed into her room and was with her and she said, "What did you do to Jamie? She's got wings like an angel."

Chapter 28

Angela and Lena

As Angela and Lena were locking up the store, Lena received a text from Sara that all members were safely home. Lena responded back with *Blessed Be*.

Lena looked at Angela, "Everyone is safe. Now we must find Paul and Peter. We are going to need the Kila, the fake Kila, and the staff for tomorrow night."

Angela said, "We need to wake them up tonight."

"I doubt any of them are sleeping. They are probably at Robert's bar, drinking in the library over there, waiting for us."

Angela said, "Lena, did you text them all prior to tonight's events?"

Lena said, "I might have had the idea while I was putting on my robe tonight. Intuition is a great thing to trust."

Angela smiled at Lena, "I have so much to learn, don't I?"

Lena smiled, "One lesson at a time, my dear, one lesson at a time." They walked, elbows interlocked, across the street to Casseneta's, and were giggling as they walked up to the door and could hear the men laughing in the library. As they were about to enter the library, Angela whispered, "I wonder how much they have already drunk?"

Lena and Angela finally walked into the library and she said, "Here we are. Let's get down to business."

Robert and Paul were in the library drinking a bottle of wine

Chapter 28: Angela and Lena

and Angela said, "We also need Peter to bring the Kila and staff. Where is he?"

Paul said, "We called him, he should have been here by now. Let me text him again." As Paul was texting, Peter walked into the library carrying the Kila, the fake Kila, and the staff.

Peter said, "I am sorry about the delay. Paul hid the fake in a weird place in his house, but I found it." He placed all three items on the table in front of them.

Paul said, "Excuse me?"

Peter said, "You're excused. Now let's talk about what happened tonight with Lena and Angela. Where is Jamie?"

Lena said, "Let's all sit at the table and talk tactics in what we need to do tomorrow night. During tonight's coven, Samael made an appearance and demanded the Kila, and then he took Jamie as collateral and also, Nera. We will need to exchange the Kila for Jamie tomorrow. Do we have any concerns or questions?"

Peter calmly said, "If you don't mind, I would like to recommend something first." Everyone agreed and let Peter continue. He said, "Lena is going to be in charge of the coven meeting tomorrow night. She will have the attention of everyone. Angela, you will need to be close to Lena during this time. The three of us are not permitted, but I can have special access. What that means is, I need Paul and Robert to be on the next roof watching with night vision devices for other visitors. If you don't have any, you can borrow mine. Angela, you need to have the fake Kila to give to Samael, but I will bring the real Kila and attach the staff, and will hold it until you need it. When you need the real Kila, I will get it to you. I will feel it. Angela, please make sure you have the special crystal in your pocket that Joe gave you. It will come to be handy tomorrow night. Robert and Paul, I also need one other thing from you that we will discuss later."

Lena said, "Peter, I agree with all. We just do not know what Samael will do and he is unpredictable. We also have no idea of Nera's mental stability. If her curse is not taken away, she might cross all lines in frustration. She could be the most dangerous. We will just have to see what happens and trust our intuition."

Peter said, "I think that is enough to discuss tonight. Does anyone have any questions or comments? We should all get plenty of rest, as we do not know how long tomorrow night will last. Let's call it a night."

Everyone agreed and started to get up from the table. As Peter was standing up he whispered to Angela, "Please stay for a private discussion with me after everyone leaves. Just take your time getting your things together."

Lena walked over to Peter, "Peter, this will be like old times."

Peter said, "Well, I hope so. We will see what happens. Our old times were not always successful."

Everyone started leaving until it was just Peter and Angela alone in the library. Peter said, "Angela, are you ready to fulfill Joe's quest tomorrow night?"

"Yes, I am."

Peter said, "That is all I wanted to hear. I will assist you. Trust your feelings, you have done this before. You have the courage from your past lives. Courage is in your veins."

Angela gave Peter a hug and said, "I am not afraid."

Chapter 29

The Coven Revisited

Lena and Angela drove together to the store and got out of their car. They looked at each with confidence as they walked across the street to enter the building. Other women of the coven were parking their cars on the empty main street and walking into the building. As some women took the outside fire escape ladders up to the roof, Lena and Angela walked over to the old rustic elevator and pushed the number three button again, until it lit up. As the elevator came to the main floor and opened, the woman inside said, "Welcome, Lena and Angela. Shall we join the rest of the coven."

Lena said, "Yes, it is time."

Lena and Angela walked into the elevator and waited patiently until it reached the third floor and the doors opened. As they exited the elevator, there was only one flight of stairs to go to the roof where the coven was going to convene tonight. A full moon shone brightly from the southeast. A woman came up to Lena and Angela and handed them their robes for the evening. As they were putting on their assigned robes, Sara came up to Lena, "Lena, everyone is here and I have told them that you will lead the session tonight. I recommend 10 pm, when the moon will be at its fullest, in about twelve minutes."

Lena walked over to the edge of the roof to collect her thoughts. She also wanted to look at the full moon, and she looked out into a far neighboring park. She saw five people walk out of the park, walking toward their building, and she knew who they were and she smiled. As she smiled, a man and women, who were both green, smiled up to her. She then turned toward the coven and walked into the center of the roof and started to convene the circle. She scanned the room looking for Angela and waved her to stand next to her. All the coven became silent and formed two circles, one inner and one outer, and all the women were holding hands. The outer women were holding torches and the dancing started in a circle. On cue from the singing, the women with torches would twirl and the singing grew stronger as it went on.

* * *

Merc, Lilith, Jack, Angel, and Kilas left the inner temple and walked a trail to a huge tree, down through a tunnel underneath it, and now they were in a park in a foreign city, in a foreign land.

Merc said, "Please, follow me. I know where we are going to assist in the matter tonight." As they were departing the park, Jack and Kilas both looked up toward the roof of a building, and saw a woman looking at them behind the moon light and smiling back to them.

Merc walked behind a building toward the fire exit stairs and Kilas said, "Merc, where are we?"

Merc said, "We are in the past and we are returning the athame to the owner before you. We are here to witness something and to finally settle some scores. Is that enough? We will return back as soon as the ceremony is complete."

Kilas said, "Thank you. That is enough for me."

Lilith touched both Kilas and Angel. "Do not be afraid. Merc, Jack, and I will protect you if there is any harm toward you."

Angel said, "Thank you."

They started walking up the fire escape exterior ladders to come up to the roof of the building. As they were coming onto the roof, a young woman approached them with robes and said, "We are expecting you all. These robes are for you to keep your identity hidden until the proper time, when you need to make an

Chapter 29: The Coven Revisited

appearance."

Lilith said, "Thank you, my dear."

The young woman handed robes to everyone and when finished said, "It is an honor to meet you, Lilith. You are an inspiration for me."

Lilith took her hand and said, "We shall talk later. Please find me after the ceremony."

Lilith helped Merc with his robe, because he always had issues putting it on, like showing up for dinner late. It was just what it was. She helped zip up the robe and then put the hood over his head and said, "They are not expecting us. We will observe until it is the time not to."

Merc smiled back, "It's always an adventure with you." He gave her a wink.

Angel and Kilas were putting on their robes, together, still confused where they were and why they were there. They both helped Jack with his robe because he was such a large man.

Lilith walked up to Kilas, "Do you still have the athame?"

Kilas said, "Yes, it is attached to me, but it is glowing right now."

Lilith smiled, "It will probably glow the rest of tonight because the enemies of several of its past owners are here."

Lilith looked at all of them. "Stay close and we will stay in the back and try to be unnoticed until it is time. Just watch and listen."

They all agreed and walked to the corner of the roof and watched the dancing circles. They were not noticed at all, except for Lena, who had anticipated their visit and had had her assistant bring them robes.

Lena hit a large gong to make everyone stop dancing and singing. She said, "We shall wait for Samael to arrive. I feel that he is close." There was silence for a long pause and everyone was in anticipation. Then there was a cold mist on the roof and it turned purple, and Samael appeared from the mist with Nera and Jamie. Samael had his black wings out in full as he walked toward Lena. Next to him was Nera, in a robe. And what surprised everyone was Jamie, walking behind them, and who also had wings, but hers were blue and white and looked new. Jamie's hair was also tinted blue, and now curly. Jamie had a smile on her face and waved at Lena, signaling, trying to say through her facial expression 'look what happened to me last night' without actually saying it with words. She was walking a little awkward, trying to get used to her new wings.

Samael said out loud so everyone could hear him, "I have brought Jamie back as promised, and you owe me the Kila. You did not inform me that Jamie was partially an angel. That was low, Lena, even for you. I could not hurt her, even if I wanted to, because of the ancient code."

Lena smiled, "Samael, you never asked about her when you took her last night or we might have told you, but this is more fun. Jamie, you look awesome with your new wings."

Jamie just gave two thumbs up and smiled back, trying to avoid any confrontation.

Samael said, "Nera, go to Lena and take the Kila from her. Then we will release Jamie."

Nera walked over to Lena, with an arrogance about her that she was about to open a present early, but as she approached, Lena said, "Nera, I do not have the Kila. But I do know someone who has that athame that you seemed a bit interested in."

Nera stopped in her tracks as the idea of the athame being so close, and her curse might be broken made her rethink her actions. At the same time, Kilas touched the athame that she was holding in her robe to assure it was still there, and she looked at it and it was still glowing.

Nera said, "What do you mean? The athame is hidden and will not be found for over many centuries. That is what the latest cards foretold. What do you mean that you have the athame? You can't have it here."

Lena just smiled, "There is a woman who is right here, tonight. She is the new rightful owner of the athame and has portaled tonight to be here. You see, this is not what it seems to be, because Samael has also another agenda on his mind, more than the Kila. Don't you Samael?" Lena gave a look at him and so did Nera.

Chapter 29: The Coven Revisited

Samael said, "Lena, I always have multiple plans on the table at the same time. It's waiting time for the Grim Reaper, or Angel of Death, whichever you want to refer to me as tonight. So, let's have the Kila, so we can be finished with this, tonight."

Nera yelled, "No, I want the athame! I deserve the athame and I deserve this curse to be released from me. The stupid Kila can't do anything for me. Now show me the athame, right now!"

Samael walked up to Nera and yelled out, "The Kila first, because I want to be reunited with my friends who are trapped inside it and are seeking to return. The athame is your small problem, Nera. It is just a trinket in this big picture of the cosmos. The Kila is the prize."

* * *

As the discussions were happening on the roof, the three angels were on another roof watching, how they usually do, and sharing a flask between them. Senoy said, "Look at her wings. They really grew last night. She will need training on how to use them and how to, most importantly, hide them when not necessary." The other two just laughed and kidded him on actually being a proud father type of figure. Senoy just kept smiling and watching, "If Samael, or anyone, tries to hurt Jamie, we are jumping over this street and making things right and just." They all kept watching.

* * *

On the opposite building, Paul and Robert were watching with Peter's night vision goggles. Paul said, "Why does Peter have night vision goggles? Like, why would a normal person have them at all?"

Robert just smiled and said, "Paul, have you not noticed yet? Peter is not a normal person. He is one of the most unique and mysterious persons that I know. Have you ever been to his house?"

Paul said, "No, I have no idea where he lives."

Robert said, "I have known him for over thirty years and have no idea where that man lives. He likes his solitude for sure. Now let's keep watching and see what happens. By the way, where is the fake Kila?"

Paul said, "It was right here next to me, but it's not there anymore. Where did it go?"

Robert just smiled, "Oh my friend, I assume Peter has it and he has a plan for it."

* * *

Samael looked sternly at Lena, "Lena, I will not ask for the Kila twice. Now give it to me now or you will regret your next actions for a long time."

As Lena was looking coldly at Samael, standing firm and strong as she also did, Peter stood behind Angela and quietly, without anyone noticing, handed Angela the Kila into her robe. She heard his voice like a whisper, "Angela, do not move or move your eyes. I am going to slide the fake Kila into your hands without anyone knowing. Please be perfectly still." He was standing right behind her and she could feel him, and he had slid his hand into her robe and placed the fake Kila into her hand backward, so the blade was hidden in her robe sleeve. He then whispered to her, "Now, walk up to Lena with this Kila and hand it to her so she can give to Samael. Move slowly and steadily. You will do great."

As he walked away from her into the crowd, Angela slowly walked over to Lena and held the Kila in her hand, ready to give it to Lena. Samael quickly looked at Lena and said, "Well, it's about time."

Lena took the Kila from Angela and winked at her and said, "Blessed be," quietly and softly while holding the fake Kila, but showing reverence and full respect. Lena held it in both hands and bowed, and reached out to hand it to Samael. He walked closer to her and picked up the Kila from her hands and raised it near his face to inspect it. "Lena, thank you for being reasonable with all of this. Now I can release my friends from the blade. Jamie, you are free to go."

Jamie walked over to Angela and they hugged each other like

Chapter 29: The Coven Revisited

they had never hugged before. Angela said, "I was worried about you."

Jamie said, "I was worried about you, too, but once I grew these wings, I was not afraid anymore. A bit uncomfortable, but not afraid. There has to be a way to put them away."

Angela said, "We can discuss that later. Let's see what happens next."

Jamie and Angela held hands as they watched Samael with the Kila.

Samael was saying some ancient text and then knelt down and stabbed the fake Kila into the roof. Nothing happened. Samael stabbed the Kila again into the roof, expecting something to happen, but nothing did. Nera walked over to the Samael and knelt down at the Kila and examined it and said, "They fooled you. It's a fake. You are playing the fool."

Kilas was in the back, but felt the athame in her hand talk to her and she slowly walked through the silent crowd of robed women. She was now in the front row, holding the glowing athame that was now warm to her touch. Angel was right behind her, trying to protect her, and watch for any threats in the room. Kilas was being called internally to protect the woman next to the woman called Lena. She felt this instant connection with the petite brunette that handed the Kila to Lena.

Nera took the Kila out of the floor and stood up, and with anger, threw the Kila toward Lena. Angela ran to cover Lena and the blade went deep into Angela's left shoulder. The blade slipped between the upper back ribs and went full into her heart, and she screamed so loud that everyone could hear from the rooftop. The three angels stood up in concern, and Paul and Robert fretted, helpless witnesses. Angela fell into Lena's arms and was in excruciating pain. The dark red blood was running down her back and Lena could not hold her. Jamie went to her, to hold her and try and save her. Jamie's wings stretched full, and she stared down Nera, who stood with pure evil toward the group of women.

Lena yelled, "Someone help us! She is fading fast! I can't stop the bleeding. Pray to the gods to help us now. She did not deserve this."

As Nera was looking at Jamie with her wings fully outstretched, Kilas had walked behind Nera and tapped her on the shoulder, Nera turned around and looked at the strange woman and said, "Who the hell are you?"

Kilas just said, "This blade calls for you, you bitch!" Kilas took the athame and stabbed Nera straight into the heart, which took Nera by full surprise. And as she fell onto the roof, she looked at the knife, which was the athame, which she had been wishing to save her. As she was lying on the roof, she felt the blade that was deep into her heart and she started to laugh and said, "Thank you for releasing me from my curse. I am finally free. I have been waiting so many past lives to be free of this curse." As the blood was spitting out of her mouth as she was talking, she was laughing hysterically and looking at the woman holding the athame and said, "Thank you, whoever you are. I am free from all of my deeds of evil. You have freed me." She started to cry and laugh at the same time.

Angel went to Kilas and said, "Why did you do that?"

Kilas said, "The blade told me to do it. There is another reason, but I do not know what it is yet."

Samael, irate with the events, shouted, "Where is the Kila? Lena, I want it now or you might be next."

A man walked next to Angela as she was bleeding out, and kneeled next to her and started to touch her hand. Samael yelled at the robed person and said, "I order you to stop helping that women, or you will be hurt."

The man stood up and turned toward Samael and took off his hood to reveal himself.

Samael took a step back, "Merc, what are you doing here? You are not involved in this situation. You need to keep to you own business, this has nothing to do with you."

Merc said, "Samael, my friend, I have been watching this too long, and there are a few of us who are now putting things right, you see. You wanted Nera to try to kill my beloved Lilith and well, I do not tolerate threats to my love. It's a good thing Nera has the athame she seeks, because your control over her has been severed, and she can think on her own, and she is free from the

Chapter 29: The Coven Revisited

curse."

Samael said, "Merc, I have no quarrel with you. I only have a quarrel with Lilith."

Merc said, "Well, if you have an issue with Lilith, why don't you tell her in person? She is right behind you."

Samael went pale and looked down, and then turned around to Lilith, who was taking her hood off, and totally shocked Samael. Lilith said, "Why, it is so nice to see you." Samael looked upset and scared at the same time, "Lilith, why are you here? This has nothing to do with you, or Merc. You both need to leave. This is my business, not freaking yours."

Lilith walked closer to him, "Samael, you see, I do not appreciate death threats or having plans to have anyone try and kill me who is too cowardly to do it themselves. It proves such low character, but then you have always been that type of person. So pathetic."

Samael was upset and took off his jacket and let his dark wings stretch out and he looked at Lilith, "You may just get what you want tonight." As Samael leaped toward Lilith, Jamie leaped in front of Lilith to protect her and held him off with just one hand. Samael could not move her hand from his chest, he could not move her. He said, "You are just a stupid new-born angel. How do you have these powers over me? That's impossible. It can't happen. I am the strongest."

Lilith just said, "Samael, you mean this simple new angel is stronger than you? Well, how is that possible? I wonder who she really is?"

Samael was vividly upset and using all his power against Jamie, but to no avail. She finally pushed him back and he went falling onto the roof floor about ten feet, sliding another five feet. Samael quickly got on his feet, and his claws came out of his hands, and he leaped toward Jamie. But as soon as he leaped, he was suspended and could not move and he said, "Who are you?" As he was screaming at her, he could see that her eyes were yellow and black, and he stopped cold at that sight. "That is not possible."

There was a loud voice in the background, "Peter, it is time."

Peter walked up with the real Kila on the staff and drove it into the roof and all of a sudden, everything froze. The only people who were not frozen were the angels and gods. All of the other women with robes on were frozen in time. There was a figure, walking from the back toward the front, in an old-English 18th century suit, with blue round glasses, and no shoes. The man walked up to Peter and said, "It is always nice to see you, Peter. Thank you for doing that."

Peter said, "Anytime, Louis, anytime."

Louis said, "Please hold it in place until I say so, because we do not want to release anything, but only add to the blade tonight."

Louis walked over to Samael and said, "Samael, Samael. I am sure I am the last person you expected to see tonight. You probably expected the other guy. You see, you can bullshit her, but you can't bullshit me, because I know your true character."

Louis looked at Nera and woke her from the freeze and her bleeding continued. Nera looked at the stranger and looked confused. Louis pulled the athame out of her heart, and then put his other hand on her heart to heal the wound. He said, "Lilith, please take the athame and make sure we keep it out of people who align with types like Samael. Can you do that for me?"

Lilith said, "Louis, I give you my word."

Louis said, "Thank you my dear. I can always count on you."

Louis stood up and put his hand out to help Nera up since he had healed her. She took his hand and stood up. He would not let go of her hand. "It is so nice that so many of my friends are here. I have not seen so many of you in so long. Lilith, my dear, and Merc, please visit me more. Peter, as always it is a pleasure. My three cowardly angels over there, I see you there, yes, please wave back. And Jack, it is always an honor in your presence. I think we have seen enough tonight, if anyone objects. Merc, I want you to heal that brave woman Angela over there, who would give her life to save Lena. That is an honorable soul that deserves to live." Merc immediately went to help Angela.

Louis started walking, still holding Nera by her hand. Nera yelled, "Let go of me! I am free from my curse." Louis looked

Chapter 29: The Coven Revisited

at her, "You are free from this curse, but now you have deeds owed, and you are coming with me." Louis looked at everyone, "Does anyone mind if I take this evil and wretched woman back to my domain, my home? Are there any objections? Samael, do you mind if I take this one with me?"

Samael snarled, "You can take whoever you desire, Louis. Nera means nothing to me."

Nera started to scream, realizing she had been released from the curse to be going to a much worse scenario. Nera looked back at Samael, "Samael, save me. I have been a devoted servant to you and I did all your deeds. You bastard!"

Louis kept dragging her by her hand. As she tried to go limp to prevent from going with him, he said, "My Nera, all the things you think Samael made you do, you actually did them without his guidance or orders. You see, your nature only belongs in a special place and I am taking you with me tonight. Payment is due for all your deeds, and you can't blame anyone but yourself."

Louis then picked her up over his shoulder as she was screaming and kicking, and as he got closer to the edge, there were four dark winged entities that flew up and he said, "Boys, take this one to the special place. I will be right behind, no delay." They grabbed her as she was screaming and he kissed her forehead and said, "I will see you soon."

The four dark winged entities took her and flew off the roof and disappeared.

Louis took a pause and looked at everyone. "When I leave, please tell them all, all the people, that your actions in your past and current lives will catch up with you someday. Teach them. Teach them well. Hell keeps score and is not discriminatory. We come for all who deserve it. One last thing. Samael, please apologize to Lena and never threaten her again, or I will come for you next time, no matter what the other one says. Jack, teach those two brave women everything you have learned, they are your legacy. One last thing, tell Lena that Dr. Louis C. Pffiefer sends his regards. She will know what that means. Well, my friends, it is time to depart. Peter, you know what to do."

As Louis jumped off the roof, Peter pulled the Kila and the

staff out of the roof and everyone came back to life and were unfrozen.

As Peter was looking around he saw Samael had departed, also, which was his usual, and he saw Merc and Lilith healing Angela's wound. He could account for the staff, the Kila, and he saw that Lilith had the athame. He walked over to Lilith and asked, "How is Angela going to do?"

Merc said, "I have healed her, but she has a nice scar. She might want a tattoo to cover it up someday." Jamie just smiled at Angela.

Peter waved for the three angels to join them, in which they did, and they started talking with Jamie about her wings and her new experiences. It seemed she now had three father figures. He walked up to Lilith, "I would like to give the athame to the rightful owner, who will be trained by Jack."

Lilith smiled and gave him the athame, and she said, "She will be a good student for Jack. They both will."

Peter walked over to Kilas and Angel and Jack, and said, "Kilas, here is your athame. I want you to take it back to your time. You have earned it and it communicates with you." Kilas hugged Peter and he smiled. He looked at Jack and said, "Train them well. Please take them back through the portal in the woods that you came through. The portal will remain open until you depart."

Jack said, "Thank you, Peter." They shook hands and the three of them departed down the back-building fire exit.

Peter pulled out his cellphone and texted Robert, *Robert, could you open up Cassenetta's for a small party of ten, they need fellowship and lots of whiskey and hugs?*

Robert texted back, *Paul and I will go open it up now for anyone interested.*

Peter texted *Thank you my friend.*

Finally, Peter walked over to Lena, "Lena, it has been quite a night with this full moon."

Lena said, "I account for everyone except for Nera. Did she escape?"

Peter said, "Well, Dr. Louis C. Pfeiffer sends his regards and

Chapter 29: The Coven Revisited

he departed with Nera tonight."

Lena smiled, "That is too bad for Nera, but when *Lucifer* calls, there is no discussion. Well, that is deserved. We must be kind to one another. It is so nice to see you, Peter. Can you visit more? I miss my teacher."

Peter said, "I will visit more, and it seems that I have new friends who I can trust again."

He sat with her and he started to tell her what had happened in great detail.

Chapter 30

The Tattoo

A few days, later Angela and Jamie are at a tattoo artist getting tattoos and holding each other hands. They were on tables next to each other, talking through the pain. During the time, Jamie had told Angela about the pain of her past tattoos, on her inner thigh, the top of her foot, and her gigantic angel wings. Jamie kept talking to keep Angela's mind off the pain of her new tattoo.

George, her tattoo artist said, "Angela, I think we are done, and you can't see the scar anymore, and I hope you like it."

Jamie was finished, also, with her tattoo additions and they both got off their tables, and walked over to the mirror to admire Angela's new tattoo. It was a sunflower tattoo, consisting of three sunflowers together and colors of orange, yellow, some purple and rose on the flowers. The new tattoo had covered up the Kila scar that was made when Nera had thrown it toward Lena and Angela had protected her by blocking the blade. With her new tattoo, Angela could see, through the mirror, that the colors completely covered the new scar and you could not tell there was a scar at all. Jamie looked at it and totally loved it. George looked at Angela, waiting patiently as an artist, hoping that the client loved her tattoo. Angela looked at George with tears in her eyes and said, "George, I so love it." Angela gave him a hug and he started tearing up, too. Jamie joined in with the hug.

Jamie smiled and said, "We are now twins. It matches mine."

Chapter 30: The Tattoo

Angela did not know what she was talking about, until she showed that her tattoo artist had put the exact same sunflower tattoo on her left shoulder, also. Angela pointed to it and smiled. Jamie started to cry again, and hugged Angela again.

Angela said, "Where are your angel wing tattoos? What happened to them?"

Jamie said, "When I had the transformation and received my actual wings, my wing tattoos disappeared. It was a surprise for me, too. So, I thought we should get matching sunflower tattoos."

Angela just said, "That is so cool, it's freaking awesome. I love you."

Jamie smiled and said, "I love you, too."

Angela asked, "Why did you get the angel wing tattoos in the first place?"

Jamie smiled and said, "I got the large angel wing tattoo when I was a teenager to cover up my birthmark on my back."

Chapter 31

Louis and Nera

Nera was in a straight-jacket, in a white room, with white walls. A team of medical students were looking through the one-way glass at her, discussing her diagnosis.

One of the students said, "She looks schizophrenic."

Another student said, "Delusional."

While another student said, "She is not in touch with reality."

A strong male's voice said, "Maybe she is merely crazy?"

The students with their white medical coats all watched as Nera sat up and screamed, "I am going to find you Lucifer! I am going to find you and you will release me from this hell of yours! I am going to escape and kill the people who put me in here. I swear I will." Nera started banging her head against the padded wall and kicking her feet on the wall. Full furious force.

The medical students were all in agreeance that Nera could never be released back into society. She would be a danger to other people, and to herself. The professor in charge of the psychology medical students allowed them all to comment about what to do with the patient. Then one of the students said, "Dr. Louis, how did you find this patient?"

Dr. Louis C. Pfeiffer said, "I found this patient, named Nera, a couple days ago, screaming in the streets about Lucifer, Sameal the Angel of Death, Lilith—Adams' first wife, and the god Mercury, and then she was violent about wanting to kill one of our

Chapter 31: Louis and Nera

professors at this university. That's right, Nera was an employee here at the university and she had a complete mental breakdown and lost touch with all reality. After I discovered her in the streets, we medical professionals quickly had her committed here at our university behavioral health facility. She even thinks that I am Lucifer. Delusional is quite a gifted mind."

Dr. Pfeiffer looked down at his clipboard, smiled and said, "Shall we look at our next patient, my students? The next one has been here at our hospital for almost twenty years. He claimed to look at an artifact he had collected and looked at too long and thought it was a portal to another dimension. Let's see if he is awake. This shall be more fun than patient N." Dr. Louis led the students out of the hallway into another wing of the hospital. He kept talking about the cases and the medical students willfully followed him down the corridor.

As Nera was alone in her room secured by a straight-jacket, Sameal appeared in her room and squatted down and looked at her to get her attention.

Nera was lying on the padded floor, with her head on the floor, and smiled and said, "I knew you did not forget me."

Sameal said, "I would never forget my most faithful follower throughout the millennia."

Nera whispered, "What do we do next?"

Sameal said, "My dear friend, I will help you escape in the grandest of styles, in time."

Nera said, "Thank you. I knew my loyalty to you would not be misunderstood or forgotten."

Sameal said, "My dear, your day is soon to come and to be revealed. You just have to be patient and stay here awhile longer. I promise you escape when the time is right. Be a good patient here and cause no trouble and soon I will come to take you. I give you my solemn word." As he said this he put some fingers on her hair to remove them from her eyes, gently and caressing.

Nera said, "I knew you would never forget me, thank you."

As she said this, Sameal slowly disappeared from her room to leave her alone in her thoughts.

Chapter 32

The Artifacts Secured

A few days after the events on the roof, Robert telephoned Paul and said that they should meet at the security vault behind his academic building. The last time they visited the storage facility, many artifacts had been taken by who they thought was Nera as she was looking for the athame. Robert just had a gut feeling they should do an accountability check to make sure nothing else was missing, now that Nera should be out of the picture for the near future.

Robert drove up to Paul's house and picked him up in his convertible jaguar because it was such a beautiful day. Paul said, "It is always nice to ride in your convertible, but you never drive over 50 miles per hour. Why don't you let her go someday?" He opened the side door and got in passenger seat.

Robert said, "With a car like this, you never have to prove you can go fast. Everyone on the road already knows and silly stunts like that are for the young, full of their hubris. I don't need to prove anything to anyone." As he finished his sentence, Robert put on his sunglasses and his driving gloves and slowly cruised down the block to the university. Since it was a weekend, the parking lots were empty and there was almost no traffic on campus as they pulled behind the academic building to visit the security facility that 99 percent of the faculty had no idea existed. As they pulled into the back parking lot, they both noticed Peter's

Chapter 32: The Artifacts Secured

beast Jeep, from some science fiction movie, parked next to the entrance. They both looked at each other funny and now were curious why he was here.

Robert asked, "Paul, did you tell Peter we were coming here today?"

Paul said, "No. I did not tell anyone."

Robert said, "Well, that is odd. Let's see what he is doing."

Robert parked his convertible next to the Jeep and they both got out and walked to the entrance of the security facility. Robert put in his PIN code and the first door opened. They walked inside the warehouse and continued walking to the more highly secure area. There was no sign of Peter. As they walked up to the vault door, the door was open, so they walked in and OSCAR, the artificial intelligence security guard, sounded, "Welcome professor Dr. Robert and Mr. Paul."

Robert said, "Thank you OSCAR. Is Peter here?"

OSCAR said, "Yes, Dr. Peter is in the main vault."

Robert said, "Thank you."

OSCAR then said, "Mr. Paul, you still need to pay your parking ticket from Texas that remains unpaid."

Paul just looked at Robert, "Thank you, I promise I will."

Robert smiled and they continued walking to the main storage room. That's where they found Peter putting artifacts back on the wall from a bag on the floor.

Robert said, "Peter, it is a surprise to see you here. Are you putting back or taking our artifacts?"

Peter said, "I am putting them back."

Robert said, "Did you go to Nera's townhouse and find them there? We assumed she was the one who stole them and that's when we sent Paul and Maggie to Colorado with the athame."

Peter looked up at Robert, "Nera never stole them. How would she get inside this vault? She has no access. I took them for safekeeping until these events played out. I stored them in my private vault and now that Nera is gone, I can bring them back for safe keeping."

Paul said, "Why didn't you tell us that you took them?"

Peter said, "It was not necessary and I was not in the equation of events yet until Lilith and Merc actually brought me in. You see, Nera was also guided to find me, but it took her quite a bit longer and they had to use crayons and draw a map with an "X", but then that is another story, for another time. All that is important is that all your artifacts are back in your facility and under your guard."

Robert said, "Where is the Kila?"

Peter said, "Well, that is not yours to keep. I am keeping that and following my guidance."

Robert said, "What about the staff?"

Peter said, "Same principle. I will secure them both. If there is a time that we will need it, you will know where to find me on 18th Street." With that last statement, Peter picked up his bag and said, "Gentlemen, it has been a pleasure, but it is time for me to depart." He shook Paul and Robert's hands and left the vault. He said, "I know the way, OSCAR, thank you."

Paul said, "Well at least everything is as it should be. You have all your artifacts that no one knows about."

Robert looked around and said, "Yes, everything seems to be as it should be and so I guess our task is complete. Let's head out and do dinner. Maybe we can stop by Angela and Jamie's place and see if they are free for intellectual discussion."

Paul said, "I think you are trying to create another adventure?"

Robert said, "That's not my style. Usually adventures find me."

* * *

Peter departed and drove out of the parking and drove back to his remote home in the woods. He pulled out his duffle bag and carried it into his own vault in his basement. He used his thumb print to get the access for the door to open and the light automatically turned on. He pulled out the Kila from the duffle bag and placed it on the wall next to the staff with his other collectibles throughout the ages. As he was about to depart, he looked over at his Scottish broadsword and it was glowing and he smiled. He said, "Lilith, are you here?"

Lilith walked in behind him, "Yes my friend, I am here and

Chapter 32: The Artifacts Secured

was curious where you would store the Kila and I am glad you still have the broadsword. It wants to talk to us."

Peter said, "Not tonight, my beloved, let's have dinner like old times, back in the 12th century."

Lilith smiled "But I preferred the 8th century, when you were much younger." She stopped and looked at a particular disheveled sword in the corner with dust on it. "It is good you have the Sword of Destiny still."

Peter said, "You are the only one who knows where it is. I hope to keep it a secret for another couple of centuries. The world is not ready for it to be public yet."

Lilith said, "I agree the world is not ready. Let's have dinner, I am starving. Are you cooking or are we eating out."

Peter said, "I know a nice place downtown with a small library, if you are interested?"

Lilith looked at Peter with a smirk and laughed.

About the Authors

P.E. Berg has a doctorate in adult education and served in the government for 29 years. Paul has written military history and adult education journal articles over the past 15 years and The Birthmark Scar is his first novel. He is currently a university professor, tries to write full-time, and lives on Sentinel Hill in Kansas on his five wooded acres.

Amanda Hemmingsen: Tantra, Ayurveda, and energy healing are Amanda's 3 core metaphysical disciplines. She has a master's in English, and works full time as an editor. You can reach her via www.amandahemmingsen.com.

A Warrior's Path is the second book of their trilogy.

Other Books by Ozark Mountain Publishing, Inc.

Dolores Cannon
A Soul Remembers Hiroshima
Between Death and Life
Conversations with Nostradamus, Volume I, II, III
The Convoluted Universe -Book One, Two, Three, Four, Five
The Custodians
Five Lives Remembered
Horns of the Goddess
Jesus and the Essenes
Keepers of the Garden
Legacy from the Stars
The Legend of Starcrash
The Search for Hidden Sacred Knowledge
They Walked with Jesus
The Three Waves of Volunteers and the New Earth
A Very Special Friend
Aron Abrahamsen
Holiday in Heaven
James Ream Adams
Little Steps
Justine Alessi & M. E. McMillan
Rebirth of the Oracle
Kathryn Andries
Time: The Second Secret
Will Alexander
Call Me Jonah
Cat Baldwin
Divine Gifts of Healing
The Forgiveness Workshop
Penny Barron
The Oracle of UR
The Oracle of UR, Book 2
P.E. Berg & Amanda Hemmingsen
The Birthmark Scar
The Birthmark Scar, Book 2
Dan Bird
Finding Your Way in the Spiritual Age
Waking Up in the Spiritual Age
Julia Cannon
Soul Speak – The Language of Your Body
Jack Cauley
Journey for Life
Ronald Chapman
Seeing True
Jack Churchward
Lifting the Veil on the Lost
Continent of Mu
The Stone Tablets of Mu
Carolyn Greer Daly
Opening to Fullness of Spirit
Patrick De Haan
The Alien Handbook
Paulinne Delcour-Min
Divine Fire
Holly Ice
Spiritual Gold
Anthony DeNino
The Power of Giving and Gratitude
Joanne DiMaggio
Edgar Cayce and the Unfulfilled Destiny of Thomas Jefferson Reborn
Paul Fisher
Like a River to the Sea
Anita Holmes
Twidders
Aaron Hoopes
Reconnecting to the Earth
Edin Huskovic
God is a Woman
Patricia Irvine
In Light and In Shade
Kevin Killen
Ghosts and Me
Susan Linville
Blessings from Agnes
Donna Lynn
From Fear to Love
Curt Melliger
Heaven Here on Earth
Where the Weeds Grow
Henry Michaelson
And Jesus Said – A Conversation
Andy Myers
Not Your Average Angel Book
Holly Nadler
The Hobo Diaries
Guy Needler
The Anne Dialogues
Avoiding Karma
Beyond the Source – Book 1, Book 2
The Curators
The History of God
The OM
The Origin Speaks

For more information about any of the above titles, soon to be released titles, or other items in our catalog, write, phone or visit our website:
PO Box 754, Huntsville, AR 72740|479-738-2348/800-935-0045|www.ozarkmt.com

Other Books by Ozark Mountain Publishing, Inc.

Psycho Spiritual Healing
James Nussbaumer
And Then I Knew My Abundance
Each of You
Living Your Dram, Not Someone Else's
The Master of Everything
Mastering Your Own Spiritual Freedom
Sherry O'Brian
Peaks and Valley's
Gabrielle Orr
Akashic Records: One True Love
Let Miracles Happen
Nick Osborne
A Ronin's Tale
Nikki Pattillo
Children of the Stars
A Golden Compass
Victoria Pendragon
Being In A Body
Sleep Magic
The Sleeping Phoenix
Alexander Quinn
Starseeds What's It All About
Debra Rayburn
Let's Get Natural with Herbs
Charmian Redwood
A New Earth Rising
Coming Home to Lemuria
David Rousseau
Beyond Our World, Book 1
Beyond Our World, Book 2
Richard Rowe
Exploring the Divine Library
Imagining the Unimaginable
Garnet Schulhauser
Dance of Eternal Rapture
Dance of Heavenly Bliss
Dancing Forever with Spirit
Dancing on a Stamp
Dancing with Angels in Heaven
Annie Stillwater Gray
The Dawn Book
Education of a Guardian Angel
Joys of a Guardian Angel

Work of a Guardian Angel
Manuella Stoerzer
Headless Chicken
Blair Styra
Don't Change the Channel
Who Catharted
Natalie Sudman
Application of Impossible Things
L.R. Sumpter
Judy's Story
The Old is New
We Are the Creators
Artur Tradevosyan
Croton
Croton II
Jim Thomas
Tales from the Trance
Jolene and Jason Tierney
A Quest of Transcendence
Paul Travers
Dancing with the Mountains
Nicholas Vesey
Living the Life-Force
Dennis Wheatley/ Maria Wheatley
The Essential Dowsing Guide
Maria Wheatley
Druidic Soul Star Astrology
Sherry Wilde
The Forgotten Promise
Lyn Willmott
A Small Book of Comfort
Beyond all Boundaries Book 1
Beyond all Boundaries Book 2
Beyond all Boundaries Book 3
D. Arthur Wilson
You Selfish Bastard
Stuart Wilson & Joanna Prentis
Atlantis and the New Consciousness
Beyond Limitations
The Essenes -Children of the Light
The Magdalene Version
Power of the Magdalene
Sally Wolf
Life of a Military Psychologist

For more information about any of the above titles, soon to be released titles, or other items in our catalog, write, phone or visit our website:
PO Box 754, Huntsville, AR 72740|479-738-2348/800-935-0045|www.ozarkmt.com